KANDY AT WAR

Indigenous Military Resistance to European Expansion in Sri Lanka 1594–1818

Channa Wickremesekera

MANOHAR
2004

First published 2004

ISBN 81–7304–547–X

Published by
Ajay Kumar Jain for
Manohar Publishers & Distributors
4753/23 Ansari Road, Daryaganj
New Delhi 110 002

Typeset at
Digigrafics
New Delhi 110 049

Printed at
Lordson Publishers Pvt. Ltd.
Delhi 110 007

To my brothers
SINHA and PRASANNA

Contents

Illustrations

MAPS

PLATES

Acknowledgements

This book was written under difficult circumstances that were not always conducive to research. Self-motivation was the most important resource that carried me through the research and writing of this book.

Still, the contribution of a few people was essential for its completion. Mr Victor Melder's private library in Melbourne provided many valuable and rare printed sources and was my main resource of information in Australia. Victor's extraordinary generosity with his astonishing collection of sources made a very substantial contribution towards the writing of this book. The staff at the Colombo Museum library and the Sri Lanka National Archives was very helpful in finding documentary sources. The Director of National Museum Dr Nanda Wickremesinghe and the staff at the Kandy Museum were particularly helpful in accessing weapons collections. I would also like to thank Professor Senake Bandaranayake and Manel, his wife, for providing significant encouragement and support, and Manohar Publishers & Distributors for taking up the publication of this work. Last but not least also my parents and brothers proved an enduring source of inspiration with their interest and encouragement.

CHANNA WICKREMESEKERA

Abbreviations

CALR	Ceylon Antiquary and Literary Register
CHJ	*Ceylon Historical Journal*
CJHSS	*Ceylon Journal of Historical and Social Studies*
CLR	Ceylon Literary Register
JDBUC	*Journal of the Dutch Burgher Union of Ceylon*
JRAS (CB)	*Journal of the Royal Asiatic Society (Ceylon Branch)*
JRAS (SLB)	*Journal of the Royal Asiatic Society (Sri Lanka Branch)*
SLNA	Sri Lanka National Archives

Glossary

Adigar	The highest ranking official in the Kandyan Administration.
Atapattu Nilame	Officer in charge of a body of palace guards.
Badahela Badda	Potter's department.
Badda	A department of specialised service providers.
Buth Wadana Nilame	An officer of the king's household.
Dissawa	The governor of a Kandyan province.
Gabdagam	Villages set aside for the use of the Royal household.
Gammahe	The principle landholder of a village.
Hatan Kavi	Literally 'War Poems'. Poems extolling the virtues of Kings and celebrating their victories in battle.
Kada	Two loads hanging from either end of a stick.
Kinnaraya	Weaver.
Kinnara Badda	Weaver's department.
Kodituwakku Nilame	Officer in charge of the men carrying a species of light artillery called kodituwakku.
Kottal Badda	Artificer's department.
Madige Badda	Department of fisher caste people who also provided Transport for the king's goods.
Maha Gabada Nilame	Officer in charge of the Royal store.
Muttettuva	A portion of the best productive land in the village kept for the use of the village owner.
Nindagam	Villages granted for life.
Pen Wadana Nilame	An officer of the king's household.

Pirivara	Retinue.
Ranpota	Golden chain presented by the king in acknowledgement of excellent service.
Rodiya	Outcaste.
Sannasa	A royal grant, usually written on a piece of palmyra leaf.
Tappakara Mohandiram	An officer of the king's household.
Tharam	Severed heads of enemies killed in battle, presented to the as proof of valour.
Udarata	Literally 'high country'; term for the Kandyan highlands.
Vanniyar	Local chieftain in the north and east of pre-modern Sri Lanka.

Introduction

European commercial and political expansion into regions outside Europe began in the fourteenth century and by the early nineteenth century, European dominance had spread over large areas of Asia, Africa, and the Americas. The road to this supremacy, however, was never a smooth one. Often, European expansion was fiercely and violently resisted by the indigenous peoples and war went hand in hand with commercial expansion and colonization. Armies of European nations suffered numerous reverses and defeats at the hands of indigenous forces before European authority could be securely established.

This was in spite of momentous military developments in Europe, which saw a 'revolution' in tactics and organization between the sixteenth and eighteenth centuries. On the tactical side, these developments took the form of an increasing reliance on infantry using firearms and fighting in drilled formations supported by field artillery. In terms of organization, the European armies gradually lost their feudal character and became centrally organized and controlled bodies with permanent standing.[1] These developments greatly increased the destructive potential of the European armies but by no means did they assure victory over the indigenous armies in Asia, Africa, and the Americas.

The balance of military power between the European and non-European armies in the era of European expansion has been discussed and debated by several historians. Geoffrey Parker suggests that despite numerous setbacks, overall, the odds were stacked in favour of the European armies. This was due to various reasons. In some parts of the non-European world such as Siberia and South America, European technology proved a decisive factor while in the Middle East, the Turks suffered from a combination of an inefficient utilization of resources, the incorporation of European techniques into their traditional military framework, and inferior technology. In India, European discipline and firepower initially made rapid headway but was soon seriously checked by some Indian powers adopting European techniques and tactics. However, according to Parker, this transition was incomplete, 'too little too late' to halt the ultimate triumph of European arms.[2] Jeremy Black also draws attention to the many reverses suffered by the European forces in Africa, Asia, and the Americas but he too asserts that European military power ultimately prevailed. However, Black makes the interesting point that the balance shifted markedly in favour of European arms since the mid-seventeenth century onwards due to numerous technological and tactical innovations, such as: 'the flintlock musket, accurate and mobile grape—as well as canister-firing field artillery, and warships firing a greater weight of metal'. Where non-Europeans adopted these aspects of European warfare, the European forces faced a hard struggle but like Parker, Black believes that the attempts to bridge the widening gap were only partially successful.[3]

This book attempt to position a unique case of indigenous military resistance to European expansion in South Asia within this debate about the military balance between, as Parker puts it, 'the West and the rest'. The case under investigation is the military resistance offered by the kingdom of Kandy in central Sri Lanka to European military forces. Kandy, captured by the British in 1815, was the last territory on the island to fall to European control. Prior to its conquest by the British, Kandy had survived numerous invasions and raids by three European powers based on the island's coast: the Portuguese, the Dutch, and the British themselves. Not only did Kandy survive through all these assaults, it also delivered some crushing defeats to their European enemies. Three large Portuguese armies were completely destroyed and another badly mauled in their attempts to invade and ravage Kandyan territory, resulting in the death and capture of nearly 2,000 Portuguese soldiers. Two Dutch attempts to invade and occupy Kandy met with failure, with the invaders being forced to retreat after incurring losses. During 1803–4, two British armies entered Kandy. One was trapped and massacred while the other escaped with heavy losses. However, the British conquest was seriously challenged within two years when a revolt spread across the Kandyan lands in 1817–18 and was ruthlessly put down. The Kandyans also took the fight to the enemy, invading and devastating their lands in the low country.

Earlier, in 1603 and 1630, the Portuguese suffered heavily from such invasions, with the attack in 1630 succeeding in bottling up the Portuguese in a few strongholds on the coast. In 1761, the Kandyans swept through Dutch territories in the south-west, capturing a number of outposts and the coastal fortified post of Matara.

This was a remarkable record of successful resistance. The effectiveness of Kandyan resistance even inspired a Dutch officer who took part in the Kandyan–Dutch war of 1761–6 to write an authoritative account of Kandyan warfare. Titled 'Observations on the war with the Sinhalese', this 202-page manuscript is among the earliest manuals on colonial warfare in the world. It is also testimony to the challenge posed by Kandyan military resistance to European military forces at the time.[4]

From the perspective of South Asian military resistance to European expansion, Kandyan resistance has special significance. It is a unique case of indigenous resistance in the region. On the one hand, Kandy provides the longest struggle for supremacy between a South Asian polity and European powers. European expansion into the interior in Sri Lanka began long before it began making inroads into the subcontinent. When the Portuguese were stumbling up the rugged slopes of Kandy, in India their countrymen were struggling to hold on to their coastal strongholds. When the Europeans eventually embarked on territorial expansion in India with the British conquest of Bengal in 1757 and their victory over Awadh in the 1760s Kandy was already entering into its second round of resistance to European expansion, this time against the Dutch. And when the British conquered Kandy in 1815, not only were they extending their conquests in the neighbouring subcontinent to the interior of the island, they were also finishing a struggle that had begun long before they had begun their career of conquest in India.

This long resistance is also significant for another reason. Kandy was no great South Asian power. It was very much a landlocked kingdom of rugged highlands with a small population of peasants living on subsistence agriculture. It engaged in no commerce of importance and its industry was elementary. Struggles for supremacy between European forces and kingdoms of Kandy's stature are rare in South Asia, where effective military resistance to European expansion usually came from the big states and empires, the successors to the Mughals. These were powers that could raise massive armies of men and cavalry and field large trains of artillery. They were also able to match the Europeans in technology and emulate them in discipline. These were the powers that Parker and Black have engaged with, kingdoms and empires like those of the Marathas, Mysore, and the Sikhs. Towards the close of the eighteenth century, with the help of renegade Europeans, the Maratha ruler Mahadji Scindia raised five regular brigades of infantry with field artillery.[5] Around the same time, Tipu Sultan of Mysore also embraced European-style infantry, dressed in red and green uniforms and armed with French and English muskets.[6] In the following century, the Sikhs in the Punjab raised even larger and more streamlined armies of regular infantry and artillery.[7] These armies also offered fierce resistance. It was after a bloody struggle that the British defeated the regular armies of the Maratha rulers in 1803. In 1845–9, the British paid an even higher price for overcoming the Sikhs.[8]

The European—in this case British—military supremacy on the subcontinent was achieved by defeating these and other major indigenous powers and establishing British paramountcy over them and their allies. The plethora of smaller kingdoms, with their predominantly agricultural communities, usually took part in challenging European military power as allies of the major powers. Their part in the military conflicts usually ended when their overlord was humbled. This was necessarily so. The control of a land of empires and great kingdoms was necessarily decided when its great powers were subdued. The small peasant kingdom which was but a segment of the great state's power had little scope for resisting European expansion once the great power had been humbled. As a consequence, when struggles between European forces and small peasant communities occurred on the subcontinent they were more as part of consolidation of military conquests rather than as the key to conquest itself.

The situation in Sri Lanka, however, was different. Sri Lanka was a land of little peasant kingdoms and those who strove to conquer the island had to fight it out with these tiny kingdoms to rule the island. This is how Kandy came to stand alone against the Europeans. By 1593 all other kingdoms on the island had either come under direct European rule or had succumbed to a measure of European control. Kandy in the central highlands of the island alone remained left to fend off European invasions and raids for two more centuries.

In the process, Kandy also became the best example of a prolonged military contest for supremacy between a little peasant society in South Asia and the European powers. In this sense, indigenous resistance to European expansion in Sri Lanka must stand comparison not with the neighbouring subcontinent but with indigenous resistance in Africa and the Americas. In these regions, as in the central highlands of Sri Lanka, peasant societies and tribal peoples with weak political institutions and meagre technological and material resources challenged European encroachment. Studies of indigenous resistance in these regions reveal a contest between the natural resourcefulness of the indigenous people and the technology and discipline of the Europeans. The 'natives' could scarcely expect to match the Europeans in firepower or military organization. But European technology and discipline was never a guarantee of success in these conflicts. The indigenous peoples realized that they too could offer serious military resistance, using their limited means and exploiting some of the natural advantages they possessed. These usually consisted of a sound knowledge of the terrain and the lack of encumbering baggage, which allowed them to move swiftly and surprise their enemy. The employment of guerrilla warfare often reduced the effectiveness of European firepower and discipline, while subjecting European troops to rigorous campaigns in hostile environments and unhealthy climates, thereby narrowing the gap between the two sides. Very frequently, indigenous forces also showed an ability to adopt European arms and use them in their own style of fighting.

There are many examples of such effective resistance. For instance, in 1572 in south-eastern Africa, a Portuguese expeditionary force of several hundred men moving up the Zambesi River was wiped out by tribesmen using bows and arrows.[9] On the other side of Africa, the Portuguese suffered numerous defeats at the hands of tribal armies before they succeeded in destroying the kingdoms of Kongo and Ndongo in the second half of the seventeenth century.[10] In South America, the indigenous tribes armed with bows and arrows and using their jungle-craft proved a formidable match for Portuguese colonists armed with firearms.[11] In North America, the native Indians soon acquired European firearms in their guerrilla war against the European settlers and militias, making a mockery of European tactics and techniques.[12]

The discussion on the balance of military power between the European and non-European forces has paid little attention to these conflicts. Looking at the European–indigenous clashes and struggles in North and South America, Jeremy Black draws attention to the widening gap between Europeans and indigenous peoples in the spheres of technology and manpower resources as a major contributor to the ultimate success of Europeans. In South America, the natives' failure to adopt firearms proved to their disadvantage despite their superior junglecraft. In North America where the native Indians adopted firearms with considerable success, the increasing European population proved to be the decisive factor, especially in the context of tactics, which amounted to total war. The use of indigenous manpower also contributed significantly to undermine the Indians' advantage in guerrilla warfare.[13]

Where do the Kandyan struggles against the Europeans stand in this picture? Unlike the above cases, the case of Kandyan resistance has been little investigated by historians. The only scholarly attempt to detail the military aspects of the Kandyan kingdom occurs in the form of a seven-page chapter in a work on Kandyan social organization published in 1956.[14] Geoffrey Powell's *The Kandyan Wars* has been immensely popular but does not enter into a discussion of the issues that make Kandyan resistance significant.[15] More recently, G.S. Gamage has made an attempt, in the vernacular, to describe the military strategies and tactics used by the Kandyans against the European invaders but it suffers from a woeful lack of research.[16] So is the case of a short article by M.S.C. de Silva that attempts to provide a sweeping description of the Sinhalese army from the late sixteenth to the early nineteenth centuries in less than 10 pages.[17] Apart from these, a few brief references in general works on European expansion and military innovation and in a few obscure articles is all that Kandyan resistance has received in the form of academic attention.[18] For all intents and purposes, the eighteenth-century manuscript 'War with the Sinhalese' remains the most authoritative work written on the subject.

This book aims to fill this void by examining the main elements of Kandyan resistance and its effectiveness against European military power during the period of Kandyan–European military confrontation. It begins by tracing the history of the struggle and proceeds to consider the Kandyan military organization, weapons, and tactics. Finally, it examines the balance of power between Kandyan and European military forces during different phases of confrontation.

SOURCES

What makes the lack of scholarly attention to Kandyan resistance all the more puzzling—and regrettable—is the availability of sources. It is true that there are very few indigenous sources; the Kandyans did not maintain meticulous and voluminous records of their military activities—or even of their other activities for that matter—and much of the few records they made have perished. But there are many European sources available. Even though Kandy remained closed to European penetration until its capture the Europeans had plenty of opportunities to observe Kandyan military forces in action. Indeed, the battlefield was the area in which the Europeans had the most frequent and intense contacts with the Kandyans. This resulted in a substantial output of European writing dealing with Kandyan army and warfare. The document 'War with the Sinhalese' is only the best example of its kind. There are also voluminous official and semi-official documents—correspondence, journals, reports—generated by the European civilian and military administration during the wars with Kandy. These contain a wealth of information about Kandyan warfare, particularly technology and tactics, often based on observations in the field. Even official writing during times of peace contain valuable information about European perceptions of Kandy as a potential threat.[19] Many of these are published,[20] and are readily accessible to researchers[21] while many of the important manuscript sources can be accessed in the Sri Lanka National Archives (SLNA).

The lengthy accounts of the island left by Europeans who spent many years on the island are also very useful in this regard. These include the remarkable work of Robert Knox who was one of the very few Europeans who had the opportunity to observe Kandyans closely in their own country. Knox enlarged his original work into a second edition that was never published in his lifetime. It was eventually published in 1989 and contains much new information on the Kandyan polity and people.[22] There is also the work of Joao Ribeiro, the Portuguese Captain who fought against Kandyan and Dutch troops in Sri Lanka for 18 years, while the anonymously written narrative of the ill-fated Portuguese expedition to Kandy in 1630 also provides some interesting first-hand insights into Kandyan–European military conflicts.[23]

There are also contemporary historical narratives. The history of the Portuguese conquest of Ceylon by the Jesuit Fernao de Queyroz offers a colourful view of the Portuguese sojourn in Sri Lanka.[24] The works of Barros and Do Couto are also similar narratives, dealing with the Portuguese in Sri Lanka up to 1600.[25] Written with the help of official documents and first-hand accounts, these works are replete with descriptions of wars and battles waged by the Portuguese against the Kandyans. Naturally there is exaggeration but very often it is obvious enough to make the researcher's task less complicated.

Last but not least are the works of numerous travellers who, while passing through, learnt something about the island from first-hand observation or from other Europeans already 'resident' on the island. Some of them, like Johann Wolfgang Heydt who spent a few years in the island had the opportunity to visit Kandy with a Dutch embassy in 1739.[26]

The sources available include a genre of literature called *hatan kavi* or 'war poems', really panegyrical works extolling the warfare. Some of them have been published while others are available as palm leaf manuscripts.[27] Kandyan land grants, frequently given to soldiers who performed well in battle are also of some use in this respect. There are also a few indigenous historical narratives, the *Rajavaliya*, or the 'Line of Kings', being the best known.[28] Although it rushes through the Kandyan period, its narrative on the earlier struggles between the Portuguese and the kingdom of Kotte in the low country provides some interesting information about warfare that can be of use in understanding Kandyan warfare.

These primary sources are supplemented by a number of secondary works written on the 'European period' of Sri Lankan history. A number of scholarly works were written by Paul E. Pieris during the first half of the last century, including histories of the Dutch and Portuguese periods.[29] The decades following Independence saw a number of Sri Lankan scholars departing for the School of Oriental and African Studies in London to study the Portuguese, Dutch and British periods. These scholars produced some excellent narrative histories based on painstaking archival work. These include Sinnappah Arasaratnam's *Dutch Power in Ceylon,*[30] K.W. Goonewardene's *The Foundation of Dutch Power in Ceylon,*[31] Tikiri Abeysinghe's *Portuguese Rule in Ceylon,*[32] C.R. de Silva's *The Portuguese in Ceylon*[33] and Colvin R. de Silva's classic *Ceylon under the British Occupation.*[34] Not all these excellent researches ended up as publications. The works of D.A. Kotelawela and V. Kanapathipillai remain in manuscript form.[35] All these works, while not dealing directly with military issues, provide an invaluable guidance for understanding the political and economic issues that contributed to military conflict between Kandy and European powers.

NOTES

1. Michael Roberts first advanced the concept of a 'military revolution' in Europe between 1560 and 1660 in an inaugural lecture delivered at the Queen's University, Belfast in 1956. The lecture is published in Michael Roberts, *Essays in Swedish History*, London: Weidenfeld and Nicholson, 1967, pp. 195–225. Although the broad outline of Roberts' thesis has been generally accepted by military historians, some, like Geoffrey Parker and Jeremy Black, have sought to extend the time frame to embrace the early part of the eighteenth century as well. See Geoffrey Parker, *The Military Revolution: Military Innovation and the Rise of the West 1500–1800*, Cambridge and New York: Cambridge University Press, 1998 and Jeremy Black, *European Warfare 1660–1815*, London: University College of London Press, 1994.
2. Parker, *The Military Revolution*, pp. 115–45.
3. Black, *European Warfare*, pp. 13–33.
4. '*Aanmerkingen over de Oorlog met de Singaleesen*', London, Oriental and India Office Collection, Mackenzie Ms. 39, hereafter '*Aanmerkingen*'.
5. On the Maratha regular forces, see Surendranath Sen, *The Military System of the Marathas*, Calcutta: K. Bagchi & Co., 1949; John Pemble, 'Techniques and Resources in the Second Maratha War', *Historical Journal*, vol. 19, no. 2, 1976, pp. 375–404; and R.G.S. Cooper,

'Wellington and the Marathas 1803–04', *International History Review*, vol. 11, no. 1, 1989, pp. 31–8.

6. Innes Munro, *A Narrative of the Military Operations on the Coromandel Coast against the Combined Forces of the French, Dutch and Hyder Ali Cawn, from the Year 1780 to the Peace in 1784*, London, 1789.
7. See C. Grey, *European Adventurers in Northern India 1785–1849*, Lahore: Govt. Printing, 1929, esp. pp. 17–33; George Bruce, *Six Battles for India: The Anglo-Sikh Wars 1845–6, 1848–9*, London: Arthur Baker Ltd., 1969, pp. 47–62. For a general appraisal of the 'Europeanizing' efforts of the Marathas, Mysore and the Sikhs, see Pradeep Barua, 'Military Innovations in India 1750–1850', *Journal of Military History*, vol. 58, no. 4, 1994, pp. 599–616.
8. Pemble, 'Techniques and Resources', pp. 376–9; Cooper, 'Wellington', pp. 31–8; Bruce, *Six Battles*.
9. Eric Axelson, *The Portuguese in South East Africa 1488–1600*, Johannesburg: C. Struick, 1973, pp. 158–63.
10. David Birmingham, *Trade and Conflict in Angola*, Oxford: Clarendon, 1966.
11. See David Sweet, 'Native Resistance in Eighteenth Century Amazonia: The "Abominable Muras" in War and Peace', *Radical History Review*, vol. 53, 1994, pp. 49–80 and John Hemming, *The Amazon Frontier: The Defeat of the Amazon Indians*, London: Macmillan, 1987.
12. Douglas Edward Leach, *Flintlock and Tomahawk: New England in King Phillip's War*, New York: The Norton Library, 1966; Patrick Malone, *The Skulking Way of War: Technology among the New England Indians*, Lanham, MD: Madison Books, 1991.
13. Black, *European Warfare*, pp. 31–2, Jeremy Black, *War and the World: Military Power and the Fate of Continents 1450–2000*, New Haven and London: Yale University Press, 1998, pp. 74–5.
14. Ralph Pieris, *Sinhalese Social Organization: The Kandyan Period*, Colombo: Ceylon University Press, 1956.
15. Geoffrey Powell, *The Kandyan Wars: The British Army in Ceylon 1803–1818*, London: Leo Cooper, 1973.
16. G.S. Gamage, *Mahanuwara Rajya Arakshaka Kramopaya*, Colombo: S. Godage and Sons, 1997, esp. pp. 51–85.
17. M.S.C. De Silva, 'The Sinhalese Army during the Portuguese, Dutch and British Periods 1505–1815', *Spolia Zeylanica*, vol. 32, no. 1, 1971, pp. 79–87.
18. See, for instance, the references in Jeremy Black, *Warfare in the Eighteenth Century*, London: Cassel, 1999, p. 78 and Phillip J. Haythornwhite, *The Colonial Wars Sourcebook*, London: Arms and Armour, 1995, pp. 150–4.
19. Of great importance in this respect are the numerous reports left by Dutch Governors for their successors.

20. Many important contemporary documents relating to European military campaigns against Kandy have been published in journals like the *Ceylon Antiquary and Literary Register*, *Journal of the Royal Asiatic Society* (*Ceylon Branch*), and the *Journal of the Dutch Burgher Union of Ceylon* (*JDBUC*), while many others were brought out as separate publications.
21. For instance, many key documents relating to the Kandyan–Dutch War of 1761–6 have been published. See J.H.O. Paulusz (ed.), *Secret Minutes of the Dutch Political Council 1762*, Colombo: Govt. Printers, 1954, 'Summaries of the Proceedings of the Secret War Committee of the Dutch Political Council of Ceylon during the War with Kandy, 1762–1766', trs. S.A.W. Mottau, *JDBUC*, vol. 55, nos. 1–4, 1965 and Major Roland Raven-Hart (trs. and ed.), *The Dutch Wars with Kandy 1764–1766*, Ceylon Historical Manuscript Commission Bulletin no. 6, Colombo: Government Publications Bureau, 1964.
22. Robert Knox, *An Historical Relation of the Island of Ceylon, Revised, Enlarged & Brought to the Verge of Publication as the Second Edition by Robert Knox together with his Autobiography and All the New Chapters, Paragraphs, Marginal Notes added by the Author in the Two Interleaved Copies of the Original Text of 1681*, Edited with Introduction and Notes by J.H.O. Paulusz, published as the *CHJ* Monographs series, vol. 14, Dehiwela, Sri Lanka: Tisara Publishers, 1989; 1st edn. 1681.
23. Joao de Ribeiro, *The Historic Tragedy of the Island of Ceilao*, trs. P.E. Pieris, Colombo: Lake House, 1948; *The Expedition to Uva made in 1630 by Constantine de Sa de Noronha, Captain General of Ceylon, as narrated by a Soldier who took part in the Expedition together with an Account of the Siege laid to Colombo by the King of Kandy written by Afonso Dias da Lomba*, trs. S.G. Perera, Colombo: Govt. Printers, 1930.
24. Fernao de Queyroz, *The Temporal and Spiritual Conquest of Ceylon*, trs. S.G. Perera, Colombo: Govt. Printers, 1930.
25. Joao de Barros and Diogo do Couto, 'The History of Ceylon from the earliest times to A.D. 1600', trs. and ed. Donald Ferguson, *JRAS(CB)*, vol. 20, no. 60, 1908.
26. *Heydt's Ceylon, being the relevant sections of the 'Allerneuster Geographisch und Topographischer Schauplatz van Afrika und Ost-Indien, etc. etc.'*, trs. and ed. Major Roland Raven-Hart, Colombo: Govt. Information Dept., 1952. Original published in Willendorf, 1742.
27. For instance, Kirimetiyawe Mentindu, *Maha Hatana*, ed. T.S. Hemakumar, Colombo: Samayawardene Printers, 1964; *Rajasinha Hatana*, ed. Ellepola M.M. Somaratne, Kandy: T.B.S. Godamune and Sons; date unavailable; *Ingrisi Hatana*, National Museum Colombo Palm Leaf Ms. 1859, K.11.
28. *Rajavaliya or a Historical Narrative of Sinhalese Kings from Vijaya to Vimala Dharma Surya II*, ed. B. Gunasekera, Colombo: Govt. Printers, 1954; rpt. of 1900 edn.

29. Pieris' two major histories are *Ceylon and the Hollanders 1658–1796*, Tellipalai, Sri Lanka: American Ceylon Mission Press, 1918 and *Ceylon: The Portuguese Era being a History of the Island for the Period 1505–1658*, 2 vols., Colombo: C.A.C. Ltd., 1913.
30. Sinnappah Arasaratnam, *Dutch Power in Ceylon*, Amsterdam: Djambatan, 1958.
31. K.W. Goonewardene, *The Foundation of Dutch Power in Ceylon 1638–1658*, Amsterdam: Djambatan, 1958.
32. T.B.H. Abeysinghe, *Portuguese Rule in Ceylon 1594–1612*, Colombo: Lake House, 1966.
33. C.R. de Silva, *The Portuguese in Ceylon 1617–1638*, Colombo: H.W. Cave & Co., 1972.
34. Colvin R. de Silva, *Ceylon under the British Occupation 1795–1833*, 2 vols, New Delhi: Navrang, 1995, 4th edn., 1st pub. 1941.
35. D.A. Kotelawela, 'The Dutch in Ceylon: 1743–1766', Ph.D. thesis, University of London, 1968; V. Kanapathipillai, 'Dutch Rule in Maritime Ceylon 1766–1796', Ph.D. thesis, University of London, 1969.

ONE

The Frontier

Kandy: Its Origins and an Outline of its Struggle against European Expansion

Although Kandy was the last indigenous kingdom to fall under European power it was also one of the last kingdoms to emerge on the island. Until the fifteenth century, the central highlands of Sri Lanka feature little in the island's historical chronicles. The ancient and medieval rulers of the island seem to have generally avoided the rugged region for obvious reasons. It was inaccessible and inhospitable, 'a country which was difficult to penetrate owing to the inaccessibility of the many mountains and on account of the danger from wild animals', according to the Sinhalese chronicle *Culavamsa*.[1] Accordingly only those who had a good reason to remain inaccessible—rebels and bandits—took the risk of settling among the jungle-clad hills. It is only in the mid-fifteenth century that we first hear about the highlands with regard to their place in the political configuration of the island. At this time, we are told, *Udarata*, or the 'high country', was paying tribute to the kingdom of Kotte in the south-west of the island.[2] Then, in the second half of the century, Kotte's grip slackened and around 1473 a new kingdom arose in the hills with its capital at Senkadagala. This is generally accepted as the beginning of the kingdom of Kandy.[3]

The political context to the emergence of Kandy had much in common with politics elsewhere in the region. In ancient and medieval South Asia, political authority was highly localized, with local rulers and chiefs enjoying considerable political and economic autonomy. Local rulers would often offer a degree of allegiance and submission to greater rulers or overlords that was neither absolute nor permanent. Submission was largely symbolic and ritualistic, which allowed overlords to claim authority over a large number of local rulers who remained effectively in control of their local areas. As Burton Stein writes with reference to the state in medieval South India:

> Localized political units were capable of being linked, loosely and symbolically, to kings whose sovereignty might for a time be recognized by local chieftains. Kings whose overlordships were so recognized were in all cases effectively in control of but a small portion of the macro region, but the legitimacy of their hegemonic claims—which were ceremonial rather than real in any case—could be recognized by those far-removed from this core of real power.[4]

This type of political and territorial control was perhaps the only kind feasible at a time when modes of communication were primitive. But it was a far cry from the modern state with strong central control extending over an area marked by fixed boundaries. Territorial control—and boundaries—in the medieval South Asian state was constantly changing as rulers moved in and out of the larger networks of allegiances. Kingdoms rose and fell and empires expanded and contracted as alliances were made and unmade and submission was offered and withdrawn.

In Sri Lanka, this kind of 'segmentary' state was much in evidence from ancient times. There is little evidence of the existence of strong centralized government before the establishment of British rule in the early nineteenth century. In its place existed a fragmented system of political authority placing several rulers in control over areas, which they could, effectively, control with the means at their disposal. Regional and local autonomy was strong and submission to overlords was offered and expected in the form of an acceptance of paramountcy and the offering of material tokens of submission.[5] As elsewhere in the region, strong local rulers could set themselves as virtually independent of their overlords while powerful overlords could extend their control at the expense of neighbouring overlords. Sometimes one kingdom, under a particularly vigorous ruler, would attain paramountcy over other rulers on the island for a brief period, but it was a rare occurrence rather than commonplace. On the other hand, any weakening of the overlord's power could result in the greater independence of local elites.

Kandy emerged out of such a realignment of political power in the fifteenth century. Since the eleventh century, a combination of south Indian invasions and internal turmoil had gradually pushed Sinhala rule southward from its heartland in the north-central plain while giving rise to a Tamil kingdom based in the Jaffna peninsula in the north. The frontier of the Sinhala and Tamil controlled regions came under the rule of local chieftains called the Vanniyars who enjoyed a virtually autonomous status.[6] In the south, Sinhala authority suffered further fragmentation, but in the fourteenth century, the kingdom of Kotte in the south-west emerged as the most powerful Sinhala kingdom on the island. In the fifteenth century, under King Parakramabahu VI (1415–66), Kotte reached the zenith of its power, succeeding for a brief period in extending its control over the entire island including the kingdom of Jaffna and, as we have seen, *Udarata*. But with the death of Parakramabahu VI in 1466 Kotte's authority contracted. Jaffna reverted to Tamil rule and, as noted earlier, *Udarata* too made a successful bid for freedom from its tributary status, emerging as a new kingdom.[7]

At this early stage, the kingdom of Kandy embraced a large area of land. Its heartland was in the central hills but its effective control and influence extended far into the eastern seaboard.[8] In the west and south-west, Kotte remained dominant, its lands reaching deep into the interior. In the north, Kandyan territory extended into the thickly forested and sparsely populated lands controlled by the Vanniyars. Beyond the Vanniyars' land lay the kingdom of Jaffna, again ruled by a Tamil dynasty.

This was the state in which the Portuguese found the island when they arrived there in the early sixteenth century.

THE ADVENT OF THE EUROPEANS

The arrival of the Portuguese in the Indian Ocean in the late fifteenth century opened an era of European commercial and political expansion in Asia. The Portuguese, and the European nations that followed them, entered the complex systems of indigenous political, commercial, and military networks, creating tensions and conflicts and altering these networks in the process. Sri Lanka too was not spared the change and turbulence.

European commercial expansion into Sri Lanka began in the early sixteenth century. In 1505 Dom Laurenco de Almeida landed in Colombo *en route* to intercepting a Muslim fleet and established contact with the local ruler, the king of Kotte.[9] This first contact resulted in an agreement by the Kotte king to supply a substantial quantity of cinnamon to the Portuguese. For several years after this the Portuguese made annual trips to the Colombo port to collect their cinnamon but in 1518 they went a step further and obtained from Kotte the permission to establish a fort in Colombo.[10] The fort was soon dismantled in 1524 after the authorities in Goa deemed it unnecessary but the Portuguese continued to maintain a foothold in Colombo through their trade.

This was the beginning of European commercial and military presence in Sri Lanka but not the beginning of the 'European' frontier on the island. That emerges only towards the end of the century when the Portuguese began to extend control over territory in south-west Sri Lanka. The stage was set by the bloody overthrow of the Kotte king, Vijayabahu, in 1521 by his three sons. This event, known as *Vijayaba Kollaya* or the sacking of Vijayabahu led to the division of the kingdom of Kotte between the three brothers. The eldest son, Buvanekhabahu, became the paramount ruler reigning at the capital Kotte while Mayadunne and Dewarajasinha were placed in control of the peripheral areas.[11] But this division of the spoils settled nothing; it only prepared the ground for a monumental struggle between the two brothers to gain the upper hand in the south-western region of Sri Lanka.

The Portuguese came to play a major role in this struggle as allies of Buvanekhabahu who requested their aid. To Buvanekhabahu, the apparent military and naval might of the Portuguese was just the antidote for his brother's aggression. For their part, the Portuguese saw, in an alliance with the Kotte ruler, an opportunity to consolidate their position in Colombo. Since their arrival in the port, they had not had an easy relationship with the local population that comprised a large number of Muslim traders with links to the Mappilla Muslims in Kerala. The Mappillas were a thorn in the side of Portuguese commercial interests on that coast and were proving to be troublesome in Colombo also. In 1518, they had staged localized armed resistance to the Portuguese in Colombo and then in 1519, had gone so far as to persuade the Kotte ruler, Vijayabahu, to lay siege to the fort.[12] The siege failed but it clearly showed the Portuguese the obstacles they faced in Colombo. So when Buvanekhabahu sought their aid to face Mayadunne's challenge they saw in it a valuable opportunity to further strengthen their position.

As the Portuguese came to Buvanekhabahu's aid, Mayadunne turned to the Samudri of Calicut—an inveterate enemy of the Portuguese and the patron of the Mappilla Muslims. The struggle between the two brothers and their foreign allies continued intermittently until 1539 when the Portuguese defeated Mayadunne and forced him to hand over the Malabari captains.[13] This ended the Sitawaka–Calicut alliance but not the Sitawaka–Kotte conflict. Within a few years of the Malabaris' betrayal, Mayadunne was back threatening his brother's kingdom. Kotte came under ferocious assault and, in 1565, the attacks forced Buvanekhabahu's grandson and successor, Dharmapala, to abandon the city and take refuge with the Portuguese in Colombo. Mayadunne promptly annexed the devastated Kotte.[14]

With the abandonment of Kotte, the power of Sitawaka reached new heights. But an equally significant outcome of these events was the rise of Portuguese influence in the island's politics. The successful alliance between Buvanekhabahu and the Portuguese paved the way for the latter's entry into the network of local alliances as a major player. This status was largely due to the military contribution of the Portuguese who bore a major share of the battles against the Malabaris. This status continued to grow in the years that followed with Mayadunne's repeated attempts to dominate Kotte, which made the latter continue to depend on the Portuguese. Dharmapala's retreat to Colombo obliterated any pretensions the Kotte ruler had to independence from the Portuguese and raised the latter from being the foreign power behind a local power into a major local power. Their growing influence in Kotte politics also led to a gradual build-up of Portuguese troops in Colombo and Kotte. Only a few dozen Portuguese soldiers had battled against Mayadunne and the Malabaris in the 1530s; but by the early 1550s there were several hundred supporting the beleaguered king of Kotte. In 1554 they also rebuilt their fort in Colombo on a larger scale.[15]

Sitawaka's annexation of Kotte and the emergence of the Portuguese as a major power turned the conflict into one that was directly between the Portuguese and Sitawaka. The contest was intense and bloody and turned the south-west region of Sri

Lanka into a flaming, ravaged country.[16] Sitawaka, increasingly under the influence of Mayadunne's warlike son, Rajasinha, turned its attention to bringing Colombo under control. With the ascendance of Rajasinha to the Sitawaka throne following Mayadunne's abdication in 1578, Colombo suffered the young king's fury, surviving with great difficulty two major sieges in 1579 and 1588–89.[17]

The struggle between Sitawaka and the Portuguese finally ended in 1593 when Rajasinha died from an infected wound. His death removed the most virulent enemy the Portuguese had known in Sri Lanka since their arrival in the island. It also marked the demise of Sitawaka. With Rajasinha dead, Sitawaka experienced a power vacuum that was hard to fill. A brief succession struggle further weakened the kingdom and paved the way for the Portuguese to take control.

Thus, finally, the Portuguese emerged as the only real power in the south-west part of Sri Lanka, acquiring the mantle of the Kotte kings. During the struggle with Sitawaka they had also extended their influence over the northern kingdom. The Portuguese had built a fort on the island of Mannar in 1560 to control the pearl fishery and protect converts to Christianity among the fisherfolk.[18] In 1591, the Portuguese also succeeded in forcing the Jaffna rulers to accept their overlordship. Their power was seriously challenged only in one quarter—in the kingdom of Senkadagala.

KANDY, SITAWAKA, AND THE PORTUGUESE 1521–1593

What was Kandy's place in all the struggles between Sitawaka and Kotte? Ever since breaking free from Kotte's control Kandy had not had an easy relationship with Kotte. Naturally, the Kandyan ruler was more than happy to see Kotte destabilized by internal turmoil, and to this end he provided active support to the three brothers in their struggle against Vijayabahu. The outbreak of the struggle between Sitawaka and Kotte also meant that Kandy could have some respite from their expansionist designs. But it also signified that when the two were not fighting, Kandy was in danger of drawing their attention as a potential prize. Thus, when the two brothers were at peace in 1545, Mayadunne threatened to march on Kandy, which was only averted by the payment of a huge bribe by the Kandyan ruler to Mayadunne. Then, after taking over the Kotte lands in 1565, Sitawaka again turned to Kandy, Rajasinha making an attack on the highlands in 1574. The attack failed but, undeterred, Rajasinha struck again in 1582 with a bigger force and succeeded in forcing Kandy into submission.

The threat from Sitawaka also brought Kandy into contact with the Portuguese. The first Kandyan–Portuguese contact was far from hostile. The pressure from Sitawaka made Kandy look for allies and who else was around but the Portuguese who seemed to be providing good support to Kotte? As early as 1542 the king invited the Portuguese to establish a factory in Kandy. A small Portuguese party arrived in Kandy but nothing came out of the mission due to internal problems in Kandy. Four years later the Kandyan king again sought the help of the Portuguese against Mayadunne who was again spoiling for a fight but before Portuguese help arrived, the Kandyan king had made his peace with the Sitawaka ruler. But within a year Mayadunne was again making threatening noises and the king of Kandy was back on his knees before the Portuguese. However, the 100 Portuguese soldiers sent in aid of Kandy found that the Kandyan king wanted them to conquer Sitawaka for him! Disagreement over the issue led to the Kandyans gathering their forces and fearing a terrible fate, the Portuguese hurried back to Colombo.[19]

This rupture with the Portuguese led to the first ever European assault in force on Kandy. To avenge the insult to their expeditionary force, the Portuguese sent a much bigger force of several hundred Portuguese supported by Kotte troops to Kandy in 1550. But just a few miles from Kandy, they were assailed by the Kandyan forces and forced to beat a hasty retreat, losing 200 men and all their baggage.[20] This was the first real military victory obtained by Kandy over a European foe.

The rupture, however, was not permanent. The Kandyan king had to seek Portuguese help again when Rajasinha attacked in 1574. A small force of Portuguese arrived in Kandy to thwart the invader. Then, when Kandy finally succumbed to Rajasinha, the Kandyan king, Karaliyadde Bandara, took refuge with the

Portuguese in Mannar. But Kandy did not remain under Sitawaka for long. Rebellious Kandyans soon threatened Sitawaka's hold on the highlands and capitalizing on that the Portuguese took Kandy in 1592 and installed Yamasinghe Bandara, the heir to the Kandyan throne, in Kandy. The Portuguese sought to rule Kandy through Yamasinghe but their plans were dealt a severe blow when the young prince died in the following year. The power vacuum was filled by Konappu Bandara, a Sinhalese nobleman who commanded the Portuguese expedition to Kandy. Konappu Bandara, brought up by the Portuguese and baptized as Don Juan of Austria, quickly turned against his Portuguese mentors, renounced Catholicism, and established himself in Kandy in 1593 as Vimala Dharma Surya I. Kandy was free again.

Kandy's new-found freedom was given great significance by events unfolding in the low country where, as noted earlier, the Portuguese had consolidated their power by bringing Sitawaka under control. This, and the establishment of a puppet regime in the north, made Kandy the only kingdom on the island outside the influence of a European power. This status was enhanced shortly after Vimala Dharma Surya's accession. The Portuguese, stung by Konappu Bandara's affront to their prestige, launched a major expedition against Kandy in the following year under Captain-General Pedro Lopes de Souza. De Souza's main objective was to install Karaliyadde's daughter, Kusumasana Devi, now baptized as Dona Catherina, on the Kandyan throne. De Souza entered a deserted Kandy and placed the princess on the throne but the desertion of the majority of the Sinhalese auxiliaries that marched with the Portuguese soldiers and increasing Kandyan resistance in the countryside forced him to retreat with the newly-crowned queen. On the way, the Kandyans struck, killing or capturing hundreds of Portuguese soldiers. Among the killed was de Souza and among the prisoners was the teenage queen of Kandy, Dona Catherina.

The defeat of de Souza's expedition and the capture of Dona Catherina marked the emergence of Kandy as the centre of indigenous resistance to European dominance. Konappu Bandara had won Kandy with the sword. He and his successors were to have frequent resort to the sword to keep Kandy free of European dominance.

KANDY *VS.* THE EUROPEANS 1594–1818

The establishment of direct Portuguese rule in Kotte and the survival of Kandy as an independent kingdom in the central highlands set-up a European–Kandyan frontier that was to play a crucial role in determining the status of European power in Sri Lanka. For the next few decades following de Souza's defeat, the Portuguese sought to consolidate and expand their power over the interior and the coastal areas of the island. Their main thrust in the interior was in the south-west of the island, mainly the lands of the former kingdoms of Kotte and Sitawaka. At the height of their power, in the early seventeenth century, this area extended right up to within a few miles of Kandy. The Portuguese also made gains elsewhere on the island. In 1619, direct Portuguese rule was finally established over Jaffna which was placed under a Captain-Major and in the 1620s, the Portuguese also established themselves at Trincomalee and Batticaloa on the east coast of the island. All this territory was ruled from Colombo, where the Portuguese had their main fortress and trading centre. The Captain-General who came to head the government in Sri Lanka had his residence in Malvana on the *Kelani* river while numerous fortified posts were established in strategic places in the interior.

The Portuguese control over the south-west and the coast had a commercial as well as a military significance. The south-west of the island was rich in the coveted commodity of cinnamon and was also more densely populated than other parts. Therefore control over this area ensured a steady supply of a valued commodity as well as large land revenues. The defeat in 1594 had not ended Portuguese hopes of conquering the hills; it only made them prepare for the conquest more systematically. Controlling the interior in western Sri Lanka with its back to the port and fort of Colombo was very important in this regard. The numerous fortified posts in the interior were meant as a means of strangling the highland kingdom. In 1611, the Portuguese extended their reach as far as the pass and also established a large post at Menikkadawara within striking distance from Kandy. This was meant to act as a launching pad for raids and invasions into Kandy.[21] At the same time, control over the coast, especially the ports on the east coast, was aimed at preventing Kandy from obtaining foreign aid.

For several decades after De Souza's defeat in 1594 the Portuguese and Kandy waged a bloody struggle across the frontier. Within a few years after De Souza's defeat the Portuguese, under the new Captain-General Dom Janome de Assessed, launched a fresh offensive to take Kanday. It failed, with Azevedo's force narrowly escaping annihilation. This reverse was a watershed in the Portuguese policy towards the conquest of Kandy. Thereafter, the Portuguese would invade Kandy only to burn and ravage rather than to conquer and occupy. Accordingly, from 1605 until 1638, Kandy was subjected to numerous raids, which killed its people and destroyed its crops. The destruction was most systematic under Azevedo and his immediate successors who launched raid after devastating raid into Kandyan lands. Their aim was to burn, kill, and plunder until the kingdom submitted. As Azevedo explained to his successor, it was with 'this regime of war that kingdom is to be bled to death, until it is entirely depopulated and laid waste, and in such manner that life of no male of fourteen years or above is spared'.[22] It was total war in contemporary terms.

Needless to say, Kandy suffered terribly from these ravages. But it was also not an abject victim in this war. The kingdom hit back frequently and the blows sometimes fell hard. As noted in the Introduction, two more Portuguese armies were completely destroyed. In 1630, an army under Captain-General Constantine de Sa was trapped in the valleys of Uva and wiped out while, in 1638, another under Diogo de Mello was annihilated on the banks of the Mahaveli river that skirts the Kandyan capital. The Kandyans also took the battle to the Portuguese. Their territories in the south and the west were frequently raided, most notably in the wake of the Portuguese reverses in 1603 and 1630 when many of the Portuguese forts in the interior were taken. Colombo itself was besieged in 1630.[23]

However, it must also be noted that the contest was not only between the Portuguese and the Kandyan kingdom at this time. True, Kandy was the main indigenous challenger to Portuguese authority but there were also numerous local chiefs who rose against Portuguese rule. Many of them took advantage of Portuguese defeats by the Kandyans in 1603 and 1630 to rise against the Portuguese. The Kandyans were also not loath to throw in their lot with these rebels on many occasions, recognizing the potential their uprisings had for destabilizing Portuguese power.[24] But sometimes, such revolts could also turn into a campaign against both Kandy and the Portuguese. This is what happened in 1617 when a major revolt broke out in the provinces of Sabaragamuwa and Seven Korales. The revolt turned into a grave threat for both Kandy and the Portuguese, with the threat being so serious that the two arch enemies entered into a treaty to deal with the 'common enemy'![25] while the treaty recognized the Kandyan king's rule in the highlands, it also reduced Kandy to a degree of submission as the king agreed to pay the Portuguese an annual tribute of two elephants and have no dealings with any enemies of Portugal.[26] The rebels were eventually defeated by the Portuguese who were now freed from fighting Kandy by the treaty. But the accord between the Portuguese and the Kandyans was shortlived. Within a few years hostilities broke out again and Kandy was once more subjected to Portuguese raids.

Portuguese struggles with Kandy and the local chiefs showed how flimsy the European control over the interior was, in spite of all the devastation they caused. A massive Kandyan invasion or a widespread uprising could very quickly confine the Portuguese to their forts. It is fair to say that for the Portuguese the frontier with their enemies really began outside their coastal strongholds and outposts in the interior and expanded with their military operations and retracted when Kandy counter-attacked. On occasion, the outposts themselves had to be evacuated, limiting European power to their coastal fortresses, as it happened in 1630.

Portuguese power on the island ended with the entry of the Dutch into the equation between Kandy and Colombo. The Dutch had entered the Indian Ocean at the beginning of the seventeenth century as commercial and religious rivals of the Portuguese, and Kandy was only too willing to enlist their help against the Portuguese. Kandy made several attempts to engage Dutch assistance in the early years of the century but it was only in 1638 that a treaty could be signed between two parties. According to the treaty, the Dutch agreed to eject the Portuguese from Sri Lanka in return for trading concessions and the expenses of the campaign. The Kandyan–Dutch alliance led to a combined assault on Portuguese possessions on the island. The Kandyans took on the enemy in the interior while the Dutch attacked their coastal strongholds. The coastal forts of Trincomalee and Batticaloa were taken in 1638 and Galle was stormed in 1640. Negombo was taken in the same year but was lost and recaptured in 1644. After a brief truce the war began in earnest in the 1650s and the Portuguese were finally ejected from Colombo in 1656. The last two Portuguese strongholds on the island, Jaffna and Mannar, were taken in 1658 and the Portuguese power in Sri Lanka was finally extinguished.[27]

The Dutch took over the Portuguese coastal possessions against the wishes of the Kandyan king who expected them to be handed over to him. The Dutch interpreted the Kandyan-Dutch treaty in favour of their continuous presence to hold on to the Portuguese possessions. However, the initial Dutch possessions on the island were much smaller than that controlled by the Portuguese. The Dutch held the ports and forts on the northern, western, and southern coasts but little territory in the interior. This, however, changed in 1665 when internal instability in Kandy gave the Dutch the opportunity to expand into the interior. The revolt, led by a noble called Ambanwela Rala, succeeded briefly in forcing the king to flee the capital but the ringleaders' indecisiveness allowed the king to gather support and strike back. Though the revolt was crushed and Rajasinha's authority re-established, the brief upheaval in Kandyan politics tempted the Dutch to extend their sway over a large area in the interior in the south and south-west of the island. They also occupied Trincomalee and Batticaloa and by 1669, strategic look-out posts were also set-up in Panama and Magama in the south-east.[28]

These events led to the first major war between Kandy and the Dutch. In August 1670, Rajasinha hit back and in a re-enactment of the Portuguese response to such offensives, the Dutch power rapidly contracted. The Kandyans took the Dutch fort at Arandora and pushed the Dutch back from many districts in the interior. Forces were also sent against Kottiyar, Batticaloa, and Panama on the east coast. The Dutch counter-attacked and pushed back the Kandyans but were unable to reoccupy all the lands they had previously held. Then, in August 1675, Rajasinha launched another, bigger offensive, again driving out the Dutch from the interior. They succeeded in capturing the Dutch fort at

Bibilegama with 70 Dutch soldiers, 20 Topasses, and 200 lascarins. The Dutch counter-attacked but only succeeded in establishing a precarious hold over a part of the territory they had previously held.[29]

For the next ninety years, the frontier enjoyed a measure of stability. The Dutch held on to their limited gains in the interior in the south and the south-west and the ports in the east. They still had to contend with a hostile Kandyan court that continued to consider them to be intruders. The major point of dispute was the Dutch control of the ports. Dutch possession of these ports placed severe restrictions on the Kandyan economy and external relations. The Kandyan population was self-sufficient in most basic needs but they depended on external trade for items like salt, cloth, and dried fish that were obtained by either barter or purchase. The kingdom also exported a few natural resources of commercial value like elephants, areca nut, and precious stones, which were all royal monopolies. This trade had been traditionally centred on ports like Puttalam on the west coast and Kottiyar on the east coast, but by 1670 all these ports were under European control and the Kandyans dependent on their goodwill to carry on an uninterrupted trade. European control did lead to a flourishing smuggling trade, especially around Halawatha on the west coast and it was never possible to place absolute controls over trade.[30] But smuggling could never compensate for free trade. Moreover, the Kandyan state also used to derive a considerable income from customs dues from the ports.[31] European control completely dried up that revenue. Last but not least, the loss of the ports also threatened to isolate Kandy from external political contact, sealing it off from the world.

Therefore, getting the ports open to Kandyan trade was the main objective of the Kandyans after the war in 1670–5. The main concern for the Dutch was gaining access to the rich cinnamon lands in the interior, which required the king's permission every year. For much of the first half of the eighteenth century, these two issues dominated Kandyan–Dutch relations. The Dutch concentrated on making commercial gains while the Kandyan court's major focus was on getting the ports opened to Kandyan trade. The Dutch kept the Court in good humour with annual presents and flattering behaviour but held on to the ports and their control on trade. The relationship was never easy but there was greater stability on the frontier than existed during the time of the Portuguese and no major wars took place between the two sides for nearly a century. Rather than resort to open war, the Kandyans used other means to put pressure on the Dutch. The favourite Kandyan ploy was to encourage the local population in Dutch controlled territories to defy Dutch authority and to offer sanctuary to those who fell foul of the Dutch authorities. The peasantry in Dutch territories often used this support from Kandy to push their grievances in an aggressive fashion, frequently resorting to open rebellion.[32]

Towards the mid-eighteenth century, the Kandyan demands for a piece of the overseas trade began to grow louder. When a particularly serious rebellion broke out in the south and south-western regions of the island in 1759 they decided to take the fight to the Dutch more aggressively than ever before.[33] In 1761, Kandyan armies descended from the hills to capture Dutch outposts. A number of frontier garrisons succumbed to the onslaught while Matara on the coast had to be abandoned to the rampant Kandyans and their low-country allies. The Dutch hit back in 1762–3, retaking all the lost territory and pushing back the Kandyans. Rebellious and frontier districts were punished with devastating raids while a ban on the importation of dried fish and salt into Kandyan territories was imposed. This was not all. The Dutch also invaded Kandy for the first time. In early 1764, a large Dutch force of 1850 fighting men marched on Kandy from Negombo while a number of other small detachments made incursions into Kandyan territory from several directions. The main force made its way deep into the Seven Korales but was halted by heavy resistance; of the other detachments, one lost its way and was captured and the rest recalled or quickly withdrawn. Undeterred, the Dutch launched another invasion, sending another army of about 1,800 soldiers under Baron Van Eck in April 1765. This time the Dutch entered Kandy and occupied the town for several months while detachments roamed the countryside burning and killing. The occupation came to nothing as the Kandyans chose to resist rather than succumb and the Dutch were forced to fight a long guerrilla campaign in the heart of the highlands. Fearing for the safety of the expeditionary force, the Dutch also despatched a small relief force under Major Medeler in September 1765, but by the time Medeler reached the outskirts of Kandy, the Dutch had already evacuated their garrison and had to fall back on Colombo. Eventually, both the main force and Medeler's column arrived safely in the low country but the conquest of Kandy had again failed.[34]

Hostilities continued in various parts of the frontier, with the Kandyans attempting forays into the Dutch lands. The Dutch launched a fresh invasion in the following year but by then, the Kandyan court was ready to negotiate. The negotiations left the Kandyan sovereignty over the hills intact but the court had to cede the control of the entire coastline to the Dutch East India Company. The treaty of 1766 established a new European frontier in Sri Lanka: one that truly encircled Kandyan territory. It made Kandy a virtual prisoner of the Dutch but still far from a conquered state.[35] However, there was no further conflict despite the occasional sabre rattling by the Kandyans.[36]

The British took over the Dutch territories in Sri Lanka in 1795. The British, already well established in India, had shown an interest in cultivating ties with Kandy since the 1760s. The earliest contact was made in 1762 when a British embassy requested a harbour and a monopoly of the cinnamon trade on the island. The negotiations came to nothing largely due to the king's insistence on armed British assistance against the Dutch. The British did not wish to commit themselves to a war against a country they were at peace with. Another embassy in 1782 proposed an offensive and defensive alliance but was rejected by the king. The occasion for the next treaty was brought up by the aftermath of the French Revolution. In 1795 when Holland allied itself with revolutionary France, the Stadtholder fled to Britain and ordered the Dutch in Sri Lanka to admit British troops into their forts. Despite some resistance, caused by the existence of elements of Jacobite sympathizers within Dutch ranks, the Dutch possessions in Sri Lanka were taken over by the British by February 1796.[37] While the British troops proceeded with their campaign in Sri Lanka, Madras sent an embassy to Kandy to draw up a treaty. It offered the Kandyan king limited trade concessions and protection in return for a cinnamon monopoly and the right to build forts and trading posts. The treaty ran into difficulties due to the Indian government's insistence on it being ratified by London and the king's insistence on his not signing any revised treaty.[38]

When the British took over the Dutch possessions in Sri Lanka in 1795–6, Kandyan independence became a British problem. The existence of an independent kingdom in the centre of the island, however subdued it may be, was a constant irritant to the British government in the lowlands, especially when that kingdom continued to see the Europeans as intruders. The British decided to end the problem once and for all and, in 1803, sent a military expedition of nearly 3,400 troops to install a puppet regime in Kandy. The British entered Kandy and placed their protégé, Muttusami, on the Kandyan throne but their plans ended in disaster. A force of about 1,000 men, left in Kandy to prop up the new regime, became holed up in the mountains and plagued by illness and Kandyan attacks. An attempt to negotiate with the Kandyan court resulted in the surviving British troops being taken prisoner, the majority of whom were massacred. True to form, the Kandyans followed their success with an assault on British possessions in the lowlands. In a repetition of Portuguese and Dutch behaviour the British abandoned some of their outposts, in many places the frontier contracting again up to the walls of the British forts.[39] The invasion was beaten back, with the main Kandyan army comprehensively defeated at Hanwella on the Kandyan–British frontier. Like the Portuguese and the Dutch before them, the British launched retaliatory raids on Kandyan territories. The countryside was mercilessly ravaged while all trade across the frontier was suspended. Another British expedition was also planned for the following year but was later cancelled at the last minute. However, one detachment of about 300 soldiers under Major Arthur Johnstone that did not receive the order of cancellation in time and marched into Kandy. Realizing their error, they fell back on Trincomalee on the east coast in the face of heavy Kandyan attacks.

The British did not attempt to annex Kandy again until 1815, and when they did, Kandy offered no resistance. The king had antagonized all his powerful nobles who were only too willing to see his back. In 1814, a powerful Kandyan noble, Ehelepola, revolted against the king and defected to the British. The British were quick to take advantage of this situation and, in February 1815, despatched two expeditionary forces into the hills. The fleeing king was captured with the help of his estranged nobles and banished to Vellore fort in south India. On 2 March 1815, the

Kandyan nobles signed the Kandyan Convention, handing over the sovereignty of the Kandyan kingdom to the British Crown.[40] Thus ended 221 years of Kandyan independence.

However, this 'conquest' of Kandy was seriously challenged within three years. In late 1817, a revolt occurred in the province of Uva in the east in protest against the appointment of a Moorish man to an office hitherto held by a Kandyan noble. The revolt soon spread to other provinces and assumed the form of an uprising to remove the British from the highlands. A new 'king' was brought forth and coronated. The rebellion, however, was crushed within a year by the British who again employed ruthless methods. The countryside was devastated 'the dwellings of the inhabitants were burnt, their fruit trees cut down, and the country was scoured in every direction by small detachments, who were authorised to put to death all who made opposition or were found with arms in their hands'.[41] By late 1818, all the rebel leaders were captured and either executed or banished.[42] Kandyan resistance was over; the frontier had finally ceased to exist.

To recapitulate, the establishment of direct Portuguese authority over the kingdom of Kotte and the survival of Kandy brought into being a European–Kandyan frontier in Sri Lanka. Except in the south-west region of the island, European power was limited to their coastal strongholds. In the south-west, the Europeans exercised a measure of control over the interior where rich cinnamon lands lay. Across this frontier in the south-west—and occasionally elsewhere as well—Kandy and the Europeans clashed in an attempt to gain advantage over each other. The Kandyans often pushed back the Europeans from the interior, limiting their control to their strongholds. Sometimes, the European strongholds in the interior had to be evacuated and the frontier contracted right up to the coast. For their part the Europeans raided and invaded Kandyan territory, devastating the land and sometimes occupying the interior. An economic blockade was also maintained to cripple the Kandyans' livelihood. However, neither side succeeded in delivering a decisive blow until internal dissension allowed the British to march in without opposition in 1815. Armed resistance to this occupation was brutally crushed in 1818, consolidating European authority over the territory.

NOTES

1. *Culavamsa, being the more recent part of the Mahavamsa*, trs. into German by Wilhelm Geiger, trs. from German into English by C. Mabel Rickmers, London: Pali Text Society, 1973, p. 287, Ch. 70, verses 3–5.
2. G.P.V. Somaratne, *Political History of the Kingdom of Kotte*, Colombo: Somaratne, 1975, p. 193.
3. Ibid., p. 193; A.S. Hettiarachchi, 'Mahanuwara Rajaparapura', *JRAS(CB)*, New Series, vol. 12, 1968, pp. 123–4.
4. Burton Stein, *Peasant State and Society in Medieval South India*, Delhi: Oxford University Press, 1980, p. 5.
5. As explained by H.L. Seneviratne: 'The model of political organization of the traditional order was what Tambiah has called "galactic". Here the units are not centralized, but centre oriented. They enjoyed substantial autonomy. Centralization was more symbolic than real, with the king styling himself as universal emperor, receiving ritual homage from the units which in reality managed their own affairs'. H.L. Seneviratne, 'The Buddhist Historiographical Tradition in Sri Lanka', unpublished paper, quoted in David Little, *Sri Lanka: The Invention of Enmity*, Washington, D.C.: United States Institute of Peace, 1994, pp. 127–8. Also Elizabeth Nissan and R.L. Stirrat, 'The Generation of Communal Identities', Jonathan Spencer (ed.), *Sri Lanka: History and the Roots of Conflict*, London: Routledge, 1990, p. 25, K.M. De Silva, *History of Sri Lanka*, London: C. Hurst & Co., 1981, p. 23.
6. On the southward retreat of Sinhala rule see K. Indrapala (ed.), *The Collapse of the Rajarata Civilization and the Drift to the Southwest: A Symposium*, Peradeniya: University of Ceylon, 1971.
7. Somaratne, *Political History*, pp. 151–3, 193.
8. Hettiarachchi, 'Mahanuwara Rajaparapura', p. 124.
9. Somaratne, *Political History*, p. 204.
10. Fernao de Queyroz, *The Temporal and Spiritual Conquest of Ceylon*, trs. S.G. Perera, Colombo: Govt. Printers, 1930, p. 188.
11. C.R. de Silva, 'The Rise and Fall of the Kingdom of Sitawaka 1521–1593', *CJHSS*, New Series, vol. 7, January–June 1977, p. 3.
12. Joao de Barros and Diego do Couto, 'The History of Ceylon from the earliest times to AD 1600', trs. and ed. Donald Ferguson, *JRAS (CB)*, vol. 20, no. 60, 1908, pp. 49–50. Queyroz, *The Temporal and Spiritual Conquest*, pp. 199–200.
13. Ibid., pp. 90–107.
14. Ibid., pp. 240–2.
15. Ibid., p. 154.
16. Much of the fighting during this period was restricted to the present Colombo district, a small area to play host to intense fighting and the attendant devastation.

17. Barros and Couto, 'History of Ceylon', pp. 288–354.
18. Between 1536 and 1544 the Portuguese had converted a considerable number of fishermen from the paravar caste on the so-called fishery coast in south India and the north-west coast of Sri Lanka. These were under constant threat from their Hindu overlords. C.R. de Silva, *Sri Lanka: A History*, Delhi: Vikas Publishing House, 1987, pp. 116–17. Also P.E. Pieris, *Ceylon: The Portuguese Era*, vol. 1, p. 175 and Jeyaseela Stephen, *Portuguese in the Tamil Coast: Historical Explorations in Commerce and Culture*, Pondicherry: Navajothi, 1998, pp. 75–6. On the Portuguese reduction of Jaffna, see T.B.H., Abeysinghe, *Jaffna under the Portuguese*, Colombo: Lake House, 1986, pp. 1–3.
19. T.B.H. Abeysinghe, 'The Politics of Survival: Aspects of Kandyan External Relations in the Mid-Sixteenth Century', *JRAS(SLB)*, vol. 17, 1973, pp. 12–19.
20. Barros and Couto, 'History of Ceylon', pp. 140–2.
21. Abeysinghe, *Portuguese Rule in Ceylon*, pp. 28–31.
22. T.B.H Abeysinghe (trs. and ed.), *A Study of Portuguese Regimentos on Sri Lanka at the Goa Archives*, Colombo: Dept. of National Archives, 1974, p. 49.
23. C.R. de Silva, *The Portuguese in Ceylon 1617-1638*, Colombo: H.W. Cave & Co., 1972, pp. 111–33.
24. Abeysinghe, *Portuguese Rule in Ceylon*, pp. 24–5.
25. The uprisings put the Portuguese on the back foot, making their hold on many parts of the west and the south-west precarious. The Kandyan king initially supported the rebels but was soon forced to reconsider his position when the leader of the rebellion in the Seven Korales, Nikapitiye Bandara, claimed royal descent from Rajasinha I. Faced by a potential competitor to his position, Senerath now decided to withdraw support from the rebels and sought an alliiance with the Portuguese. Left to their own devices, the rebels were doomed and after much fighting and devastation of land and property, especially in the Seven Korales, the Portuguese reasserted their control in the lowlands. De Silva, *The Portuguese in Ceylon*, pp. 22–30.
26. Portuguese attempts to lay claim to Batticaloa and have Balana fort—which the Kandyans had recaptured in 1617—returned to them were successfully resisted by the Kandyans. De Silva, *The Portuguese in Ceylon*, pp. 32–5.
27. For a comprehensive description of these events, see K.W. Goonewardene, *The Foundation of Dutch Power in Ceylon 1638–1658*, Amsterdam: Djambatan, 1958.
28. The Dutch had captured Kalpitiya on the west coast in 1659. Sinnappah Arasaratnam, 'Ceylon in the Indian Ocean Trade: 1500–1800', in A. Das Gupta and M.N. Pearson (eds.), *India and the Indian Ocean 1500–1800*, Calcutta: Oxford University Press, 1989, pp. 233–4. See also W. van

Damast Limberger, 'A Short History of the Principal Events that Occurred in the Island of Ceylon, Since the Arrival of the First Netherlanders in the Year 1602, and Afterwards, From the Establishment of the "Honourable Company" in the Same Island till the Year 1757', ed. P.A. Leupe, trs. F.H. de Vos, *JRAS(CB)*, vol. 11, no. 38, 1889, pp. 64–6.

29. Sinnappah Arasaratnam, *Dutch Power in Ceylon*, Amsterdam: Djambatan, 1958, pp. 55–72; Limberger, 'A Short History', p. 69.
30. De Silva, *The Portuguese in Ceylon*, p. 135.
31. Lorna Srimathie Dewaraja, 'Revenues of the Kings of Kandy', *JRAS(CB)*, New Series, vol. 16, 1972, p. 21.
32. S. Arasaratnam, 'Vimala Dharma Surya II (1687–1707) and His Relations with the Dutch', *CJHSS*, vol. 6, no. 1, 1963, pp. 59–70, T.B.H. Abeysinghe, 'Embassies as Instruments of Diplomacy in Sri Lanka in the First Half of the Eighteenth Century' *JRAS(SLB)*, vol. 30, 1985–6, pp. 1–40; D.A. Kotelawela, 'The Dutch in Ceylon: 1743–1766', Ph.D. thesis, University of London, 1968, p. 32; Linberger, 'A Short history', pp. 125–37.
33. Rebellion had started in mid-1757 in some of the southern Korales but had died down by the middle of the following year. But it flared up again in June 1759. Later in the same year the Siyane, Hapitigam, and Alutkuru Korales in the west also boiled over. Kotelawela, 'The Dutch in Ceylon', pp. 190–220.
34. On later narratives and analyses of this war see, W. Zwier, *Het Verdraag van 1766 Tusschen de O.I. Compagnie en de Vorst Van Kandi,* Amsterdam: H.J. Paris, 1927, pp. 22–87, Kotelawela, 'The Dutch in Ceylon', pp.192–282; Raven Hart, *Dutch Wars with Kandy*, pp. 3–18; E. Reimers, 'Old Matara and the Rebellion of 1760-61', *JDBUC*, vol. 15, no. 1, July 1925, pp. 7–14; vol. 15, no. 2, Oct. 1925, pp. 59–64; vol. 15, no. 3, Jan. 1926, pp. 88–95; J.H.O. Paulusz, 'The Outbreak of the Kandyan Dutch War of 1761 and the Great Rebellion: Secret Minutes of the Dutch Political Council', *JRAS(CB),* New Series, vol. 3, 1953, pp. 28–55.
35. On the treaty between the Dutch and the Kandyans in 1766, see Kotelawela, 'The Dutch in Ceylon'; Zwier, *Het Verdraag*, pp. 88–93.
36. The Kandyans continued to demand a share in trade and refused to recognize the treaty of 1766. V. Kanpathipillai, 'Dutch Rule in Maritime Ceylon 1766–1796', Ph.D. thesis, University of London, 1969, pp. 108–216.
37. Lennox A. Mills, *The Advent of the British to Ceylon*, London: Frank Cass, 1964, pp. 8–15; Colvin R. De Silva, *Ceylon under the British Occupation 1795–1833*, 2 vols, New Delhi: Navrang, 1995, vol. 1, pp. 21–44; George Nypels, *Hoe Nederland Ceilon Verloor*, S'gravenhage: Martinus Nijhoff, 1908, pp. 38–95.
38. Mills, *The Advent*, pp. 1–7; Colvin R. de Silva, *Ceylon*, vol. 1, pp. 57–70.

39. On this Kandyan war, see James Cordiner, *Description of Ceylon containing an Account of the Country, Inhabitants and Natural Productions with a Narrative of a Tour around the Island in 1800, the Campaign in Kandy in 1803 and a Journey to Ramisseram in 1804*, 2 vols., Delhi: Navrang, 1983; rpt. of 1807 edn., vol. 2, pp. 155–259.
40. Colvin R. de Silva, *Ceylon*, vol. 1, pp. 129–67; Mills, *The Advent*, pp. 139–67.
41. John Davy, *An Account of the Interior of Ceylon and of its Inhabitants with Travels in that Island*, Dehiwela, Sri Lanka:Tisara Publishers, 1969, rpt. of 1821 edn., p. 246.
42. For details of the rebellion and related events see P.E. Pieris, *Sinhale and the Patriots*, Delhi: Navrang, 1995; rpt. of 1950 edn.; R.L. Brohier, *The Golden Age of Military Adventure in Ceylon: An Account of the Uva Rebellion 1817–1818*, Colombo: Plate Ltd., 1933; and Davy, *An Account*, pp. 244–8.

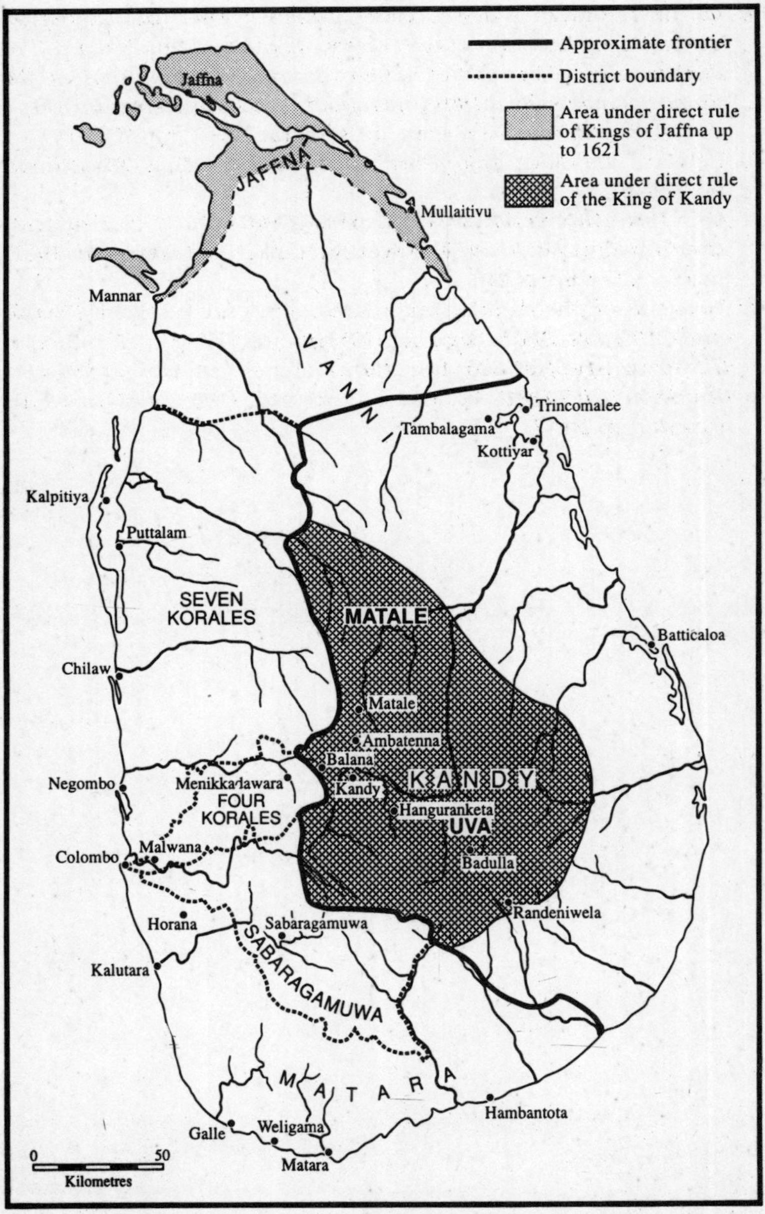

Map 1: The Portuguese in Sri Lanka in the Seventeenth Century

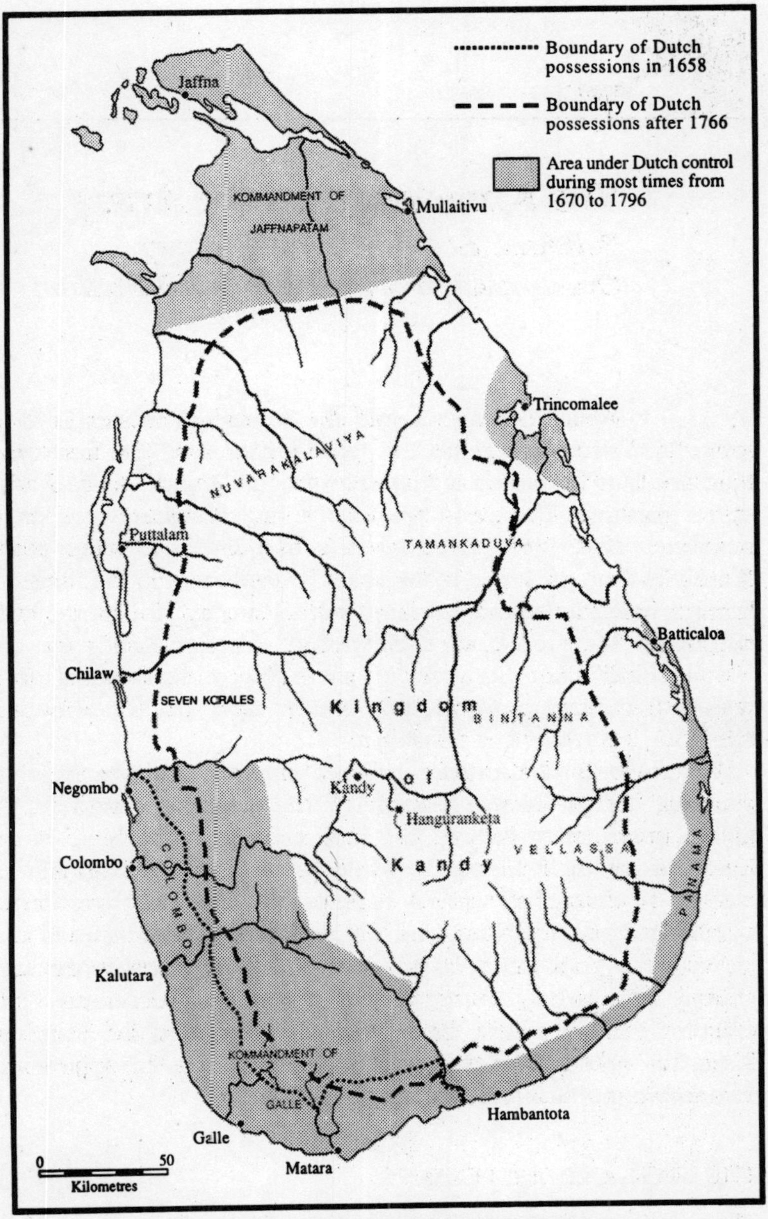

Map 2: Sri Lanka in the Eighteenth Century

TWO

The Kingdom and the Army

Political, Economic and Military Organization of the Kandyan Kingdom

What resources could the Kandyans muster in their long, hard struggle against European expansion? The first thing that needs to be noted is that even though Kandy clashed with three maritime European powers, it had absolutely no naval resources of its own. Even when it had access to some ports, Kandy had no presence in the sea. The trade was in the hands of foreign merchants and Muslims settled around the ports, with whom the Kandyans traded. Therefore, although Kandy was not always landlocked, its activities were always land-based. So it was with military power. Kandy had no navy and the army was the main instrument of resistance.

To understand Kandyan military organization we need to examine the political economy of the Kandyan kingdom. To give a preliminary outline, the king reigned at the head of the Kandyan political hierarchy while below him were numerous nobles in charge of various aspects of central and provincial administration. The king and the aristocracy administered and governed a population of peasants, living by subsistence agriculture and largely untouched by a monetary economy. This chapter examines how the relationship between the Kandyan king, his nobles, and the peasants operated in the spheres of economic, political, and military organization.

THE STATE AND THE PEASANT

The process of Kandyan government basically amounted to ensuring a steady supply of revenue and keeping order in the country—not much different from the objectives of many governments, past and present. The political economy of the kingdom was based on a system of property relations, enmeshed by a complex web of obligations and privileges. The ideological framework for this was provided by the concept of kingship. Theoretically, the king was divine.[1] He was the owner of all land and as such had absolute command over the inhabitants of that land. In practice however, this meant that the king had the right to extract the services of his subjects—and tenants—and a portion of what they produced. In return, the people were given a measure of control over areas of land. The duty of the people based on this relationship was called *rajakariya* or 'king's service'.[2]

The services and produce extracted from the peasantry depended on the economy of the Kandyan territories. Rice was the staple diet while *chena* or slash and burn cultivation and garden cultivation provided a number of dry grains like *kurakkan* and *meneri* and vegetables. These provided the basic necessities for the people. As rice was the staple food, Kandyan villages had an extent of paddy land which the peasantry worked. The paddy land had its appurtenance, which included gardens and forestland which could be cleared for *chena* cultivation. The paddy land and the highland were divided among the families in the village.

The produce of their paddy land and highland made the Kandyan peasant remarkably self-sufficient. As noted earlier, their main requirements from outside their villages were confined to cloth and salt and, sometimes, dried fish. The Kandyan peasant's trading activities were largely limited to obtaining these essentials which were exchanged for paddy and areca nuts. Itinerant Muslim traders operating from the coastal areas acted as middlemen in this exchange of goods while a brisk trade between the ports of south India and the Sri Lankan coast ensured the supply of cloth and other articles.[3] There was little circulation of money; barter seems to have been the chief method of economic transaction.[4]

The state obtained the fruits of the peasant labour in several ways. A number of fertile and productive villages in the kingdom were set apart as *gabdagam* or store villages. The inhabitants of these villages cultivated a portion of the paddy land called *muttettuva* for the king's storehouse. Apart from this the paddy land in most Kandyan villages was assessed in units of pingo loads or *kat* and the landholders were required to pay the required amount to the royal store annually. For example, in the province of 4 Korales a sowing extent of 3 amunams equalled one pingo load and villages having more than this extent were required to pay a pingo load annually. This was a collective responsibility of the villagers. In the case of smaller fields, the fields from several villages were grouped together to form one pingo.[5]

However, not everybody was required to pay *kada*. Paddy fields in villages granted to Buddhist and Hindu temples were exempt from the *kada* payment. The people who performed various services were also free from this duty. These services basically amounted to those required by a subsistence economy, and included the services of potters making pottery and iron-smiths and other craftsmen producing and mending tools, etc. They belonged to separate castes associated with these services. In return for their land they were required to serve the king regularly in Kandy, producing whatever pottery was needed in the king's kitchen and attending to any construction work that was required in the palace.[6] To regulate these services, the castes were organized into *baddas* or departments. Thus, the *badahela badda* comprised potters, the *Kottal badda* all the craftsmen in the kingdom, and the *Kinnara badda* all the weavers. However, not all *baddas* were strictly based on caste. For instance, the *Madige badda* comprised both karava or fisher caste people and Muslims settled within Kandyan territory who were not a part of the caste system. The task of the *Madige badda* was to supply dried fish to the palace and to provide pack cattle for transporting the king's goods. They also purchased arecanut from the villagers and sold them on behalf of the king.[7] Thus the *Madige badda* was a convenient way of mobilizing the services of two different communities—fishers and traders—that worked closely in the pursuit of their livelihoods.

Apart from performing pingo duties and providing all these services attached to the land they held, the peasantry was also obliged to provide certain general services for the state. One was to provide labour for public works. We hear of the last king utilizing this service to construct a lake in Kandy. The other area in which general services were required was in the sphere of military service, which will be discussed later in the chapter.

Given the subsistence economy of the peasantry, the king's

cash revenues were limited. Much of it was derived from trade. As noted earlier, the king had a monopoly over the sale of areca nut, precious stones and elephants while customs duties were levied on ports.[8] The king also received money upon the appointment of officials to their positions, all appointees having to purchase their appointments by paying to the treasury a fixed sum of money. All this revenue depended on the control over or access to at least a few ports; even the money paid for appointments was largely realized by selling the areca nut in the lands of the appointees. When it was possible to maintain control over the ports these sources provided a considerable income for the king. For instance, when Kandy enjoyed access to almost all the ports in the east and west of the island in the first half of the sixteenth century the king had enough monetary resources to offer payment to the Portuguese forces he was soliciting in the 1540s.[9] It was probably in the hope that the ports would revert to his authority that the king agreed to pay the expenses of the Dutch campaign against the Portuguese. But as explained earlier, the Dutch simply took over the Portuguese coastal possessions. And as Kandy's struggles with the Europeans continued, the ports came to be first blockaded and then captured, 'the whole coastline dotted with strategic points of control and inspection'.[10] As a result, the economy contracted and the cash flow into the treasury dwindled, leaving the Kandyan government with little more than the revenue that was extracted in the form of the produce and labour of the peasantry. By the early nineteenth century the cash flow had dried up to such an extent that when the British took over Kandy the last king's annual cash income was calculated at only about 1500 pounds sterling.[11]

THE KING AND HIS RETINUE

The officialdom mentioned earlier organized and administered the system of revenue and services. Here again caste played a major role; the higher officials were all drawn from the upper 'radala' caste. The two Adigars were the chief advisers to the king and signed orders issued in the king's name. They were the main channels of communication between the king and his other chiefs. They were also responsible for the administration of the city of Kandy.[12] There were also numerous palace officials who were entrusted with all aspects of the administration of the palace and the organization of all services within the royal household. Some of them looked after the day-to-day administration of the household and the king's stores. For instance, the Maha Gabada Nilame supervised the delivery of the *kada rajakariya* while the Tappakara Mohandiram and his staff kept the exterior of the palace clean.[13] Others provided personal services that were concerned with the king's individual needs. The Buth Badana Nilame served the king his food at mealtime while the Pen Wadana Nilame poured the water.

A large number of people attended the palace as guards. There were several categories of them. One was called the Atapattu and was under an official called the Atapattu Lekam.[14] The Kodituwakku Nilame was in charge of a small number of people who carried a piece of light artillery called *kodituwakku.* In the late eighteenth century, another branch of palace guards called the Maduwe people came into existence. This department was formed after the Dutch wars in 1761–6 and consisted of a body of young men who served as palace guards on a rotational basis. The *baddas* had their own chiefs who were responsible for mobilizing their services for the state and ensuring a regular supply of their services.[15]

Mention must be made here of a small number of Europeans employed by the king. They were acquired in a number of ways. Many were prisoners. These included prisoners of war as well as 'detainees'—shipwrecks like Robert Knox and members of European missions to Kandy who were detained in the highlands indefinitely. Rajasinha II who showed a keen interest in 'collecting' exotic animals and people was largely responsible for this practice. Among his more distinguihed 'captives' were the Dutch ambassador, Ensign Draak, who was kept in Kandy from 1663 until his death in 1673 and the French ambassador and his retinue sent by Admiral De La Haye in 1672.[16] There were also a considerable number of deserters who left their countrymen for various reasons.[17]

The king appointed Europeans to various posts. Ensign Draak in particular is said to have been a favourite of the king and took up office in the King's administration.[18] According to Knox, the king employed some of the Europeans, organized in two companies, one under a Dutchman and another under a Portuguese, to guard one of his magazines. In the late seventeenth century, a Frenchman named Jean Bloom was appointed to look after the king's horse, while a descendant of a French detainee and a Portuguese woman was raised to the rank of First Adigar by King Narendrasingha (1706–39).[19] Many of the European detainees intermarried with local women and founded lineages that continue in Sri Lanka to this day.

The officials known as the Dissawas had an important role in the Kandyan government. Also drawn from the aristocracy, their main function was to administer the various parts of the kingdom and to regulate the flow of revenue and services to the state. The Kandyan kingdom was divided into a number of provinces districts (rata) and provinces (dissawa). The districts formed the heartland of Kandyan rule—the central highlands—while the provinces were the areas that lay at the periphery of this core area and in most cases bordered on the European controlled areas in the low country. During the reign of the last king of Kandy, there were 9 districts and 12 provinces.[20] The administration of these divisions were headed by the Dissawas or provincial governors. An Adigar always held one or more of these offices so that his duties as Adigar and Dissawa overlapped. The Dissawas administered justice within their provinces and also collected the revenue from the provinces. In all this they were assisted by a number of subordinate officials.[21]

The officers were remunerated in various ways. They had considerable extents of land called *nindagam* granted to them. The peasantry inhabiting these granted lands cultivated their *muttettus* for the land grantee and also provided various personal services.[22] The Dissawas also enjoyed all the services due to the king from the different categories of service providers in his province. Thus they received pingo loads of food from the Gamwasam people, pots from the potters while the ironsmiths provided their services to them. The Atapattu people in the dissawa kept watch at his residence. When they travelled in their provinces they and their attendants were provided with all the necessities by the inhabitants. Those Dissawas who were also Adigars enjoyed additional honours. For instance, when travelling they were preceded by people cracking whips and people were to leave their verandas and give way to his retinue. No one except those from the royal family could sit while the Adigar was standing and when a Dissawa visited the Adigar's province he was to cease the beating of tom-toms.[23]

Revenue and service ensured the king and his nobles as comfortable a life as possible under a subsistence economy. They were ensured a steady and abundant supply of the basic necessities and a few luxuries along with the availability of specialized services and general labour.[24] The life of ease it provided for the elite is nicely explained by a nineteenth-century British observer in this frequently quoted passage:

A chief with several villages will draw his cook or his bath boy for two or three months a year from one village, from another for four months, and a third for one month, etc., carefully arranging to have one throughout the year. There are the potters to make the tiles and supply earthenware; the smith to clean the brass vessels and repair and make agricultural implements; the cunam weaver (*kinnaraya*) and the outcaste *rodiya*, who buries the carcasses of animals that die on the estate, and supplies ropes, etc., made of hide and fibres. Others supply pack bullocks for the transport of the produce of the fields, and for bringing supplies of salt and cured fish from the towns on the coast.[25]

But the extraction of surplus produce and labour was not only about providing sustenance to the elite. It was also about the assertion of power over the peasantry. The whole system of land tenure sustained an idea of power based on command over men and material. The relative significance of the members of the Kandyan political and social hierarchy, from the lowest official to the king, was demonstrated by the degree of command they had over men and material in the kingdom deriving from their land. The lowest officials enjoyed an abundant supply of grain and vegetables from their *muttettus* and the labour of the people in their *nindagam* while the higher officials had the services of a larger number of people and the surplus produce from a greater extent of land. The king asserted his control over over all the people and resources in the kingdom by extracting surplus produce and services from everybody. As for the peasantry who toiled in the land, the offering of produce and services was not simply a matter of supporting their chiefs and king but also a token of submission, an offer of tribute by the individual as a mark of his subservience.

An important point about having this command over men and material was the display of this command. The people who attended the Dissawa's house and provided labour in his kitchen and fields formed a group of followers or hangers-on at the service of the chief and maintained out of his resources. As such, they were a visual statement of his abundant means as well. The best time to demonstrate this command was when the chief travelled about. On such occasions the attendants and servants formed his retinue or *pirivara*[26] which accompanied him. Some members of the retinues of bigger chiefs performed tasks which were clearly ceremonial, such as carrying insignia of honour. The Atapattu people, for instance, carried the Dissawa's main banner and his ceremonial arms in public[27] while the Hewawasam people bore smaller banners.[28] But the most important function of the *pirivara* was the display of numbers. The more important the chief and the bigger the landlord, the bigger the retinue. Naturally, the king had the biggest retinue. This included his large household staff, his palace and bodyguards, as well as his Adigars and Dissawas with their own retinues of attendants. The perahera or annual procession in Kandy showcased the Kandyan political–economic hierarchy and also displayed, in full ritual splendour, the king's complete retinue.[29]

THE ARMY

How did the Kandyan army fit into this system? It was stated earlier that the king required the Kandyan peasantry to provide general military service during war. However, the Kandyan military organization was a bit more complex than this statement would suggest. Basically, kingdoms in pre-modern Sri Lanka used two types of soldiers in their wars: foreign troops and local soldiers. The foreigners functioned as a small, elite contingent, leaving the local peasantry to contribute the bulk of the army. Only the foreigners enjoyed the status of a standing army, the peasant troops being mobilized during war. The Kandyan army was no different.

FOREIGN TROOPS

Kandyan kings obtained their foreign troops from a number of sources. Queyroz speaks of the king's guard of about 400 troops, the majority of them 'Badagas from the opposite coast'.[30] *Badagas* was a corruption of Vatuka, a common name for Telugus at the time. They seem to have been very active in Vimala Dharma Surya's wars against the Portuguese in the late sixteenth and early seventeenth centuries; Queyroz speaks of 800 of these warriors, 'renowned in India for their valour', fighting alongside the Kandyans in 1597.[31] Their continued presence in the Kandyan ranks prompted the Portuguese to keep a close surveillance of the island's east coast to prevent their induction.[32] However, that did not make the Badagas disappear from Kandyan campaigns. A Telugu contingent also took part in King Senerat's abortive attempt to wrest Jaffna from the Portuguese in 1629.[33]

Many of the Telugus that fought in Vimala Dharma Surya's army earlier in the century were probably military adventurers seeking employment. It was common practice at the time for contingents of warriors on the Indian subcontinent to offer themselves as mercenaries to rulers.[34] Interestingly, Queyroz at one point describes the Telugus in the Kandyan service as mostly fugitives.[35] There is little doubt that the Kandyan king was only too glad to accept such mercenaries in his time of need. It also further underlines the healthy state of the royal treasury at a time when the ports were still under the king's control.

However, not all Telugus were adventurers. Some of them were also sent as military aid by the Nayak rulers on the opposite coast.[36] This was quite understandable. The Nayaks of Madura and Tanjore had been very hostile to the Portuguese in south India, especially on the Fishery Coast where their missionary and trading activities posed a threat to the Nayaks' political and economic interests. The Nayaks' hostility had prompted the Portuguese to move their base on that coast to Mannar in 1565 and the help extended to the Kandyans was a further demonstration of this determination to keep the Portuguese out of the Fishery Coast and south India.

With the loss of the ports and the control over the coast, the access to Vadugai troops was restricted. But an alternative source of Indian troops was opened when a change of guard occurred in the Kandyan dynasty. Since the time of Rajasinha II (1630–80), it had become common practice for the Kandyan kings to obtain brides from south India, particularly Madura.[37] In 1739, the Kandyan king Narendrasinha died childless and was succeeded by his Tamil wife's brother.[38] With this, the Kandyan kingdom passed under a Tamil dynasty leading to a considerable influx of Tamils into the Kandyan kingdom as the kinsmen and retainers of the ruling dynasty. Some of them also functioned as personal guards to the king. A number of them carrying swords and wearing large turbans appeared in a guard of honour drawn up to receive Major-General Mcdowall's embassy to Kandy in 1800.[39] Their numbers were not large; Ehelepola, the Kandyan noble who defected to the British in 1814, reckoned there were only 82 of them in the king's service at the time.

But it was the enemy forces that provided the best source of foreign troops! In the seventeenth and eighteenth centuries, the European civil and military establishments in the coastal areas became another fertile source of foreign troops. We have already seen how some of the Europeans who were in Kandy either as prisoners or deserters were made to serve the king as guards. Some of them were also required to fight for the king. Some did it willingly. Emmanuel Dias, a Portuguese who was captured during De Souza's rout in 1594 later served Vimala Dharma Surya as a Mudaliyar and was implicated in the massacre of the Dutch envoy Sebald de Weert and his entourage in 1602.[40] The king appears to have held him in high esteem; according to the Dutch writer Baldeaus, Dias was 'much beholden to the emperor for many favours heaped on him'.[41] According to Knox, during the campaign against the Dutch fort at Bibilegama in August 1675, the king armed about 30 of his European prisoners belonging to various nations and ordered them to march against the fort. Many of these men were deserters from the Dutch while others were captives. They agreed to fight on condition that in the event of their deaths their families would be looked after.[42] According to a late seventeenth-century French observer, a number of Frenchmen also took up the king's request to train his soldiers, 'which office they filled so well that a part of his subjects are so perfected in warfare that they now go boldly against the very gates of Colombo and many other places led by the French'.[43]

Others, however, did so unwillingly. During the war in 1761–6, several European prisoners taken from the Dutch were forced to fight for the Kandyans. Phillip Hartman, who was with the detachment sent to evacuate Hakmana in January 1761, was taken by the Kandyans when the detachment was annihilated and forced to serve Kandyan batteries at Katuwana and Matara.

Hartman managed to escape to his countrymen during the fidgeting at the latter place.[44] Many others escaped to the Dutch at the first opportunity they received during the Dutch invasion in 1764.[45] A British captive, Ensign Greeving, was also similarly pressed into service in 1803 but slipped through the Kandyans during their incursion into British-held territories in August 1803.[46]

Some Europeans also deserted to the Kandyans during campaigns and fought for them. In January 1763, during the war with Kandy, as many as 19 European deserters were reported to be with the Dissawa of the 3 and 4 Korales.[47] In the following year, two Europeans were seen with a Kandyan force confronting the Dutch near Gonawila.[48] These were no doubt some of the above-mentioned deserters. When one of the Europeans in Kandyan service was killed and his head brought in during the invasion in 1765, it was identified as that of a Frenchman in Dutch service who had deserted earlier.[49] In 1803, the British were alarmed when one of their European artillerymen named Benson crossed over to the Kandyans. Benson was gladly received by the Kandyans and later put in charge of supervising the making of gunpowder in Kandy. He accompanied the Kandyans on the ill-fated expedition against Hanwella and reportedly died of a wound received in the action.[50]

The Europeans, however, never seemed to have formed a significant portion of the Kandyan army. At best, they formed a ragtag band of individuals who added little more than variety to the Kandyan army. The British ambassador, Robert Andrews, who visited Kandy in 1796 found them presenting a sorry and amusing sight, dressed 'in a most whimsical style—their uniform resembling what the Portuguese wore some centuries ago'.[51]

Asian and African troops deserting from the European armies, or pressed into service after capture, formed the largest contingent of foreign troops in the Kandyan army, particularly since the mid-seventeenth century. According to the nineteenth-century Sinhala war poem *Ingrisi Hatana*, they were commanded by Kandyan nobles—the Malays coming under the command of Dehigama Dissawa while the Africans were commanded by Vattawe.[52] Of these troops, the Malays formed a very significant force. The Dutch forces in Sri Lanka included a considerable number of troops from Indonesia and the Malay archipelago, generally called 'Easterners' or 'Malays'.[53] They figured prominently in the Dutch campaigns against the Portuguese and later against Kandy.[54] When the Dutch evacuated their posts in the island the Malays joined the British military establishment in Sri Lanka.[55]

A number of Malay soldiers deserted from the Dutch and the British and found their way into Kandyan service. The Kandyan–Dutch war of 1761–6 and the British occupation of Kandy in 1803 provided ample scope for this. Several Malays deserted during the return of Medeler's relief expedition in 1765 while during the British occupations of Kandy in 1803, there were more frequent desertions, Malays and lascars deserting 'by the dozen'.[56] For their part, the Kandyans also attempted to detach the Malays from the Europeans, offering inducements to those who deserted. Interestingly, soldiers were not the only Malays who entered Kandyan service. Some of the 'Kandyan Malays' were criminals escaping from Dutch custody![57]

The Kandyans also coerced Malay soldiers to join their service. A large number of Malays with the Kandy garrison in 1803 were intimidated into taking service with the Kandyans. Many of them, however, deserted back to the British during the abortive Kandyan attack on Hanwella just a few months later.

But whether deserting soldiers or escaped criminals, the Malays came to play a prominent role in Kandyan military operations. Major Dufflo describes how the Malays spurred on the Kandyans during an action at Gonawila in 1764 shouting 'amok' to encourage the 'timid Sinhalese'.[58] Every major Kandyan army during the campaign in 1803 seems to have had a number of Malays, probably as a leavening. For instance, British spies reported the army of the Dissawa of the Seven Korales being accompanied by a body of Malays estimated between 300–400[59] while around the same time 100–50 Malays were reported with the Kandyan troops in Matara.[60] Even the Kandyan army that invaded Mullaitivu included a number of Malays.[61] But perhaps the most notable action involving Malays occurred in June 1803 when the Kandyans attempted to storm the British garrison in Kandy. The attack was led by a Malay chief named Sankilan who was killed after he had stabbed a British officer to death.[62]

Along with the Malays, Indian troops of different ethnic and cultural backgrounds also crossed over to the Kandyans. When

Prince Vijayapala, the brother of the king, deserted to the Portuguese in 1640 he brought with him 2000 men, among whom were two companies of Canarese.[63] These soldiers were either deserters or prisoners taken from the Portuguese army that was defeated in 1638. The Portuguese began employing Canarese and African troops in Sri Lanka in the early 1630s and the Portuguese Captain-General Diogo De Mello took with him several hundred of these troops on his disastrous expedition in 1638. Those who returned to the Portuguese fold with Vijayapala were no doubt soldiers taken captive or those who deserted at Gannoruwa. In the following century, Indian troops or sepoys in the Dutch service also deserted to the Kandyans, but not in large numbers. In May 1764, a number of sepoys deserted to the Kandyans, with their commanding officer and some arms complaining of ill-treatment.[64] During the Dutch occupation of Kandy in 1765, more desertions occurred but only in small numbers.[65] Small numbers of sepoys also deserted to the Kandyans during the Kandyan-British war in 1803–4. Like the British Malays, some British sepoys were also coerced into serving the Kandyans and, like their Malay counterparts, many of them found the opportunity to rejoin their former masters during the action before Hanwella.

The 'Kaffirs' or Africans formed another interesting group of foreign troops. Africans had been employed as slaves by the Portuguese from an early time but they were first employed as troops in substantial numbers only after 1631 when reinforcements of African and Canarese soldiers arrived to boost the Portuguese army in Sri Lanka. Several hundred African troops took part in the subsequent Portuguese campaigns against Kandyan forces and about 300 took part in De Mello's ill-fated expedition in 1638. It is possible that a number of them either deserted to the Kandyans or were captured during the battle of Gannoruwa because when Prince Vijayapala defected to the Portuguese in 1640, 50 Africans also accompanied him along with the Canarese troops mentioned above.[66] It is likely that they, like the Canarese, were the remnants of the Portuguese army annihilated in 1638. However, Africans have been reported from Kandy many years before that. When the Dutch envoy, Spilbergen, visited Kandy in 1602 he saw a number of Africans serving with the Kandyan forces, suggesting that some

Portuguese slaves may have taken the opportunity to seek refuge with the Kandyans.[67] After the Portuguese were expelled from the island, the number of Africans in Kandyan service continued to be boosted by the desertion of slaves from Dutch employ. By the time Knox was detained in Kandy the Africans had become trusted bodyguards of the king. They continue to be mentioned with Kandyan forces in the eighteenth and nineteenth centuries.[68] About 80 of them, 'fellows resembling giants', were reported with the Kandyan army that surrounded the retreating British force in 1803[69] while about 200 of them were reported to be in Kandyan service in 1810. Their duties, however, were sometimes not pleasant; it was they who were assigned the task of butchering the British captives in 1803.

It is not clear as to how all these foreigners were remunerated. With a limited cash income, it is unlikely that the Kandyan kings were able to offer their foreign troops money, at least not in the eighteenth and nineteenth centuries. The payment was probably made in land, the way everybody else in the kingdom was paid. According to Ehelepola, the Malabar troops of the king were given land in return for their services. No doubt the Africans and the Malays were also similarly rewarded.[70]

As noted earlier, these foreigners formed only a fraction of the army, which the Kandyan kings commanded. They rarely exceeded a few hundred, with the vast majority of soldiers in the Kandyan armies being raised from the numerous peasantry that inhabited the highlands.

LAND TENURE AND MILITARY SERVICE

As noted earlier, the Kandyan peasantry was under a general obligation to provide military service for the king. This service, however, was a general service required in emergencies. For more general needs the state had at its disposal a smaller core of regular militiamen. It was earlier pointed out that the Dissawas could call upon a considerable retinue. Among the various categories of people who formed this retinue were some who had military designations. So were the Kodituwakku, Atapattu, and the Hewawasam people. The Kodituwakku people carried a species of light artillery called kodituwakku when the Dissawa went on circuit and also apprehended criminals.[71] As explained earlier, the Atapattu people mounted guard at the palace and at the Dissawa's house. The term 'atapattu' itself was derived from a Tamil term for 'care-takers or watchers'.[72] The Hewawasam people, literally meaning military landholders, performed in peacetime a similar duty to the Atapattu people—that is, to keep watch at the Dissawa's house. However, the Hewawasam people seem to have been something more than mere watchers. There is evidence suggesting that they were treated as a militia who had to maintain themselves in armed readiness while performing their peacetime duties. This is suggested by the fact that the Hewawasam people of Sabaragamuwa were expected to maintain firearms.[73] A seventeenth-century *sannasa* or land grant also speaks of the military services performed by the grantee as service attached to his land.[74]

When they accompanied the Dissawa on circuit, this militia carried their arms. The Kodituwakku people bore their gingals and the hewayas carried muskets and other weapons. There are a number of reports from British spies of such armed attendance. For instance, in September 1810, two of the spies reported seeing the Second Adigar at a rest house near Batugedera in the Sabaragamuwa province with about 350 people in attendance. The people were armed with guns, swords, and casthanas (a kind of small sword), while 7 kodituwakku were also placed near the rest house.[75] Less than a month later in early October we hear of a meeting of a number of Dissawas with their retinues, the Dissawa of Tamankaduwa arriving in Katugastota in a palanquin attended by 6 kodituwakku bearers and 1 man with a musket while the Dissawa of Nuwarakalawiya was seen with 6 kodituwakku and 2 muskets. Rakwatte Nilame of the Four Korales had with him about 100 men, about 10 kodituwakku, and 4 or 5 muskets.[76]

Such demonstrations were mostly aimed at inspiring in the people respect and awe for the chiefs. But during wartime these people no doubt formed the backbone of the peasant army of their province. At least in the sixteenth and seventeenth centuries, the Atapattu people seem to have enjoyed a prominent place in the army. According to Couto, the 'atapata' were the 'king's guard', picked and brave soldiers. Ribeiro also describes the Atapattu as the king's personal guard.[77] A Dutch document of the late seventeenth century also speaks of these service holders in the same vein.[78] The Atapattu and Hewawasam people probably functioned as the core or the elite of the Kandyan army in wartime by virtue of their usual role in the Kandyan political and social structure.

But the militia formed only the core of the army, not the whole. They could not satisfy all the manpower needs of the state during wartime, especially at times when large armies were needed. This is where the general mobilization of the peasantry took place by appealing to the basic obligation of the peasantry to serve the king in war. As Knox explains:

> Here one Ceylone the Kings Army consists of standing regiments only, who are all and every one free holders of land that they hold from the King for that service and are required to serve no longer then they keepe possession of that land. . . . But if the King goes himself in person to the War, then those they call Gommoies who are free holders also till the Kings land and pay him Corne, etc. must goe armed along with him to the Wars, but not else unlesse the King goes himselfe.[79]

Here, Knox is clearly speaking of two types of Kandyan soldiery. On the one hand are the soldiers who are maintained as regular 'regiments'. These were the ordinary provincial militia. On the other hand we have the 'gommoies' who are mobilized when the king himself goes to war. The 'gommoies' are the *gammahes* or principle landholders in villages. The connection made between their mobilization and the king taking the field is very interesting. It probably signifies a different kind of emergency which involved the state rather than a province. As such it was to be met by resorting to mobilization that went beyond the provincial militia.

The peasant troops were mobilized from the Kandyan heartland as well as all the outlying provinces of the kingdom.[80] It seems—as Knox seems to be saying—that the general mobilization mainly targeted the peasantry in the Gabada villages, particularly from the Govigama caste or principle landholders. Knox's observation is supported by other sources. In a petition made by the Portuguese auxiliaries or lascarins in 1636, the Gamwasam people who were of the Govigama caste claimed that it was their duty during peacetime to till the land and plant the seeds while in wartime they had to watch and guard their korales.[81] According to an early nineteenth-century British observer, although the king could call up all men in the kingdom without caste distinctions, the Govigama people received priority.[82] As reported by a British spy, thousands of men were being assembled for service from the gabada villages in 1810. This was just another way in which the gabada villages contributed to the king's resources. But other villages were also not totally exempt. *Nindagam* holders were also required to supply a quota of men during war.[83]

The enforcement of this aspect of 'rajakariya' ensured a large pool of manpower that could be mobilized at short notice. However, despite the availability of this large pool of potential soldiers it is likely that care was taken not to denude villages of all the available manpower. We have already noted above how quotas were set for nindagam holders. This seems to have been the general case, villages providing a number of men according to their population. Thus we hear the Dissawas requesting two men from each Vasama in 1810 while other observers too speak of a systematic approach to collecting men,[84] a measure probably motivated by the drastic implications that large-scale mobilization had for agriculture in a peasant society.

While the great majority of the Kandyan army was drawn from the peasantry, military mobilization also reigned in a people living on the margins of Kandyan society. These were the Veddahs or the aboriginal hunter-gatherers of the island. The Veddahs inhabited a large area in the periphery of Kandyan territory stretching from Uva and Wellasse in the east to Puttalam and the Wanni in the north and the north-west. The Kandyans frequently made use of these people in their campaigns. In 1675, Tennekoon Dissawa made a foray into Dutch possessions in the north-west of Sri Lanka guided by Veddahs[85] while in 1762 they were even reported in the escorts of Kandyan Adigars.[86] The Veddahs became very prominent during the rebellion of 1817–18. During the uprising they were considered to be the 'closest adherents' of the Kandyan rebel leader Keppetipola.[87]

The Dissawas had overall command of the men in their provinces[88] and the soldiers from the different provinces rallied around their respective banners.[89] In mobilizing the people, the Dissawas relied heavily on their subordinate headmen to gather the men under their jurisdiction. Orders were sent out to inferior chiefs to assemble their men and bring them to specific locations for further orders on the conduct of operations. Sometimes the

Dissawas themselves toured their provinces, gathering men as they went. An account of a seventeenth-century land grant by Rajasinha II speaks of Giragama Dissawa gathering *Sinhale Sarapurushayo* or the 'fierce people of Sinhale' to fight the Portuguese in 1638.[90] Dutch and British sources speak of numerous similar instances.

The letters of Lewis Gibson, the Collector of Matara in 1803, about the progress of the Kandyan army towards Matara provides a good picture of the mobilization of a provincial Kandyan army. Gibson obtained his information from Kandyan spies who carefully reported the advance of the Kandyans under the Dissawa of Sabaragamuwa. On 8 August, a couple of months after the massacre of British troops in Kandy, Gibson was informed by his spies that the Adigar was in Kolonna in the Sabaragamuwa province and that he had ordered the people in the surrounding areas to assemble.[91] On 10 August, the Adigar was still in Kolonna while his headmen were gathering men in different parts of the surrounding country.[92] Three days later it was reported that two of the Adigar's headmen had advanced beyond Kolonna and had arrived at Katuwana and that they had called the inhabitants to join the army by beating tom-toms.[93] Those who did not join were threatened with the destruction of their houses. As a result of this threat the people of Katuwana and Udubokke had joined the Kandyans.[94] By the fourteenth day they had gathered about 1,500 people in Katuwana with more people constantly coming in.[95] While his headmen were raising this army the Adigar had himself set out for Katuwana but by the 12 August, he had reached only Wallalgoda, a place on the way to Katuwana. He was expected to leave Wallalgoda for Katuwana on 14 August and then finally to Matara via Hakmana.[96] After reaching Wallalgoda, the Adigar had sent instructions to one of the headmen at Katuwana to proceed to the rest house at a place called Dompahale while the others were ordered to proceed to the rest house at Maracadde.[97] Both were places beyond Katuwana, closer to the British controlled territory. On 16 August, a chief called Gallegoda Bandara was reported to have arrived at the rest house at Maracadde with about 1,000 men while some others had left Katuwana for Hakmana.[98] On the same day, Saram Mudaliyar informed that a headman called Heeralu Aratchi had joined the Kandyans who were hoping to enter Gangabaddapattu in British territory on 17 or 18 August. He also reported that the Adigar finally reached Katuwana on 15 August with about 3,000–4,000 armed Kandyans and that the Kodituwakku Nilame with 700–800 people had advanced further to the rest house at Maracadde.[99]

The Adigar continued at Katuwana, while there is conflicting information about his future movements. Some reports suggest that he was to go to Maracadde while others speak of Morawaka as the possible destination.[100] In the meantime the Kandyans who were in Maracadde were calling on the people in the neighbourhood to assemble with arms if they did not wish to suffer flogging and their houses destroyed. According to the informant, there were by this time about 5,000 Kandyans assembled in the whole district with more coming in daily. There were also unconfirmed reports of 100–50 Malays with the Kandyans.[101]

While the Adigar tarried at Katuwana the Kandyan advance continued into areas beyond Katuwana. On 17 August, the Morawaka Korale Mudaliyar reported to Gibson that an advance party of two Kandyan headmen with 100 men had arrived at the rest house at Morawaka the previous night and had placed guards at Pahurutotta.[102] These men were to move forward to Akuressa the following day, and while at Pahurutotta, were joined by numerous headmen with their followers. By 17 August, some Kandyans were reported to be in Hakmana while many headmen and their people in the areas approached by the Kandyans were joining them.[103] Around the same time Kandyans were reported from the neighbouring Galle district as well; several Kandyan headmen being reported in Hiniduma with about 800 men. In the meantime in Gangabadapattu in the Matara district, the people had received notice that the Kandyans were hoping to arrive there on 18 August.[104]

There is no doubt that Gibson's informants were sometimes exaggerating or playing down facts in order to please their master but it is likely that the misrepresentation was with regards to numbers and perhaps the proximity of the enemy than to the actual process of mobilizaton. As such, the information received by Gibson can be taken to present a comprehensive picture of a Kandyan army gradually brought into being. The army advances and is assembled in stages and as it advances. The commander of the army, the Adigar, is seen moving leisurely—most probably in stately procession with his numerous retinue—towards the district to be invaded while the minor headmen busy themselves raising troops and bringing them to different points, usually ahead of the Adigar. The headmen bivouac at rest houses, probably constructed in advance, and the populace is summoned by the beat of tom-toms.[105] The men assembled include those brought from Kandy as well as people raised in areas entered by the advancing Kandyans.

The use of the threats in the case of the latter is significant. These areas were outside Kandyan control under normal circumstances and threats were aimed at gaining their doubtful allegiance. This was a common practice whenever the Kandyans entered European controlled territory or were reoccupying territory that had briefly passed under European control. For instance, in February 1764 we hear of the First Adigar ordering people who had submitted to the Dutch during their invasion that year to return to the Kandyan fold on pain of having their houses burnt and the degradation of their families.[106]

SUPPLY

The mode of supplying troops in the field was as cheap as the process of mobilization. The soldiers brought their own supplies, enough to last them for a short period of time, usually 15–20 days.[107] This was probably the maximum quantity an individual could carry with him. According to a British officer the supplies consisted of a small quantity of rice, a few rotis made of *kurakkan* and a few coconuts.[108] Once his supplies ran out the Kandyan peasant returned home to fetch more, so that 'after a month or so, the majority of the army is always absent from the field'.[109]

Each soldier also carried a small cooking vessel while a talipot leaf provided him shelter from the sun and rain. When the army encamped the soldiers set-up makeshift huts with their talipot leaves, several soldiers combining together to form a hut while the officers had more spacious lodgings constructed with the same material.[110] According to Queyroz, it was the custom for the people in the surrounding villages to bring in bundles of talipot leaves or palms to cover the barracks of the troops but it is not certain if this was the usual case or something which happened on special occasions.[111]

This mode of supply greatly relieved the state of the burden of feeding and housing the troops. The Kandyan organization of logistics appears strikingly similar to that of the contemporary Burmese army. The Burmese soldiers were also peasants and carried all their supplies, which according to a European observer, consisted of a mat, a blanket, a small cooking vessel, and a provision of rice, salt, and a piece of dried fish or meat. When they camped they built crude shelters from the branches of trees.[112] It was a system, which ensured minimum expense to the state while bestowing the army with remarkable mobility.

However, there is also some evidence to suggest that, despite expecting the troops to supply themselves, to some extent the state also took the burden of supplying its troops. In 1652, the king was reported to have erected a strong stockade in Wewuda in the Seven Korales and collected all the supplies from the district.[113] The king's granaries, filled with the paddy from his *gabdagam,* functioned as valuable sources of grain for armies in the field. During wartime, European armies frequently stumbled upon such granaries containing large stocks of paddy and rice. In 1764, the Dutch came upon a massive hoard of 480,000 pounds of paddy stored in four storehouses in Ettambey while two years later they stumbled upon about 200,000 pounds of rice that had been collected by the Dissawa of Matale.[114] Some of this rice may have been collected during the military campaigns then in progress as it was not unusual to collect supplies just prior to or during a major campaign. In August 1803, it was reported that the Migastenna Dissawa of the Seven Korales had 'erected a very large barracks and collected a large quantity of rice for the use of his army' not far from Halawata[115] on the coast in north-west Sri Lanka. When the British reached the place to destroy it they found five godowns with 1,500 parrahs of rice and paddy.[116] When the chieftain Pandar Vanniar was defeated in the following month the British found a large depot of supplies stocked with rice, dried fish, and tobacco, sufficient for about 5,000 people.[117]

In 1810 and 1811, John D'oyly heard from his spies that there was a mobilization of people in Kandy and that along with that, rice was also being collected. However, there were conflicting reports as for whom the rice was meant. One informant spoke of the people in Ruwanwella being ordered by the Dissawa to beat out rice for a large number of people expected from Kandy but did not specify if they were part of the Dissawa's retinue or people already mobilized.[118] Others were more specific and spoke of rice being collected for the Dissawa's attendants but, as we have seen, these people also contained a good number of militiamen.[119]

TRAINING AND DISCIPLINE

The part-time, loosely organized soldiers took the field without any formal military training. In the absence of a standing army where the soldiers learnt to fight as a part of their training, the Kandyan peasant had to learn his fighting skills in battle. Long wars rather than intense training made good soldiers out of such men. True, all armies depend to a degree on combat experience, but part-time armies like the Kandyan army depended on it more heavily than regular armies. This resulted in soldiers whose toughness depended overwhelmingly on their experience.

A Kandyan *sannasa* or land grant of the seventeenth century offers us a glimpse of the career of one such veteran soldier who fought in the armies of three Kandyan kings. According to the land grant, the soldier, called Kalu Appu, fought with distinction in the battles of Randeniwela and Gannoruwa while also performing valuable service in a number of other campaigns in diverse places in the low country, including Rakgahawatta, Ruwanwella, Sitawaka, Bibilegama, and Kottiar.[120] The campaigns involving Bibilegama, Ruwanwella, and Hanwella were probably campaigns in the Dutch wars in the 1670s because later in the grant we are told that Kalu Appu was still around at the time of the rebellion against Rajasinha in 1665. In that case we are looking at a career of almost 45 years, not impossible if Kalu Appu had entered service in his teens.

No doubt the Kandyan armies of the seventeenth century included many men like Kalu Appu who had served in numerous campaigns. Wastage in battle was also probably high at a time of intense and continuous fighting, particularly in the case of the bravest men who would have exposed themselves more often. But constant contact with the enemy also provided ample scope for the emergence of a considerable number of men who survived the ordeal of battle and were hardened by the experience. And more experienced campaigners would have also been better able to survive the hardships and dangers of campaigning than raw troops.

However, this does not mean that the rulers never took an interest in improving the fighting skills of their troops. There is some evidence to show that in the late eighteenth and early nineteenth centuries, the Kandyan state was taking steps to instruct its soldiers in some of the basic military exercises they had seen being undertaken by the European armies on the coast. According to Queyroz, the Kandyans learnt to form squadrons from the Portuguese. At Randeniwela in 1630 they are alleged to have formed at different times 'in the Turkish fashion into a half-moon, at another into a square, like the Swiss, sometimes into lines, in the French and Spanish fashion, and others they divided themselves in great battalions trying to intimidate by dexterity'.[121] We have already noted how Rajasinha II engaged his French captives to train his troops. In 1765, we find a Dutch detachment confronted by a Kandyan force with a well-drilled force of soldiers from Uva whose front ranks knelt to open fire.[122] In the early nineteenth century, British spies reported numerous instances of hundreds of Malays, sepoys, and Kandyans drilling in Kandy. On one occasion, 21 divisions of 30 men each were reported to be drilling in Kandy, wearing 'high soldiers caps, black jackets and white trousers'.[123] No doubt, deserters from European armies were responsible for these developments. However, their overall impact on the Kandyan armies remained minimal. Again, the lack of a standing army where these methods could be regularly instilled proved a major stumbling block. As a result, the average Kandyan soldier remained untutored in the European ways of fighting.

The state placed more importance on rewards in ensuring good military performance. Land was the usual reward as testified to by numerous land grants given to soldiers.[124] State offices and insignia were also given. Soldiers were encouraged to bring in the heads of the enemies they killed—called *tharam*—to demonstrate their valour.[125] However, grants were not always given for feats in combat. Many grants were given to chiefs suggesting that they were in appreciation of their role in organizing and leading the campaigns. This is quite clear from the grants of land and insignia given to a number of chiefs after the capture of Trincomalee in 1638. Atipola Dissawa was given the Matale province and a number of insignia, including a flag and 5 kodituwakku, while a number of other chiefs received additional offices and minor insignia. This campaign, however, did not involve any fighting by Kandyans. The Dutch did all the fighting. The king, however, was pleased because the chiefs had taken part in a successful campaign whereas all previous attempts in the direction of Trincomalee by other chiefs had failed.[126] Sometimes other tokens of appreciation were also given to troops who performed well. Thus, one Ulpothe Appuhamy who brought three Portuguese heads after the Battle of Randeniwela received a *ranpota* or a golden chain in addition to land.[127]

On the other hand, failure in battle resulted in punishment. In 1763, the Dutch heard reports of Kandyan chiefs being laid on the ground and beaten for having deserted their posts.[128] In 1803, after the disastrous attack on Hanwella, Leuke Dissawa who was entrusted with its organization was executed and his followers put to plough a field.[129]

NUMBERS

How many people could the Kandyans mobilize in the above fashion? Sinhala war poems provide fantastic figures for Kandyan armies. The *Maha Hatana* claims that the king collected 100,000 persons in the space of one hour[130] while according to the *Madarampura Puvatha*, Rajasinha II placed 30,000 persons to watch over Kandy while he took 40,000 men to destroy the Portuguese at Gannoruwa in 1638.[131] Considering the panegyrical nature of these works, the figures can be dismissed as hyperbole imaginary. The Kandyan Dissawa Tennekoon, who deserted to the Dutch in 1676, gave a much lower figure of 16,550, with 12,000 men from Uva alone.[132] Tennekoon was no doubt motivated by a desire to downplay the strength of his former master but he also possessed an insider's knowledge of Kandyan resources.

European sources also provided high estimates for Kandyan armies but rarely in fantastic figures. According to Queyroz, the king of Kandy could command 40,000 men within his kingdom—28,000 from Kandy and 12,000 from Uva—but only 10,000 outside it. Queyroz makes the interesting point that the people of Uva enjoyed the privilege of serving only within their province.[133] It is also significant that Queyroz's figure for Uva troops tallies with that given by Tennekoon. Robert Knox, who knew Kandyan conditions more than any contemporary European, speaks of a total of 30,000.[134] Along with such estimates made by chroniclers and resident observers must be placed the observations by Europeans on armies encountered in the field. These provide interestingly contrasting figures. On the upper end of the scale are figures that run into tens of thousands. The army that surrounded De Sa in 1630 is said to have been about 30,000 strong.[135] The Kandyan army confronted by the Dutch at Periekondomale on their way to invading Kandy in 1765 was computed at 20,000[136] while another army that opposed a detachment on its way to Hanguranketa a few days later was estimated at 10,000.[137] Ensign Greeving of the Malay Regiment was very liberal with his estimate of the number of Kandyans that confronted Major Davy on his retreat, placing it at 70,000. He also speaks of the Dissawa of the Four Korales being constantly in the field for four months with 40,000 men during the Kandyan invasion of British territories in 1803 and of the Dissawa of Walapane joining him with 18,000 men.[138] The Kandyan attack on Hanwella is said to have been made by an army of 30,000.

At the lower end of the scale are fairly small Kandyan armies numbering no more than a few hundred and occasionally exceeding a thousand. During the Dutch invasion in February 1765, the First Adigar confronted the Dutch with an army estimated at 4,000 or 5,000.[139] In March of the same year, a patrol from the Dutch base camp at Gonawila was attacked by a Kandyan force of around 900 men.[140] In March 1803, Captain Herbert Beaver estimated the Kandyan army he encountered in the province of 4 Korales to be around only 600, quite contrary to rumours about a force ten times that number.[141] As we have already seen, the army gathered by the Kandyans on their march on Matara in August 1803 did not exceed 4,000–5,000 according to the British spies. Many of the larger rebel forces encountered by the British during the rebellion in 1817–18 did not number more than 2,000–5,000.[142] Keppetipola is said to have led about 8,000 men in an attack on Paranagama in March 1818, but this was an exceptionally large force for the rebels.[143]

The first thing to note about these figures is that they do not necessarily include only fighting men. It is very likely that a considerable number of followers and mere hangers-on accompanied the fighting men for various reasons such as plunder and excitement. One is here reminded of Queyroz's wry observation that the Sinhalese had 'many seats as spectators against so few bulls [in the ring]',[144] and that the Portuguese accounts 'did not distinguish the men-at-arms from the rabble that came for the sacking, though in extreme cases they will have enough spirit to fight'.[145] But whatever their composition may have been, these contrasting figures are not difficult to understand, considering the mode of mobilization of Kandyan armies and their deployment for operations discussed earlier. The large armies represent the concerted efforts of a number of smaller bodies of Kandyan troops brought together for major operations or actions. These could easily break up into smaller bodies under the chiefs who gathered them and operate on their own. The numbers gathered also probably reflected the Kandyan perception of the military objective. A major campaign like an attack on an enemy fort or a major enemy force would require the mobilization of larger numbers while a lesser objective would call for smaller armies.

But still, we have to discard accounts of armies in excess of 10,000 as deliberate exaggerations or ill-judged overestimations. This is not because there was a dearth of potential soldiers. There is no reliable information on Kandyan population in the period from the sixteenth to the nineteenth centuries—C.R. De Silva estimates it to have been a little over 100,000 in the mid-sixteenth century but this is by no means conclusive.[146] What is very likely is that it was not very large, but still large enough to include men of arms-bearing age in excess of 20,000. The real problem, however, was one of logistics. Most certainly, an army in excess of 10,000 always included people from more than one province. If we are to believe Queyroz's statement on the privileged position of the Uva troops, any army assembling outside Uva had to reckon without them. However, such a privilege was quite redundant as serving outside their home province placed a great strain on the peasant soldiers who had to travel back home to replenish themselves when their supplies ran out. On the other hand, drawing supplies for an army of 10,000–20,000 from the locality in which it was gathered put a tremendous strain on the local population. It is also unlikely that the royal stores would have been able to support such large armies for too long. The 15-day supply limit probably signified the period an army was expected to remain 'logistically comfortable' in the field under the Kandyan system of supply. When this period was stretched the army just melted away or suffered privations. Thus, in 1814, we hear of Ehelepola's rebel force gradually drifting back to their villages in search of more supplies after only a few days in the field.[147] The Kandyan army that invaded Portuguese territories in 1655 was said to be suffering severely for want of provisions.[148] No wonder that the people of Uva refused to give up their 'privileged' position and serve in the low country in 1630 despite promises of a substantial share of the plunder.[149]

The norm, it appears, was to function in a number of semi-independent bodies of diverse strength working more or less independently towards a broad objective—for instance, the obstruction of an enemy invasion or the invasion of an enemy province, usually not very far from the areas from which the troops were drawn. This is what we saw happening in the case of the Kandyans descending on Matara in 1803. They could come together briefly for operations or actions that required the concentration of large numbers without presenting a logistical nightmare. This is probably how the large armies seen by some European observers materialized. Even then, armies in excess of 20,000 would have been extremely rare and probably non-existent, except in the imagination of European observers keen to overplay the odds against them.

THE STATE AND THE ARMY: THE BALANCE OF POWER

The Kandyan military organization reflected the limited means and aims of kingdoms in pre-modern Sri Lanka. A large, permanent standing army was not feasible due to a lack of money, in spite of a strong need for one. As noted earlier, officials, especially the provincial governors, had command over considerable wealth and power that included command over the regional military resources. This was much in keeping with the segmented power structure of the early modern state with its strong local authority. But strong provincial governors commanding the regional military resources were also a serious check on central authority and unless their ambitions were kept under control they could pose a real threat. On several occasions the nobles attempted to challenge the king's authority. As already seen, in 1664 several nobles combined to drive the king away from the capital while abortive attempts were made on the king's life in 1709 and 1760. In 1814, the First Adigar, Ehelepola, revolted in Sabaragamuwa.

These revolts demonstrated the need for—and against—a standing army. In the face of strong provincial governors, a powerful centrally controlled standing army would have been an asset to the monarchy. But at the same time the revolts demonstrated that the segmented power structure could also weaken challenges to the centre. They were always led by only a section of the elite—not the entire elite—and were always thwarted by the loyalists among the elite. Ambanwela Appuhamy's revolt in 1664 was foiled when the prince he placed on the throne turned against him and the plots in 1709 and 1760 fell apart because some of the nobles remained loyal to the king. In 1760 in particular, the plot to kill the king was revealed by a loyalist. Ehelepola's revolt in 1814 did not receive wider support from other chiefs, despite attempts to win over them.[150]

This segmented nature of the elite provided the king with many ways of checking the chiefs than by maintaining a powerful—and expensive—standing army. One was to make the officers in the king's household, the people who had immediate access to the king's person, exempt from the Dissawa's control, preventing the Dissawa's influence from extending into the royal household. The religious establishments with their large landholdings and the resident labour force were equally exempt from the Dissawa's control. This denied the provincial governors command over significant human and material resources in their provinces. The king also maintained a monopoly on external trade, preventing the governors from acquiring considerable wealth.[151] But most importantly, the king also played one Dissawa against another, often with great success. A good strategy was to reward loyal chiefs with the property of disloyal chiefs, providing an incentive to remain loyal during a crisis. Thus, the loyal noble who disclosed the plot to kill the king in

1760 received the lands of the traitors and when the First Adigar, Ehelepola, revolted in 1814 another noble Molligoda was made the First Adigar and sent against the traitor.[152] Last but not least, superstition regarding the *perahera* or the annual procession of the sacred Temple of the Tooth also acted as a deterrent to revolt. Attending the event was considered essential to ensuring the blessings of the gods and compelled all the chiefs to visit the city, making it difficult to break free from the centre.[153]

The Kandyan military organization and the role of the Kandyan army in the traditional Kandyan political structure should be viewed in the context of this balance between the centre and the periphery in the segmentary state. The mercenary troops were the king's personal guard while the peasant army was part of the segmented periphery's power. While the bodyguards' loyalty was more or less assured, in a crisis it was crucial for the king to secure the support of the greater part of this segmented army through the loyalty of chiefs. The army was meant for campaigns aimed primarily at meeting this objective—of forcing the submission of a rebellious subordinate or even a weak neighbour. Such campaigns did not last very long and consisted mainly of one major campaign forcing the issue. Usually, there was not much fighting. When Molligoda was sent against Ehelepola in 1814 the two armies met near Ruwanwella but there was no fighting, only a parley in which both sides tried to win the other over in order to tip the balance in its favour. Then both armies retired with Ehelepola crossing over to the British side of the frontier.[154] Within days Ehelepola's men were offering submission to Molligoda.[155] In 1664 too, there was little fighting but a lot of manoeuvring to secure loyalties. Bloodshed occurred after the crushing of the rebellions when the ring leaders and their families were massacred in orgies of violence.[156]

Such campaigns suited the temperament of the peasant army, which could not keep the field for a long time. When such campaigns were not taking place, which was not very often, the militia was sufficient to keep order. This, however, changed with the wars with the Europeans. Campaigns lasted for months and sometimes years. Yet, no significant change occurred in the Kandyan military organization which continued to maintain its 'feudal' character. As we shall see later, this was to create considerable problems for the Kandyans.

NOTES

1. H.L. Seneviratne, *Rituals of the Kandyan State,* Cambridge Studies in Social Anthropology, Cambridge: Cambridge University Press, 1978, p. 2; Ralph Pieris, *Sinhalese Social Organization: The Kandyan Period,* Colombo: Ceylon University Press, 1956, pp. 9–11.
2. Alex Gunasekera, 'Rajakariya or the Duty to the King in the Kandyan Kingdom of Sri Lanka', in Wendy Doniger O'Flaherty and J. Duncan M. Derrett (eds.), *The Concept of Duty in South Asia,* London: School of Oriental and African Studies, 1978, pp. 134–6; Pieris, *Sinhalese Social Organization,* pp. 44–5; Lorna Srimathie Dewaraja, *The Kandyan Kingdom of Ceylon 1707–1760,* Colombo: Lake House, 1972, p. 179.
3. Sinnappah Arasaratnam, 'Ceylon in the Indian Ocean Trade: 1500–1800', in A. Das Gupta and M.N. Pearson (eds.), *India and the Indian Ocean 1500–1800,* Calcutta: Oxford University Press, 1989, pp. 231–2.
4. Andrews, the British ambassador who visited Kandy in 1795 and 1796, observed a general lack of money in Kandy and 'all necessities supplied and all commerce carried on by bartering one commodity for another'. 'Andrews Embassies to Kandy in 1795 and 1796', ed. JP. Lewis, *JRAS(CB),* vol. 26, no. 70, 1917, p. 130. A British subaltern serving in the highlands in 1820 found that nothing could be bought for money from the Kandyans 'who seem scarcely to know the value its use or value'. Lieutenant Colonel James Campbell, *Excursions, Adventures and Field Sports in Ceylon: Its Commercial and Military Importance and Numerous Advantages to the British Emigrant,* London: T&W. Boone, 1843, p. 116.
5. Pieris, *Sinhalese Social Organization,* p. 114. See also Dewaraja, 'Revenues of the Kings of Kandy', *JRAS (CB),* New Series, vol. 16, 1972, p. 19.
6. Joao de Ribeiro, *The Historic Tragedy of the Island of Ceilao,* trs. P.E. Pieris, Colombo: Lake House, 1948, pp. 28–9.
7. Sir John D'oyly, *A Sketch of the Constitution of the Kandyan Kingdom.* ed. L.J.B. Turner, published as the *CHJ,* vol. 24, Dehiwela, Sri Lanka: Tisara Publishers, 1975; rpt. of 1929 edn., pp. 66–7. Dewaraja, *The Kandyan Kingdom,* pp. 183–4.
8. According to Ribeiro, there were 25 villages in the province of Sabaragamuwa entrusted with the mining of precious stones. The inhabitants in these villages had to work fifteen days a year in the mines.' The emperor, when the season drew near, used to fix the quality and quantity of gems they had to procure to the kings, his relatives and friends on the coast of Indisa'. Ribeiro, *The Historic Tragedy,* p. 30.
9. T.B.H. Abeysinghe, 'The Politics of Survival: Aspects of Kandyan External Relations in the Mid-Sixteenth Century', *JRAS(SCB),* vol. 17, 1973, pp. 14–15.
10. Arasaratnam, 'Ceylon in the Indian Ocean', p. 233.

11. Dewaraja, *The Kandyan Kingdom*, p. 175.
12. Dewaraja, *The Kandyan Kingdom*, pp. 156–60. D'oyly, *A Sketch of the Constitution*, pp. 7–9.
13. Ibid., p. 208.
14. Pieris, *Sinhalese Social Organization*, pp. 104–5.
15. Dewaraja, *The Kandyan Kingdom*, pp. 180–8; Pieris, *Sinhalese Social Organization*, pp. 180–7.
16. Robert Knox, *An Historical Relation of the Island of Ceylon, Revised, Enlarged & Brought to the Verge of Publication as the Second Edition by Robert Knox together with his Autobiography and All the New Chapters, Paragraphs, Marginal Notes added by the Author in the Two Interleaved Copies of the Original Text of 1681*, Edited with Introduction and Notes by J.H.O. Paulusz, published as the *CHJ* Monographs series, vol. 14, Dehiwela, Sri Lanka: Tisara Publishers, 1989, 1st edn. 1681, pp. 466–71. According to some sources some of the Frenchmen in this mission are said to have been so pleased with the king's treatment of them that they sought and gained permission from De la Haye to remain in Kandy! But according to Knox, the king detained them after they refused to comply with the Kandyan conventions of paying respects to the king. Lorna Srimathie Dewaraja, *Sri Lanka through French Eyes*, Colombo, Institute of Fundamental Studies, 1989, pp. 31–3.
17. How many Europeans served the Kandyan kings it is difficult to say. Knox reports of 50–60 Europeans including 6 or 7 'Europe born' ones living in Kandy during his 19 years of captivity during 1660–79, but all of them did not serve at the court. Knox, *An Historical Relation*, p. 438. The Europeans were also treated better than the Sinhalese and were accorded privileges. They were allowed 'to wear any manner of Apparel, either gold, silver or silk, shoes and stockings, a shoulder Belt and Sword; their houses may be whitened with Lime, and many such like things, all which the Chingulayes are not permitted to do'. Ibid., pp. 271–3.
18. Sinnappah Arasaratnam, *Dutch Power in Ceylon*, Amsterdam: Djambatan, 1958, p. 54.
19. Dewaraja, *Sri Lanka through French Eyes*, pp. 33, 35.
20. D'oyly, *A Sketch of the Constitution*, pp. 9–10.
21. Ibid., pp. 36, 62–3; Dewaraja, *The Kandyan Kingdom*, pp. 169–75.
22. Ribeiro, *The Historic Tragedy*, p. 32.
23. D'oyly, *A Sketch of the Constitution*, pp. 7. Dewaraja, *The Kandyan Kingdom*, pp. 175–80.
24. How well the king was supplied can be gauged by the discovery by the Dutch in 1765 of huge stores of oil, spices, and salt in the Kandyan palace, calculated to be sufficient for their army of nearly 7000 for a year. This may well have been an overestimation but it does give a sense of the quantity of essentials that the court would have

accumulated. Diary of the Expedition to Kandy in 1765, Major Roland Raven-Hart (tr. and ed.), *The Dutch Wars with Kandy 1764–1766*, Ceylon Historical Manuscripts Commission Bulletin no. 6, Colombo: Government Publications Bureau, 1964, p. 99.

25. Quoted in Gananath Obeyeskera, *Land Tenure in Village Ceylon: A Sociological and Historical Study*, Cambridge: Cambridge University Press, 1967, p. 219.
26. Ibid., p. 219.
27. D'oyly, *A Sketch of the Constitution*, p. 12.
28. Ibid., p. 16.
29. Seneviratne, *Rituals of the Kandyan State*, p. 114.
30. Fernao de Queyroz, *The Temporal and Spiritual Conquest of Ceylon*, trs. S.G. Perera, Colombo: Govt. Printers, 1930, p. 70.
31. Ibid., p. 562, see also p. 579; Also Joao de Barros and Diogo do Couto, 'The History of Ceylon from the earliest times to A.D. 1600', trs. and ed. Donald Ferguson, *JRAS (CB)*, vol. 20, no. 60, 1908, pp. 427, 443.
32. T.B.H. Abeysinghe, *Portuguese Rule in Ceylon 1594–1612*, Colombo: Lake House, 1966, p. 43.
33. C.R. De Silva, *The Portuguese in Ceylon 1617–1638*, Colombo: H.W. Cave & Co., 1972, pp. 97–8; Queyroz, *The Temporal and Spiritual Conquest*, pp. 654–6; Philipus Baldaeus, *True and Exact Description of the Great Island of Ceylon*, trs. Pieter Brohier, published as *CHJ*, vol. 8, nos. 1–4, July 1958–April 1959, pp. 85–6.
34. On military mercenaries in early modern India, see Dirk Kolff, *Naukar, Rajput and Sepoy: The Ethnohistory of the Military Labour Market in Hindustan 1450–1850*, Cambridge: Cambridge University Press, 1990, pp. 159–92
35. Queyroz, *The Temporal and Spiritual Conquest*, p. 70.
36. Abeysinghe, *Portuguese Rule in Ceylon*, p. 36.
37. Dewaraja, *The Kandyan Kingdom*, p. 28.
38. Ibid, p. 35.
39. James Cordiner, *Description of Ceylon, containing an Account of the Country, Inhabitants and Natural Productions with a Narrative of a Tour around the Island in 1800, the Campaign in Kandy in 1803 and a Journey to Ramisseram in 1804*, 2 vols., Delhi: Navrang, 1983, rpt. of 1807 edn. vol. 2, p. 297.
40. Donald Ferguson (ed.) 'The Earliest Dutch Visits to Ceylon', *JRAS(CB)*, vol. 31, no. 81, 1928, p. 124. During an earlier visit, De Weert was escorted out of Kandy by the same officer. Ibid., p. 119. De Weert was killed as a result of an altercation with the king.
41. Baldaeus, *True and Exact Description*, pp. 31–2.
42. But the fort surrendered before they could be of any use. Knox, *An Historical Relation*, pp. 385–6.
43. Dewaraja, *Sri Lanka through French Eyes*, p. 32.

44. Deposition on Phillip Hartman, Minutes of the Secret War Committee of the Dutch Political Council, 4 March 1761, SLNA 1/747.
45. Raven-Hart, *The Dutch Wars*, p. 57.
46. Diary of Ensign Greeving. Vimalananda Tennekoon, *British Intrigues in the Kingdom of Kandy*, Colombo: Gunasena, 1973, pp. 102–14,
47. Minutes of the Secret War Committee of the Dutch Political Council, 7 January 1763, SLNA 1/4864, p. 69.
48. Raven-Hart, *The Dutch Wars*, p. 56.
49. Diary of the Dutch Occupation of Kandy 1765, SLNA 1/4944, p. 20.
50. P.E. Pieris, *Sinhale and the Patriots*, Delhi: Navrang, 1995, rpt. of 1950 edn, Appendix Z, p. 688.
51. 'Andrews' Emabassies to Kandy in 1795 and 1796', ed. J.P. Lewis, *JRAS(CB)*, vol. 26, no. 71, 1918, p. 23.
52. *Ingrisi Hatana*, Palm Leaf Ms. 1859, K. 11, verses 106–7.
53. The Malays came from a wide range of ethnic backgrounds as well as localities. According to Husainmiya, Dutch records refer to Bandanese, Balinese, Bugis, Javanese, Madurese, 'Sumanepers', and Malays. B.A. Husainmiya, *Orang Regimen: The Malays of the Ceylon Rifle Regiment*, Bangi, Malaysia: Penerbit University Kebangsaan Malaysia, 1990, p. 45. Raven-Hart reckons that they were principally recruited from Java, Madure, and Makassar. Major Roland Raven-Hart (trs. and ed.), 'Major Medeler's Relief Expedition', *JRAS(CB)*, New Series, vol. 5, 1957, p. 239.
54. Ribeiro speaks glowingly of the bravery of a small body of 'Bandanese' soldiers who fought in an action at Tebuana in western Sri Lanka in 1654: '[The Bandanese] fought with such valour that it was not possible for anyone to excel them, and it was by their swords that we sustained the greatest loss, though they were only a band of fifty'. Ribeiro, *The Historic Tragedy*, p. 172.
55. Husainmiya, *Orang Regimen*, pp. 57–61.
56. Major Davie to Colombo, 17 June 1803, Thomas Ajax Anderson, *Journal of the Proceedings of the Trincomalee Detachment commanded by Lieut. Colonel Barbut His Majesty's 73rd Regiment from their Leaving Trincomalee till their Arrival at Kandy*, London: 1809, p. 188. Also Davie' letters to Colombo, 7 and 10 June 1803, SLNA 7/43, pp. 716 and 686.
57. According to some Europeans who escaped from the Kandyans, these men were distinguishable by the brands they carried on their backs. Raven-Hart, *The Dutch Wars*, p. 57.
58. Ibid., pp. 56, 100.
59. Major Evans at Puttalam to Colombo, 14 August 1803, Governor's Military Secret Diary, May–December 1803. SLNA 7/43, pp. 901, 917.
60. Report of Tennekoon Mudaliyar, 18 August 1803, SLNA 7/43, pp. 935–6.

61. Capt. Drieberg at Mullaitivu to Colombo, 27 August 1803, SLNA 7/43, pp. 1083–4.
62. See also *Ingrisi Hatana*, verses 133–4.
63. Prince Vijayapala to the Viceroy, 1 May 1643, P.E. Pieris, *Prince Vijayapala of Ceylon 1634–1654, from the original documents in Lisbon*, Colombo: C.A.C. Ltd., 1927, p. 31.
64. Minutes of the Secret War Committee, 5 May 1762, SLNA 1/4864, p. 17.
65. For instance, the diary of the Dutch occupation in 1765 mentions the desertion of a single sepoy with all his arms on 22 August. SLNA 1/4944, p. 42. Apparently some of the sepoys that deserted during this campaign were still around in 1803 because in August 1803 we hear from a British spy that the army of the Dissawa of the Seven Korales was accompanied by 8 'old Dutch sepoys'. W.E. Campbell at Chilaw to the Governor, 10 August 1803, SLNA 7/43, p. 919.
66. Vijayapala to the Viceroy, 1 May 1643, Pieris, *Prince Vijayapala of Ceylon*, p. 31.
67. Donald Ferguson, 'Earliest Dutch Visits to Ceylon', *JRAS(CB)*, vol. 30, no. 80, 1927, p. 381.
68. For instance in February 1764 a messenger sent by the Dutch to speak to the chief Adigar reported having seen two 'unusually large Kaffirs' parading before the Adigar in what the messenger thought was an attempt to impress him. Raven-Hart, *The Dutch Wars*, p. 36. Africans were even reported with the Kandyan army that invaded Mullaitivu in 1803. SLNA 7/43, pp. 935–6.
69. Diary of Ensign Greeving, Tennekoon, *British Intrigues*, p. 507.
70. Ehelepola's report to D'oyly on the king's resources, P.E. Pieris, *Tri Sinhala: The Last Phase*, Delhi: Navrang, 1995, rpt. of 1939 edn, Appendix I, p. 186.
71. They also dug and carried earth and stoes and provided other menial services. D'oyly, *A Sketch of the Constitution*, pp. 16–17.
72. P.M.P. Abeysinghe, *Udarata Vitti*, Colombo: Dept. of Cultural Affairs, 1998; 1st pub. 1960, p. 59. In Sabragamuwa, Atapattu, and Hewawasam, people were called Hewayas. Kirielle Nanawimala, *Saparagamuwe Parani Liyawili*, Colombo: Jinalankara Press, 1942, pp. 184, 188–9.
73. The Memorandum of Hebert Wright, the Government Agent of Sabaragamuwa, to the Secretary on the administrative organization of Sabaragamuwa in 1818, in Pieris, *Sinhale*, Appendix R, p. 644.
74. K.H. De Silva, *Sinhala Hatan Kavi*, Colombo: Sri Lanka Publishers, 1964.
75. *Diary of Mr. John D'oyly*, with introduction and notes by H.W. Codrington, Delhi: Navrang, 1995, 1st published as *JRAS(CB)*, vol. 25, no. 69, 1917, p. 5.
76. Ibid., p. 55.
77. Barros and Couto, 'History of Ceylon', pp. 220 and p. 301; Ribeiro, *The Historic Tragedy*, p. 87.

78. Minutes of the Batavia Council, 23 November 1675, W.P. Coolhaas (ed.), *Generale Missiven van Gouverneurs-General en Raden aan Heren xvii Der Verenigde Oostindische Compagnie,* 9 vols, s'Gravenhage: Verkrijgbaar bij Martinus Nijhoff, 1971, vol. 4, p. 76.
79. Knox, *An Historical Relation,* pp. 171–2.
80. The Sinhala war poem *Rajasinha Hatana* lists the areas from which the army was collected. They include the Kandyan highlands as well as such far-flung areas like Trincomalee, Anuradhapura, Hiriyala, Kalaweva, Panama, Yala, Kottiyarama, Vedipattu, Tirukkovil, and the Vanni. *Rajasinha Hatana,* ed. Ellepola M.M. Somaratre, Kandy: T.B.S. Godamune and Sons, date unavailable, verses 244–55.
81. Queyroz, *The Temporal and Spiritual Conquest,* p. 1014. A Korale was a subdivision of a province.
82. M. Jonville, 'Narrative of a Journey to Kandy made on the Occasion of the Embassy of Major General Macdowall in 1800', *JRAS(CB),* vol. 38, no. 105, 1948, p. 13.
83. See for instance, the letter from Hewagam Korale Mudaliyar dated 11 November 1810 which informs the British in Colombo that 'thousands of able young men at the rate of 1 to each family' were being assembled in Kandy at the time. *Diary of Mr. John D'oyly,* entry for 24 November 1810, p. 41.
84. The British officer Arthur Johnstone writes:
    'Each village has its chief, with several inferior officers in proportion to its size. The chief, on receiving an order from his dessa [sic] or lord, summons every third, fourth or fifth man, according to the nature of his instructions and proceeds with his feudatory levies to the place of rendezvous.' Captain Arthur Johnstone, *Narrative of the Operations of a Detachment in an Expedition to Candy in the Island of Ceylon in the Year 1804 with some Observations on the previous Campaigns and on the Nature of Candyan Warfare &c &c,* London, 1810, p. 8.
85. Coolhaas, *Generale Missiven,* vol. 4, p. 79.
86. Report made by Mira Lebbe, J.H.O. Paulusz, *Secret Minutes of Dutch Political Council, 1762,* Colombo: Govt. Printers, 1954, p. 101.
87. Governor to the Secy of State, 27 November 1803, Governor's Despatches to the Secretary of State, 28 March 1817–23 December 1818, SLNA 5/9, p. 249.
88. The war poem *Ingrisi Hatana* gives a long list of chiefs and their commands: Migastenne—Seven Korales, Leuke—Four Korales, Kepetipola—Matale, Kahadava—Sabaragamuwa, Palipana—Udapalatha, Moledanda—Yatinuwara, Madugalle—Dumbara. *Ingrisi Hatana,* verses 98–107.
89. *Madarampura Puvatha,* ed. Labugama Lankananda, Colombo: Ministry of Cultural Affairs, 1996, verse 324, p. 41. According to a Portuguese soldier, the Kandyans came to attack De Sa's army in 1630 'waving

many banners of various colours to the sound of warlike instruments'. *Expedition to Uva*, p. 90.

90. The *sannasa* is reproduced in K.H. De Silva, *Sinhala Hatan Kavi*, Colombo: Sri Lanka Publishers, 1964, p. 104.
91. Lewis Gibson to Colombo, 8 August 1803, SLNA 7/43, p. 897.
92. Gibson to Colombo, 10 August 1803, SLNA 7/43, p. 899.
93. Gibson to Colombo, 13 August 1803, SLNA 7/43, p. 904.
94. Tennekoon Mudaliyar to Gibson, 14 August 1803, SLNA 7/43, p. 914.
95. Gibson to Colombo, 14 August 1803, SLNA 7/43, p. 910.
96. Gibson to Colombo, 14 August 1803, SLNA 7/43, p. 912.
97. Gibson to Colombo, 15 August 1803, SLNA 7/43, p. 915.
98. Tennekoon Mudaliyar's report, 16 August 1803, SLNA 7/43, p. 923.
99. Saram Mudaliyar's report, 16 August 1803, SLNA 7/43, p. 924.
100. Tennekoon Mudaliyar's report, 18 August 1803, SLNA 7/43, p. 935.
101. Tennekoon Mudaliyar to Gibson, 8 August 1803, SLNA 7/43, p. 935–6.
102. Report from Canda Labde Pattoe Mohandiram, 17 August 1803, SLNA 7/43, p. 925.
103. Tennekooon Mudliyar to Gibson, 17 August 1803, SLNA 7/43, pp. 932–3. Also SLNA 7/43, p. 934.
104. Report from the Vidana of Mapelgam to the Korala of Gangabada Pattu, SLNA, 7/43, p. 955.
105. The beating of tom-toms appear to have been a very common mode of collecting troops as well as conveying any type of order. See Barnsley's deposition. Also Kirimetiyawe Metindu, *Maha Hatana*, verse 48, p. 9.
106. Diary of the 1764 campaign, Raven-Hart, *The Dutch Wars*, p. 38. In 1762, similar reports were made by some minor chiefs in Matara about threats by king's officers to burn down their houses, degrade their families and lay waste their gardens and themselves punished by death. Paulusz, *Secret Minutes*, p. 51. In 1656, one of the Kandyan officers, Tudugala Appuhami, issued like orders to the people of Pasdun Korale to withhold support from the Dutch. Baldaeus, *True and Exact Description*, p. 263.
107. Ribeiro, *The Historic Tragedy*, p. 26.
108. Johnstone, *Narrative*, pp. 9–10. In his account of the Kandyan Dutch War in 1761–6, Zwier quotes a Dutch officer describing Kandyan soldiers food as 'kokers of klapperzuurzakken, wortels uit de grond, die omtrent de smaak heeben als aardappeln'. Zwier, *Het Verdraag*, p. 36.
109. Knox, *An Historical Relation*, p. 175.
110. 'The common soldiers carry every one but one piece of a Tallapat leafe—the hole is to large for one man to carry—and 2 or 3 or more of them joyne their leaves and so make a good and sufficient tent. But

for the great officers tents these Tallapat leaves are sewed together in forme that they open like the roof of a house and rowle up like a matt, so that, when they have made the frame with sticks, which here is no want of for the country is all woods, they spread these sewed Tallapat leaves over top so tight that not one drop of water can come through and are sooner set up and lighter to Carry then ours in England.' Ibid, pp. 175–6. Captain Herbert Beaver stumbled on to one of these camps, hastily abandoned at his approach, during his pursuit of the Kandyans in March–April 1803. See V.M. Methley (ed.), 'The Letters of Captain Herbert Beaver (H.M. 19th Regiment), March–April 1803', *CALR*, vol. 4, no. 2, Oct. 1918, p. 70. A similar discovery of a Kandyan camp behind their entrenchment is mentioned in the Diary of events in Matara February 1762–August 1764, SLNA, 1/4940, p. 29.

111. Queyroz, *The Temporal and Spiritual Conquest*, p. 575.
112. Vincenzo Sangermano, *The Burmese Empire a Hundred Years Ago*, with an introduction and notes by John Jarine, Bangkok: White Orchid Press, 1995; 5th edn., 1st pub. 1833, p. 99. Reverend Sangermano was a Christian missionary who lived in Ava and Rangoon between 1783 and 1806.
113. Ribeiro, *The Historic Tragedy*, p. 182.
114. Raven-Hart, *The Dutch Wars*, p. 160.
115. Capt. Evans at Puttalam to Colombo, 15 August 1803, SLNA 7/43, pp. 918–19.
116. Capt. Evans to Colombo, 8 August 1803, SLNA 7/43, p. 919.
117. Lieut. Jewell at Jaffna to Colombo, 11 September 1803, SLNA 7/43, pp. 1089–90. Another raid in November recovered large quantities of grain, areca nuts, and a quantity of salt considered sufficient for two years. Cordiner, *Description*, vol. 2, p. 257.
118. *Diary of Mr. John D'oyly*, entry 17 Sept. 1810, p. 6.
119. Ibid., pp. 9, 35, 45.
120. The land grant is reproduced in Ven. Namulle Dhammananda, *Madyama Lanka Puravrta*, Colombo: Gunasena, 1970, pp. 173–4.
121. Queyroz, *The Temporal and Spiritual Conquest*, p. 773.
122. Raven-Hart, *The Dutch Wars*, p. 100.
123. *Diary of Mr. John D'oyly*, entry for 1 Dec. 1810, p. 46. Also entries for 26 Oct. 1810, p. 32, and 13 Nov. 1810, p. 38.
124. See, for instance, the land grants which are reproduced in Kirielle Nanawimala, *Katuwana Matara Hatana*, Colombo: Gunasena, 1968, pp. 71–85 and Kirielle Nanawimala, *Saparagamuve Parani Liyawili*, pp. 51, 117, 124, 139–40, 208.
125. Abeysinghe, *Udarata Vitti*, p. 130.
126. H.A.P. Abeywardene (ed.), *Kadaimpoth Vimarshanaya*, Colombo: Dept. of Cultural Affairs, 1978, pp. 142–5, 223–33.

127. De Silva, *Sinhala Hatan Kavi*, p. 104.
128. Paulusz, *Secret Minutes*, p. 144.
129. 'The king called all the people who went with him to Hangwelle, and told them, as you cannot make war, you must make something else, and he put them to work in a largeforest of 200 acres to clear it, and they are now sowing paddy in that ground'. Deposition of Talagama Unnanse, Governor's Secret Diary, January–December 1804, SLNA 7/44, p. 160.
130. Kirimetiyawe Mentindu, *Maha Hatana*, verse, 49, p. 9.
131. *Mandarampura Puvatha*, verse 330, p. 42.
132. J.H.O. Paulusz (ed.), 'Raja Simha, His Military and Other Resources: Report by Disava Tennekoon in 1676', *JRAS(CB)*, New Series, vol. 5, 1957, p. 163. Knox gives a much higher figure of 30,000 for contemporary Kandyan manpower resources. Knox, *An Historical Relation,* p. 171.
133. Queyroz, *The Temporal and Spiritual Conquest,* p. 69.
134. Knox, *An Historical Relation,* p. 436.
135. *The Expedition to Uva* , p. 26.
136. Raven-Hart, *The Dutch Wars*, p. 91.
137. Ibid., p. 100.
138. Tennekoon, *British Intrigues*, p. 512.
139. Raven-Hart, *The Dutch Wars*, p. 91.
140. Letter from Gonawila to Colombo 11 March 1765, SLNA 1/4904.
141. Methley, 'Letters of Captain Herbert Beaver', p. 67.
142. For instance, in June 1818 the British outpost at Godamune was attacked by a force reported to be around 200-300 and again in July by a force of about 5,000. *Ceylon Gazette,* 13 June and 11 July 1818, *The Uva Rebellion: Extracts from the Ceylon Government Gazette 1817–1818,* Colombo: A.M. & J. Ferguson, 1888, pp. 31 and 34. Another force of around 3000 was reported at an action in Pasbage on 16 July. *Ceylon Government Gazette*, 25 July, Ibid. p. 37.
143. *Ceylon Government Gazette*, 21 March 1818, *The Uva Rebellion*, p. 20.
144. Queyroz, *The Temporal and Spiritual Conquest,* p. 488.
145. Ibid., p. 772.
146. C.R. De Silva, 'The First Portuguese Revenue Register of the Kingdom of Kotte, 1599', *CJHSS* , Jan.–Dec. 1975, p. 84.
147. John D'oyly to Robert Brownrigg 17 May 1814. 'The Fall of Ehelepola Maha Nilame. Documents relating to the insurrection', *CLR*, vol. 4, no. 10, p. 469.
148. K.W. Goonewardene, *The Foundation of Dutch Power in Ceylon 1638–1658,* Amsterdam: Djambatan, 1958, p. 163.
149. Queyroz, *The Temporal and Spiritual Conquest*, p. 70.
150. For the revolt of Ambanwela Appuhamy see J.H.O. Paulusz, 'Ambanwela Appuhamy's Rebellion of 1665', *JRAS(CB),* New Series,

vol. 7, no. 1, 1960, pp. 104–12. For the revolts of 1709 and 1760, see Dewaraja, *The Kandyan Kingdom*, pp. 66–9, 108–10. For Ehelepola's rebellion, see Colvin R. de Silva, *Ceylon under the British Occupation, 1795–1833,* 2 vols., New Delhi: Navrang, 1995, 4th edn., 1st pub. 1941, vol. 1, pp. 144–5.

151. Dewaraja, *The Kandyan Kingdom*, pp. 175–7.
152. Ibid., pp. 175–7.
153. Seneviratne, *Rituals of the Kandyan State*, p. 114.
154. John D'oyly to Robert Brownrigg, 17 May 1814, 'The Fall of Ehelepola Maha Nilame', *CLR*, vol. 4, no. 10, pp. 469–71.
155. John D'oyly to Robert Brownrigg, 22 May 1814, 'The Fall of Ehelepola Maha Nilame', *CLR*, vol. 4, no. 11, p. 504.
156. For instance, the king ordered many executions following the failure of the revolt in 1664. Knox, *An Historical Relation*, pp. 184–5. After crushing Ehelepola's uprising in 1814 the king ordered the execution of the ring leaders and their families, including Ehelepola's children. Colvin R. de Silva, *Ceylon*, vol. 1, pp. 148–9.

THREE

The Weapons

Kandyan Military Hardware

The Kandyan soldiers were armed with a wide variety of weapons. They ranged from the primitive club to the more modern musket and cannon. These weapons reflected a readiness to borrow technology from their opponents as well as the limitations of indigenous technology. They also further underlined the decentralized nature of Kandyan military organization.

TECHNOLOGY

Before considering the weapons and equipment used by the Kandyan forces it is instructive to look at the technological resources that were available to the Kandyans. In most societies the material culture is an index to the technology available to or in use in that society. So it was with Kandyan society. Kandyan society was not rich in material possessions as befitting a society supported by a subsistence economy. The Kandyan peasants lived in humble dwellings, 'small, low, thatched cottages built with sticks, daubed with clay' and possessed little more than a few agricultural implements and cooking utensils. Even the houses of the nobles did not appear imposing and contained just a few simple furnishings.[1] Kandy town, at least since the eighteenth century, contained broad, straight streets but the only substantial building was the royal palace. This was in a complex, 'a stupendous pile of stone buildings', but of simple construction with austere interiors.[2] As explained earlier, for Kandyans, wealth and power was measured in terms of the command over the goods and services available within a subsistence economy, and as such an abundance of food and labour, ensured by control over land, was the best index of wealth and power.

And just as no imposing edifices dominated the Kandy town and no great possessions adorned the homes of the Kandyan nobility, no complex technology aided Kandyan life. The technology in use was basic, geared to fulfil the simple demands of subsistence agriculture and the modest needs and tastes of the nobility and the clergy. The simple houses for the peasantry and their nobility, pots and baskets for their kitchens and implements for their fields did not require complex technology. Not that subtle craftsmanship was lacking. Kandyan craftsmen did produce some remarkable works of art that required specialized skill and talent. This was largely the province of silver and goldsmiths and mainly concerned decorating objects, including weapons. This work involved inlaying objects with gold, silver, and ivory and working beautiful patterns on surfaces. It was more the work of artists than those of technicians and utilized simple tools and equipment.[3] Works requiring complex mechanical knowledge was conspicuous by their absence. Even objects of daily use in European society were capable of bewildering Kandyans with their sophistication. This is clearly demonstrated by an episode concerning a watch given to King Narendrasinha by a Dutch ambassador in 1730. The watch was not working when the next Dutch embassy visited Kandy in the following year. The Kandyans told the ambassador that repeated attempts by their experts on such things failed to get the watch going. The Dutchman promptly put the matter to rest by making it work again.[4] Even in the middle of the last century, villages situated a few miles in the interior of the island employed the simplest of technology in their agriculture and cottage industries.[5]

Nowhere was this technological simplicity more in evidence than in the production of iron, the process concerned with military technology. Kandyan territories did not possess any extensive deposits of iron ore but there was an abundance of the material embedded in gneiss and found close to the surface in the ground.[6] The Kandyans extracted this iron through a simple process of smelting in a rudimentary furnace:

> Each furnace, at its mouth, was about three feet deep, and terminated in the form of a funnel, over a shallow pit inclining outwards. They were made in a bed of clay, about three feet high and three feet wide, against which a light wall about ten feet high was raised to protect the bellows and operators, who were situated immediately behind. Each

bellows consisted of a circular rim of wood, about six inches in diameter, and scarcely two high, fixed on a clay floor, and covered with moist cowhide; in the centre of which was a hole to admit air, and to receive a cross stick, to which a cord was attached, that was fastened above to an elastic stick. Each pair of bellows was worked by a boy, who rested his back against a rope, for the purpose of support, and stepped alternately from the orifice of one bellows to that of the other, at each step forcing a blast of air into the furnace, through a tube of bamboo. The furnaces were charged with a mixture of iron ore, broken into small pieces and charcoal. The fires were kept up as strong as possible, till the ore was reduced, and the fused metal collected in a cake in the ash pit.[7]

The Kandyans also manufactured a good kind of steel.[8] According to Knox, Kandyans freely engaged in producing iron from these stones and sold them to those who did not possess them.[9] Sometimes they purchased the material from low country people. Thus, in the early nineteenth century, we hear of the people in Kirama in the Matara district selling iron thus extracted to the Kandyans.[10] However, the quantity of iron and steel produced by the above method was not great. According to Ananda Coomaraswamy, Kandyan iron makers produced only about 6 pounds of iron and a few pounds of steel every three hours in their traditional furnaces in the early twentieth century.[11] This may be taken as a fair indication of the productiveness of Kandyan iron-makers during the days of the Kandyan kings as well as they were using the same technology.

But although iron was freely extracted it required the smith's expertise to fashion implements and weapons from this iron. According to Knox, several villages were served by one smith. In traditional Kandyan society, the smith's expertise was largely limited to producing the implements of peasant agriculture and household: hoes, sickles, knives, areca nut cutters, etc. They also made locks and keys, palanquin fittings, and elephant goads, which were meant for a smaller clientele connected with the nobility and clergy.[12] All this work utilized simple technology, little more than a furnace and a few instruments for beating and fashioning the implements into shape and dexterity in using them. The British surgeon John Davy favourably compared the Kandyan smith's expertise and equipment with that of the common country blacksmith in Europe.[13]

In the military sphere, Kandyan technology was capable of producing a range of simple traditional weapons such as swords, spears, arrows, and battle-axes, all of which required the same skill and processes that went into producing hoes, sickles, and knives. But the advent of Europeans for the first time brought them into contact with weapons, namely firearms and artillery, that were relatively more sophisticated than the traditional indigenous weapons. It presented a serious challenge for Kandyan technology.

FIREARMS

As the Kandyans settled down to their long struggle with the Europeans, firearms and artillery came to occupy a prominent place in the Kandyan arsenal. European sources speak of thousands of muskets and other firearms captured from the defeated Kandyan armies. The adoption of these weapons by the Kandyans, and indeed by the Sri Lankans, has a curious history. It is commonly believed that it was the Europeans who introduced firearms and artillery to Sri Lanka. The Sinhalese chronicle *Rajavaliya* has done much to establish this perception with its colourful description of the awe with which the local population of Colombo regarded the Portuguese cannon.[14] This, however, is misleading. While the Portuguese were primarily responsible for the diffusion of firearms in Sri Lanka, it was not they who introduced the new weapons to the island.

According to Queyroz, it was the Moors who first used artillery on Sri Lankan soil when they attacked the Portuguese in Colombo in 1518. And in the following year they are credited with lending some weapons to the Sinhalese when they attacked the Portuguese fort in Colombo.[15] Firearms and artillery are also mentioned in the hands of the Malabar troops that came to the aid of Mayadunne in the 1530s.[16] This is quite understandable as artillery and firearms could not have been unknown to the Indian Muslims trading with Sri Lanka. As Iqtidar Alam Khan points out, there is strong evidence to suggest that cannon and firearms had been in use in the Delhi Sultanate and the Bahamani kingdoms in the second half of the fifteenth century.[17] In the following century the Mughals employed artillery and firearms quite frequently, independent of European influence. Firearms and cannon were also being used by the Muslims on the Kerala coast at this time and it is not surprising if the Kerala Muslims who traded with Colombo possessed some gunpowder weapons and employed them against the Portuguese in the early sixteenth century.[18]

However, these guns were probably of small calibre. According to Queyroz, some of the guns used by the Moors were 'as big as *bercos*', small calibre guns firing balls of weight about one pound each.[19] The Muslims may have been using small swivel pieces taken from their ships.[20] But bigger guns seem to have been used in later battles. For instance, in 1539 we hear of a Malabar force employing field artillery against the Portuguese.[21]

However, it is also quite clear that it was the advent of the Portuguese that paved the way for the regular use of gunpowder weapons on Sri Lankan soil and induced indigenous armies to take up the weapon. After the initial confrontations in 1518 and 1519, military conflict in Sri Lanka was dominated by conflict between the Portuguese and the indigenous rulers and artillery and handheld firearms came to play a prominent role in these battles. During the early confrontations between Sitawaka and the Portuguese, firearms were being chiefly used by the Portuguese and the Malabar allies of the Sinhalese but it was not long before the latter also began to use guns. By 1552 the army of the king of Sitawaka in the low country was reported to have a great force of musketeers and archers[22] and by 1593 they were credited with the possession of a large number of kodituwakku or light artillery pieces (see below).[23] By the beginning of the seventeenth century, firearms had spread to the east coast of the island.[24]

Though it is not certain when the Kandyan armies first began using firearms, it appears to have been first used sometime in the sixteenth century. When a Portuguese expeditionary force was forced to retreat from Kandy in 1544 the Kandyan army gathered to oppose them was rumoured to have been armed with about 2,000 'very good espingardeiros'.[25] But guns are not mentioned in the hands of the Kandyans who surrounded this force later,[26] and in the ensuing fighting, we hear of only bows and arrows.[27] Queyroz describes the Kandyan army as comprising 'mostly bowmen' even as late as 1582.[28] Still, it is not unlikely that the Kandyan army may have possessed some firearms before this time because when Dom Jorge de Castro retreated from the highlands in 1551 he left a large quantity of arms and baggage in the hands of the Kandyans.[29] These no doubt included a considerable number of firearms as well.

By the end of the century, however, firearms had definitely secured an important place in the Kandyan arsenal, a substantial number of them contributing to the destruction of Pedro Lopes de Souza's army in 1594.[30] Thereafter, guns begin to figure frequently in Kandyan warfare. Hundreds and even thousands of them are mentioned in the hands of Kandyan soldiers in the seventeenth, eighteenth, and nineteenth centuries. But it is also clear that only a portion of the Kandyan army, perhaps a minority, was armed with guns. According to Queyroz, in an army of about 8,000 which confronted the Portuguese in 8,000, more than half were armed with firearms[31] and, if Ribeiro is to be believed, in the Kandyan army of 40,000 raised in 1655 there were 3,000 foot-muskets or kodituwakku and 9,000 muskets.[32] No doubt there is some exaggeration here. A more sober account was given by a Portuguese soldier who took part in de Sa's disastrous expedition in 1630, who described the Kandyan troops that attacked the Portuguese rearguard as being armed mostly with bows and spears.[33] According to a Dutch observer in the eighteenth century, if 3,000 Kandyans were collected only 500 were to be found armed with firearms.[34] But the best indication of the number of guns in circulation in Kandyan territories at any given time was provided when the British crushed the rebellion of 1817–18. The rebels yielded over 8,000 muskets to the British, from all the rebellious territories.[35] It was a large haul but still not quite sufficient to arm all the men that Kandy could bring into the field.

Where did the Kandyans get their guns from? Of course a part of them were locally produced. Unfortunately we know little about their physical appearance. According to an eighteenth-century Dutch manuscript 'Anmerkungen', the Sinhalese guns had long barrels. This is the only attempt to describe the appearance of Sinhalese firearms. It is a description borne out by the few Sinhalese firearms that survive. In addition to long barrels they also have curiously curved stocks.[36] The firearms depicted in the sixteenth-century frescoes in Kaballalena also have curved stocks.[37]

Other European observers say little about the appearance of the guns but speak admiringly about Sinhalese craftsmanship in forging them. The sixteenth-century Dutch traveller John Huyghen Van Linschoten says that the people in Sri Lanka made 'the finest barrels for peeces that may be found in any place which shine as brightly as if they were Silver'. According to the early seventeenth-century French visitor, Francois Pyrard, Sri Lankans made 'all sort of arms, such as arquebuses, swords, pikes and bucklers which are the most valued in the Indies'.[38] Sinhala sources are not very helpful either. Sinhala war poems and other chronicles list several types of firearms. The *Rajasinha Hatana,* for instance, mentions *dik tuvakku, bondikkula,* kodituwakku, *pedrenera, bogum tuvakku,* and *dhee tuvakku*[39] while the late seventeenth-century narrative, *Mukkara Hatana* speaks of *hadi tuvakku, bondikkula, ath tuvakku,* and *birangi*.[40] Of these only kodituwakku, *pedrenera, bondikkula,* and *ath tuvakku* can be clearly identified. Kodituvakku and *pedrenera* refer to types of light artillery (which will be discussed later) while *ath tuvaku,* and *bondikkula* signified pistols and flintlocks. Deraniyagala believes that *bondikkula* is a derivative of the Arabic word for musket, *bunduk,* which seems plausible. M.D. Raghavan translates *birangi* as mortars, but how he came to this conclusion we are not told. The identity of the other guns remains a mystery. It is possible that they refer to variations of the musket but we cannot be certain.

One thing we can be certain of is that some of the surviving Kandyan muskets are hardly good examples of ordinary Sinhalese guns, but are probably weapons made for a special purpose, possibly as gifts, which explains their workmanship, and, to some extent, their survival. As such, they were also special cases, produced with special care and attention. No doubt it was about such weapons that European observers spoke so glowingly about. The guns generally produced in the Kandyan highlands appear to have been of a cruder construction as shown by other surviving examples. 'The workmanship of them [locally manufactured guns] is indeed coarse and not to be praised', John Davy wrote, adding that 'still, they answer pretty well for the purpose for which they intended and give satisfaction to those unacquainted with better'.[41] The author of the '*Aanmerkingen*' however, considered Kandyan guns to be superior to Dutch muskets in some aspects, saying that the Kandyan guns, though poor in appearance, gained a longer range than Dutch muskets. But this was largely due to them having a small bore and long barrel which enabled the powder to burn longer and use all its energy to drive out the bullet.[42]

It is not clear how the transfer of technology would have taken place. The firearms reported to be in the hands of Kandyans in 1545 were supposed to have been produced by Kandyans under Portuguese tutelage. As explained above, the report appears to have been unfounded but the Portuguese reporter was no doubt allowing his knowledge of the situation in the low country—where the Sinhalese have been familiar with firearms for sometime—to colour his imagination. It is certain that individual Portuguese may have been willing to teach eager Sinhalese the craft of making firearms. But it is also not surprising if the Kandyans learnt it themselves. As explained above, the eighteenth-century Dutch traveller, Johaan Wolfgang Heydt was highly impressed with the Kandyan craftsmen's ability to copy things placed before them.[43] And the early firearms were not very difficult to copy. The firearms used by the Portuguese in Sri Lanka—arquebus and the espingarda—had a simple firing mechanism. The matchlock used in these guns consisted of a trigger forcing a slow-burning match into a pan primed with powder. Once the principle of this mechanism was grasped it was simple to copy the matchlock firearms and judging by surviving pieces, the Kandyans accomplished this well. Fashioning an iron tube was certainly within the capability of the ordinary Kandyan ironsmith.

The flintlock, however, would have been more difficult to replicate. The flintlock came to be used widely by European armies only in the late seventeenth century and the mechanism was more complex than the matchlock. It consisted of an arm holding a flint striking sparks off a metal plate. As the author of the '*Aanmerkingen*' points out, the Kandyans did use flintlocks, using pebbles instead of flints which were not naturally obtainable in the island.[44] Still, the flintlock would have been a slightly more complicated mechanism for the Kandyan craftsman to duplicate than the matchlock but not impossible. It is also interesting that in all the surviving pieces, the locks are of

European construction. It is also possible that the Kandyans used the locks from captured but unserviceable European weapons to fit their locally made guns.

But the biggest problem with producing firearms would have concerned the production of the raw material rather than the weapons themselves. Traditional iron implements and weapons required far less iron per piece than did firearms and the supply of iron ore in Kandyan lands was sufficient for meeting the very limited demand for these objects and implements within the subsistence economy. But when this supply was straddled with a demand for musket barrels that required much more iron than required by areca nut cutters, sickles, and spearheads, the supply of raw material was placed under a potential strain.[45] Furthermore, as noted earlier, Kandyan iron production was a very labour-intensive process, yielding small quantities of iron in return for hours of labouring. The production of firearms would have necessarily placed greater demands on the labour of iron producers and smiths. A correspondent for the *Ceylon Government Gazette* noted in 1818 that the Kandyans did make very serviceable firelocks 'but also surmised that their manufacture must be very slow, and it would require a long time to replace a small part of those which have been given up'.[46]

But it was not absolutely necessary to depend on traditional technology to build up an arsenal of firearms when the finished product could also be obtained from outside sources. The European settlements on the coast was an attractive source for firearms but unlike many other Asian and African peoples, the Kandyans had very little scope for buying muskets from the Europeans. This was because, unlike in Africa and many other parts of Asia, the European powers that had established themselves in Sri Lanka during the period of Kandyan resistance were always the current or potential enemies of Kandy. These powers had no commercial or political interest in selling arms to the Kandyans. Besides even if there was an opportunity for the Kandyans to buy European firearms, they were constrained by other considerations. There was little that the Kandyans could offer in return for guns. A kingdom that had little money could ill afford to purchase modern firearms. The financial constraint also applied to buying guns from sources outside Sri Lanka, particularly European and local sources on the subcontinent. The increasingly tight European noose around the coast complicated matters further.

This is not to say that the Kandyans never purchased firearms from outside sources. According to Arthur Johnstone, firearms in use in the Kandyan army did include guns purchased from the Europeans.[47] This is because if some money could be raised it was not difficult to find individual Europeans on the coast who were willing to sell guns to the Kandyans even if the European authorities frowned on such transactions. And if the blockade around the island could be penetrated there was further opportunity for laying hands on firearms. The flourishing smuggling trade between the subcontinent and some Sri Lankan ports, especially Puttalam on the west coast, helped the Kandyans in this endeavour. Thus, in early 1763 the Dutch intercepted a fleet of 13 dhonies from south India off Puttalam loaded with muskets, bullets, medicines, and linen.[48] We are only aware of the weapons seized by the Dutch but it goes without saying that a considerable number of vessels also got through the blockade. These were destined for the Kandyan market showing that the highlanders were obtaining firearms from offshore.

But it is very unlikely that the Kandyans had the money to purchase firearms in large quantities. As the seizure of the dhonies showed, purchasing was also fraught with risks. But purchasing was not the only way the Kandyans could obtain European guns. The numerous Kandyan triumphs over invading European forces yielded rich hauls of firearms. As already noted, the Portuguese retreat in 1552 would have left some firearms in the hands of the Kandyans while, according to Baldaeus, after the Battle of Danture in 1594, the Kandyans 'acquired much booty . . . of small arms and metal guns'.[49] In fact, the Kandyans may have been using Portuguese guns in this battle itself because several days prior to the final battle, a detachment of Portuguese were cut down at Halloluwa.[50] That triumph too delivered a considerable number of guns into Kandyan hands. Other major victories over the Portuguese in 1603, 1630, and 1638 enriched the Kandyan arsenal with firearms. The booty in 1630 included hundreds of kodituwakku or light artillery pieces.[51] It was a similar situation with the Dutch and the British. The many Dutch reverses during the early phase of the war in 1761–6 yielded more guns while Johnstone estimated that the disastrous British expedition in 1803 augmented the Kandyan arsenal by about '1,000 stand of serviceable English muskets'.[52]

Most firearms in Kandyan hands, whether locally produced or not, appear to have been maintained in a bad state. This is implicit in the remarks of many Europeans who saw them. The British ambassador to Kandy in 1795, John Andrews judged only about a hundred of the guns he saw with the Kandyans in 1795 to be serviceable while all 473 'country' muskets captured in 1815 were considered to be unrepairable.[53] According to another, more blunt British observer, 'the best Kandyan arms were inferior, in point of efficiency, to those of any temporarily excited European rabble'.[54] But there were also those who spoke approvingly of Kandyan treatment of their arms. According to Arthur Johnstone, the Kandyans took good care of their gun-locks, covering them with guards made of skin or wax cloth to prevent rusting.[55]

However, it is not surprising if a considerable number of the Kandyans' firearms would have been in a bad state of repair, simply because it was difficult to avoid. Many of the guns taken from Europeans would have simply deteriorated with age. It is interesting to hear Kandyan chiefs in 1810 demanding from their people firearms given to them 'during Dutch times' which refers to a time at least 14 years ago but possibly earlier than that.[56] It suggests that many Kandyans may have been in possession of very old guns, a situation borne out by Johnstone's observation that many of the Kandyan guns were 'taken at different times or purchased from their European invaders'.[57]

WS describes Kandyan ammunition as being hammered from iron and rarely if ever from lead, the Kandyans sometimes using iron rods of 1–3 inches or even pebbles in the place of bullets. The charges were carried in bamboos or small cases or even in linen cartridges.[58] According to Johnstone, the Kandyans carried their ammunition in coconut shells.[59] Large quantities of gun-powder was also carried in casks made of hollowed palmyra trunks.[60] The army that besieged the Government House in Hambantota in August and September 1803 seemed to have been well organized where ammunition was concerned. A British sortie in September 1803 came across a party of Kandyans carrying their ammunition in pouches made of spotted deer-skin.[61] Later, the British found much ammunition in the captured Kandyan batteries, all made into cartridges with iron balls 'to match the guns' taken in the batteries.[62] Sometimes, Kandyan ingenuity in craftsmanship extended to ammunition storage. During the rebellion in 1817–18, a British party in ambush in the Four Korales recovered from a rebel force an ammunition box made of a 'jaggeree' tree containing as many as 400 cartridges.[63]

ARTILLERY

The Kandyans did not use cannon widely and when used, they were usually guns of smaller calibre. When the Portuguese took Balana in 1603 they found many *roqueyras* and two iron *caes*,[64] which were pieces of medium artillery while during the siege of Talampitiya in the same year the Kandyans are said to have used an *esphera* of great length. When the Kandyans descended on Colombo in 1630 they brought with them only the few small guns taken from enemy posts overrun on the way.[65] The Kandyan deficiency in artillery in the seventeenth century is further testified to by Ribeiro who says that the walls of the Colombo fort were made of a single line of *taipa* or clay wall, 'a sufficient defence against the natives'.[66] Few cannon were used against the Dutch in 1670–5; the Kandyan army that surrounded Bibilegama in August 1675 possessed only a few light pieces.[67]

Cannon appear to feature more prominently in the Kandyan arsenal in the following century. A considerable number of them were used during the campaign against Katuwana and Matara in 1761, but even these were mostly light guns. Many of these guns fell into Dutch hands during their counter-offensive but the size of the Kandyan artillery arsenal was revealed when they captured the palace in Kandy four years later. Their booty on the occasion included 42 pieces of cannon, from 18 to 1 pounders and even two mortars.[68] The British also found the Kandyans to be in possession of a considerable number of cannon. During the campaign in 1803, 43 pieces of artillery including several mortars fell into their hands while the haul in 1815 came to 30 guns including mortars and howitzers.[69] There is no indication as to the numbers of heavy and light cannon recovered in 1765 and

1815 but the heaviest guns found in 1803 were three 12 pounders. The rest were lighter weapons, the vast majority being of 6 pounds or less. We can assume that this was the case with the cannon recovered in 1765 and 1815 as well.

The Kandyans faced several problems with the acquisition and employment of cannon. Some of these problems were similar to that of adopting firearms. They had to be either obtained from the Europeans or locally manufactured. The latter option was not very attractive. On the one hand there was the problem of resources. Artillery required large quantities of iron, much more than required by musket barrels and this was not quite obtainable in the Kandyan territories. There was also the question of expertise. Kandyan smiths were good at producing small guns and other weapons and implements but whether they had the knowhow to produce heavier weapons is a moot point. According to the Dutch visitor Johann Wolfgang Heydt, who was in the island in the 1740s, heavy cannon of Kandyan manufacture were totally unknown[70] while the defecting Kandyan chief Ehelepola, declared that no cannon was being cast in Kandy in 1815.

But there is also evidence to suggest that the Kandyans did cast cannon. A Sinhala poem, *Aldeniye Alankaraya,* speaks of an interesting contest in the early nineteenth century between the kottalbadde or artificers' departments of 'Udarata' and 'Patha rata' (high country and low country) in which two cannon cast by the two departments were test fired. The Udarata gun stood the test while the patha rata gun exploded.[71] The 'Anmerkungen' also asserts that Kandyans produced cannon but of the lightest possible kind—no heavier than 1/2 to 1 pounders.[72] Other evidence corroborates this. In 1803, the British captured one 'Sinhalese gun, mounted on a low carriage, carrying a ball of one pound and a half weight' from the forces of Pandar Vanniyar, a regional chieftain of northern Sri Lanka.[73] The only surviving Sinhalese gun, currently exhibited in the Rijksmuseum in the Netherlands, is a light piece, with a beautifully worked 39-inch barrel mounted on a carriage painted green. It was presented to the King of Kandy by Leuke, the Dissawa of the Four Korales in 1745, and was captured by the Dutch when they occupied Kandy in 1765.[74] Producing such pieces was within the technological capability of the Kandyan craftsmen. But even light guns could only be produced sparingly due to the lack of resources. And it is possible that they were produced mainly for special occasions—like Leuke's gun—than for regular use.

For heavier weapons, the Kandyans had to depend necessarily on their European adversaries. The capture of European fortifications yielded some artillery to the Kandyans. The guns brought by the Kandyan army to besiege Colombo in 1630 were all captured from Portuguese forts on the frontier. Many of the guns mentioned by Portuguese writers are referred to by Portuguese terms (like the *roqueyras*, *caes*, and *esphera* mentioned earlier), suggesting that they may have all been captured from the Portuguese in earlier battles. A number of guns fell into the hands of the Kandyans during their capture of European posts in wars in 1670–5, 1761–6, and 1803. Bibilegama fell in 1675 with a few small cannon while Katuwana and Matara yielded a considerable number of guns.[75] The Kandyans captured more guns when they ejected the British from Kandy in 1803.[76] The majority of the artillery pieces captured by the British during their occupation of Kandy in 1803 were also of foreign origin.[77]

The mode of acquisition also contributed greatly to the small calibre of the guns found in Kandyan hands. The vast majority of the guns captured from Europeans were necessarily light pieces because they were the guns used by Europeans in their outposts and carried in their expeditions into the interior. The guns taken from Bibilegama were just a few light pieces while those taken from the British in 1803 amounted to a few 3 and 6 pounders and light mortars.[78] But there were other opportunities for acquiring heavier weapons. The coastal waters of the island concealed numerous sunken European ships and if these could be located the Kandyans could count on salvaging their big guns. In 1658, it was rumoured that Rajasinha II had 24 large and 8 small guns salvaged from a sunken Portuguese ship.[79] During the Kandyan–Dutch conflict of 1761–6 the Chief Adigar, Galegoda, also obtained some cannon from sunken Dutch ships.[80]

But there were also problems associated with acquiring cannon by the above means. One was that their serviceability was not guaranteed. Many guns captured by the British in 1803 and almost all the guns captured in 1815 were unserviceable. This suggests that they were probably either abandoned by their previous owners due to their condition or made unserviceable prior to yielding them, as the Dutch did when they evacuated Matara in 1761.[81] Bad maintenance by the Kandyans cannot be ruled out either. Another problem was that once they were lost, they were difficult to replace as they were rarely manufactured by Kandyans. Almost all the guns brought by the Kandyans to besiege Colombo in 1630 were captured by the Portuguese during their counter-offensive in 1632[82] while as we have seen, the Dutch and the British captured large hauls of guns in 1765, 1803, and 1815. Even many of the guns taken from the British in 1803 were recovered when the Kandyan army was trounced near Hanwella in August 1803.[83] Of course, the guns captured during a particular campaign were not necessarily the only guns in Kandyan possession at that time. The Kandyans were yielding cannon even during Johnstone's expedition in 1804 after the rich haul of cannon in the previous year. But no doubt the captured cannon comprised the bulk of the Kandyan ordnance. The difficulty in replacing them is clearly seen from the fact that by 1815 the majority of the guns in the hands of the Kandyans were British guns surviving from the Kandyan offensive in 1803.[84] It is also significant that although thousands of muskets were captured from the Kandyans in 1817–18 there were very few cannon, a sign that the great majority of their big guns may have been lost in 1815.[85]

Problems of acquisition apart, the Kandyans also faced other obstacles in the use of cannon. One was the terrain. Whether locally manufactured or captured, cannon had limited scope for use as a weapon in the field in the rugged Kandyan highlands. The Europeans often had enough trouble carrying their guns up the Kandyan hills. As we shall see later, their sole use with the Kandyans was in static defence or in sieges.

There was also the problem of ammunition. It is very interesting that despite their frequent mention in Kandyan batteries, there are only a very few instances of cannon being *fired* by the Kandyans. The sieges of Katuwana and Matara in 1761 were perhaps the only instances when the Kandyans fired cannon intensely. This lack of 'participation in combat', can be attributed largely to a lack of ammunition. Cannon needed larger balls than muskets or gingals and producing heavier ammunition in large quantities was not easy, especially when one recalls that ammunition for the muskets were not always in plentiful supply. As noted earlier, traditional technology could produce only a chunk of iron weighing about 6 pounds after about 3 hours' labour, not a promising situation for manufacturing heavy ammunition on a large scale. According to the '*Aanmerkingen*', the Kandyan artillery ammunition was hammered and was never round, an indication of the crude technology that was at work.[86] WS is, of course, referring to of light Kandyan pieces. Producing iron balls for larger guns would have been even more demanding. It is notable that while one Dutch captive spoke of the Kandyans using 8-pounders on Katuwana, those in the fort reported only balls of 4 pounds or less falling in the fort.[87] It is possible that the sources are confused but it is also possible that the Kandyans were using lighter ammunition for heavier guns. Even at Matara where the same guns along with others were employed, no ammunition heavier than 6 pounds seem to have been fired.[88] Clearly the calibre of the weapons did not reflect the availability of ammunition. It is not surprising then to hear of the Kandyan Dissawa bragging to a British captive in 1803 that they were confident of capturing Colombo because they had acquired a few cannon and the ammunition to fire them.[89]

A partial answer to the problems of acquiring and using artillery was found in a unique weapon—the kodituwakku. This gun, called the gingal or the 'grasshopper gun' by Europeans, is really a species of light artillery unique in South Asia. It generally resembled a heavy musket or an enormous pistol and sometimes little more than an iron tube of large calibre fitted to a wooden stock. Whatever the appearance, a feature common to all gingals was the two wooden or iron legs fixed to the front part of the stock which made it appear like a grasshopper to the Dutch—hence the name 'springhaan'. The cruder specimens appeared like a gun barrel on a tripod.[90]

The Portuguese writer Ribeiro describes these guns as weighing 40 pounds and firing a ball weighing 4 ounces—only slightly lighter than a Sinhala cannon.[91] He also describes a rather intriguing way of discharging this weapon: 'they do not shoot these from the breast . . . when they wish to fire them they place them [the feet] on the ground and sit down with their legs spread out and their feet placed against the feet of the musket, the butt which is half round coming over the top of the left shoulder, and applying the match they discharge it without any trouble'.[92] Other sources provide different views on the matter. According to the author of the WS, the front legs or the butt was used to take aim[93] while the Dutch historian Zwier says that two people were required to fire a gingal.[94] Of course, different types of gingals would have required different firing methods, the heavier ones requiring the use of feet and/or a crew of two persons, with the lighter ones requiring only one person. It was extremely inaccurate because, as the '*Aanmerkingen*' explains, it jumped when fired. But it seems to have had a good reach—about 1,000 paces, according to a Zwier.[95]

The kodituwakkua or gingal, as described by Ribeiro and clearly evident from the surviving examples, did not use any firing mechanism but was fired by bringing the match to the touch-hole manually. According to Ribeiro, the Kandyan muskets were also fired with cord since they had no flint, 'yet they have a spring as if they had [flints]'.[96] He is probably talking about a variation of the matchlock mechanism. Apart from Ribeiro's observations, there is no other reference to the subject in the sources. But it is very likely that the gun was fired with a match, very much like a piece of contemporary artillery.

As mentioned earlier, sixteenth and seventeenth-century sources speak of the Kandyan armies carrying hundreds of gingals. The Dissawa of Uva is said to have brought 600 gingals to besiege the fort of Bibilegama in 1675.[97] In the eighteenth and nineteenth centuries, we do not hear of such impressive concentrations. According to Zwier who was using Dutch records, there were no more than 8 or 10 gingals per 500 Kandyans.[98] Reports from the field point to a slightly higher ratio than this. For instance on 7 July 1765, Dutch spies reported a battery near Sitawaka with 200 men and 6 gingals[99] while another spy reported in February of the same year that he saw about 100 men with 8 gingals near Wisenawe.[100] On 16 July 1765, another spy spoke of having seen 1,000 men with 200 muskets and 15 gingals.[101] According to Ehlepola there were only about 100 gingals in the entire Kandyan kingdom in 1814 and while 8,000 muskets were captured in 1817–18 only 91 gingals were recovered. Clearly in the eighteenth and nineteenth centuries the number of gingals in the hands of Kandyans were to be counted by the score rather than by the hundred.

The gingal overcame many of the above problems associated with cannon. It was cheap, easily manufactured locally, and because of its light weight, was eminently suited for use in the rugged Kandyan terrain. It could easily be carried by a single man. A British officer remarked how the Kandyans carried them 'from one bush to another with great celerity as occasion required'.[102] It was also perfectly suited tactically for the kind of challenge they had to face often—from invading armies in the field rather than from fortified posts which would have required the use of heavier artillery. True, the gingal was highly inaccurate and was no cannon in terms of its destructive power. But its other advantages more than amply compensated for this drawback. Its one real problem was that it was of no use against the lightest of fortifications.

Interestingly, Europeans also took a fancy to gingals as a kind of light artillery. The Portuguese demanded a regular supply of gingals from workshops in their territories[103] and during the Portuguese raid on Kandy in 1611, 200 gingals were used to command the passage of the Mahaveli river.[104] Some of the lascarins in Dutch territories were also armed with gingals[105] while the Dutch carried several with them on their expedition in 1764.[106] Like the European muskets and cannon, some of their gingals also ended up in the hands of the Kandyans. As noted earlier, hundreds of them fell into the hands of the Kandyan army when they routed the Portuguese invaders in 1630.[107]

GUNPOWDER

There is no doubt that a considerable quantity of the gunpowder that was needed to fire these weapons came from captured European stocks. But gunpowder was also locally manufactured. The making of gunpowder requires three ingredients: charcoal, sulphur, and saltpetre. Of these, the Kandyans obtained charcoal from the Parwatta tree but sulphur had to be imported from south India.[108] South India was also a source for saltpetre.[109] This was particularly so in the seventeenth century when Madura became a major supplier of the ingredient.[110] The European control over the ports and sea routes was a potential threat to the supply of these ingredients but this was offset by smuggling and local production.[111] Saltpetre in particular was widely

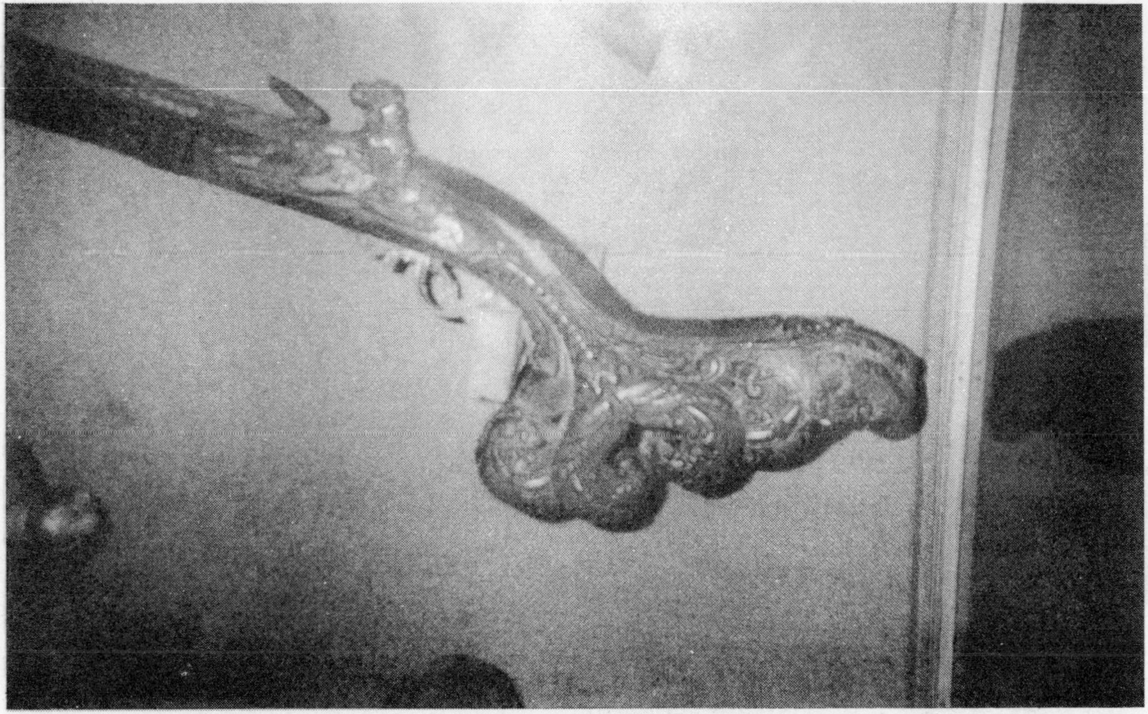

Plate 1: The ornately carved curved stock of a Kandyan flintlock belonging to Sri Wickreme Rajasinha, the last king of Kandy. Colombo Museum.

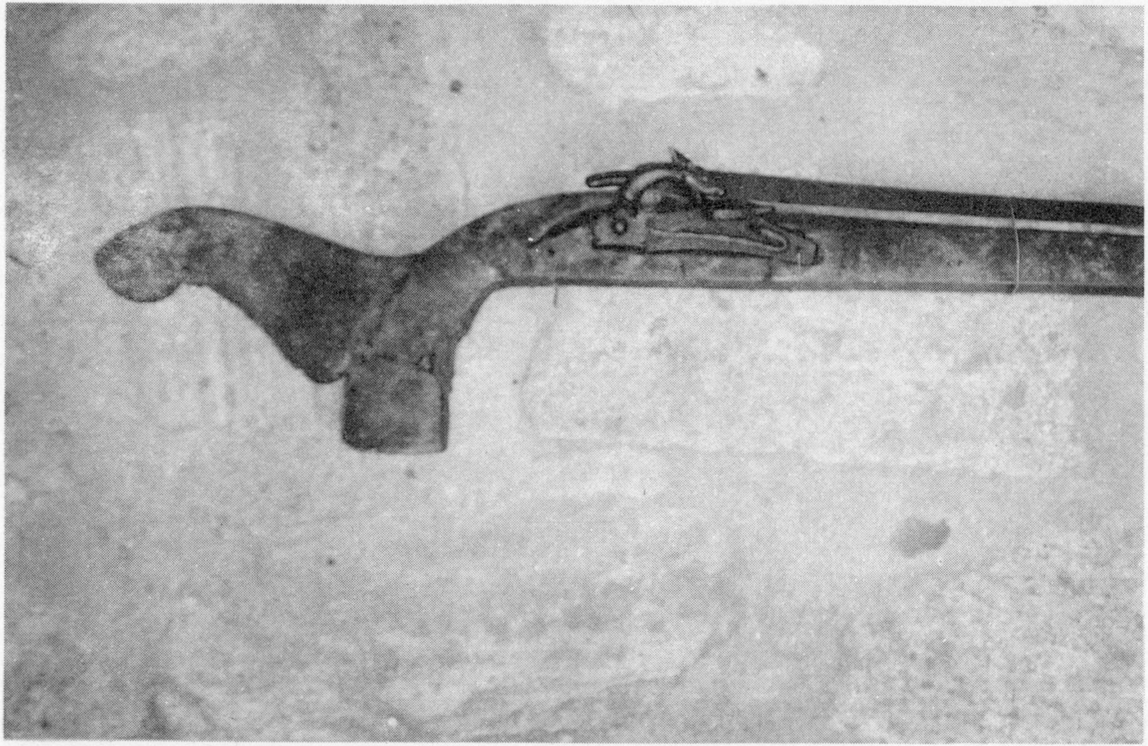

Plate 2: A more crudely constructed matchlock. Kandy Museum.

Plate 3: A late eighteenth century cave painting from Degaldoruwa in Kandy district showing a demon armed with a musket. The gun is a flintlock musket and lacks the curved stock of Kandyan Muskets, suggesting that the artist used a European piece as a model. Colombo Museum.

Plate 4: A gingal. Kandy Museum.

produced by the Kandyans who made it by scraping or chipping the salt off the rocky surface of certain caves and then putting it through a process of washing, boiling, and filtering.[112] Even sulphur was locally obtainable as it was produced as a result of iron smelting albeit in very small quantities.[113]

According to Dr John Davy, who was a keen observer of Kandyan crafts, the process of manufacture and the quality of Kandyan gunpowder left much to be desired:

> In their mode of manufacturing powder, which is very generally understood, there is not the least refinement. To proportion the constituent parts, scales are used but not weights. The proportions commonly employed are, five parts of saltpetre, and one of each of the other ingredients. . . . The ingredients, moistened with very weak lime water and a little of the acrid juice of the wild yam (arum maerorhizsn), are ground together between two flat stones, or pounded in a rice mortar. After the grinding or pounding is completed, the moist mass is exposed to the sunshine to dry. Nothing further is done to it; no attempt is ever made to granulate it: and it is used in the state of a very coarse powder, or impalpable dust. Considering the rudeness of the method, the gunpowder is better than could be expected: some specimens of it that I have examined have inflamed readily, exploding pretty strongly, and have left little residue.[114]

Like iron, gunpowder also seems to have been freely produced in the countryside, albeit in small quantitities. The annual emoluments received by the Dissawa of Sabaragamuwe from subordinate headmen included, in some instances, bottles of gunpowder, most certainly from stocks locally produced, the small quantity suggesting that these stocks were very limited.[115] When Knox was on the run in 1680, he carried with him several charges of gunpowder. How he obtained them, we are not told, but it is reasonable to assume that it was locally manufactured.[116] The gunpowder used during the Great Rebellion of 1817–18 would have been certainly manufactured locally in response to the outbreak of the insurgency. One Kandyan headman interrogated by the British during the rebellion said that when the Uva province rose in revolt the people were put to collect and make ammunition.[117] British detachments combing the countryside often came across small quantities of gunpowder, sulphur, and gunpowder-making equipment in the possession of rebels.[118] It was reported that the rebels were grinding gunpowder in mortars, beating them with rice pounders.[119] The practicability of producing gunpowder locally was clearly shown when, in 1842–3 during a feeble attempt by some Kandyan leaders to incite Kandyans into rebellion, gunpowder was locally manufactured in quite large quantities, two parrahs being made at a place called Bogamuwa.[120] Gunpowder was often stored in pots,[121] and there were also reports of gunpowder being carried in casks made of hollowed Palmyra trunks.[122]

It not certain how much gunpowder the Kandyans were capable of producing. According to a Kandyan noble, the Royal stores did not possess more than 750 pounds of the ingredient in 1803.[123] But in 1766 the Dutch captured and destroyed a massive haul of 15,000 bags of saltpetre in Matale. The stock was said to have been collected over a period of years and gives an indication of the productivity of the Kandyan methods.[124] During the Rebellion the British recovered some 750 pounds of sulphur from the Kandyan territories,[125] quite a large quantity for that ingredient considering the small proportion of sulphur required in making gunpowder.

OTHER WEAPONS

As noted earlier, only a proportion of the Kandyan peasantry was armed with guns. Those who were not armed with guns, that is, the majority of the Kandyan army, were armed with more 'traditional' weapons mentioned earlier in this chapter, namely bows and arrows, spears and swords. Of these, the bow and arrow was the premier missile weapon in the pre-gunpowder era and continued to supplement the firepower of muskets and gingals even during the seventeenth century, the Portuguese often being met by 'clouds of arrows'.[126] According to the Portuguese writer Sa y Menezes, the Kandyans were very dexterous in using their bows. He also mentions poisoned arrows obtained by 'rubbing certain herbs on them'.[127] According to Queyroz, the Sinhalese arrows were made of areca wood 'with the point hardened in the fire whereby they became sharper and do as much harm as those of iron'.[128]

The bow and arrow seems to have declined in popularity in

the eighteenth century. It was rarely used during the Kandyan–Dutch War in 1761–6. The weapon regained its importance during the rebellion in 1817–18 when arrows as much as bullets stalked British detachments. A British subaltern, Colour Sergeant Calladine, speaks of a march from Batticaloa to Uva 1817 during which his party was attacked only with arrows.[129] The prominent place enjoyed by the bow in the Rebellion was largely due to the inclusion of a large number of Veddahs in the rebel forces. These aboriginals who inhabited the thickly forested areas of eastern Sri Lanka featured prominently in the revolt, especially in the Uva province. Their chief weapon was the bow, in the use of which they were considered quite dexterous.[130] Interestingly, Queyroz also says that the Kandyan troops of Uva were all armed with bows and arrows.[131]

Not much is known about Kandyan swords and spears. Portuguese observers speak of a type of sword called *calachurros* that is described by Ribeiro as a short weapon two and a half palms long.[132] Queyroz describes them as 'either scimitars with a curve at the point and very broad or straight in the same way with a cross at the hilt'. It is described as being very heavy, the weight making up for the force. 'All the skill consists in protecting oneself well with the shield and trying by light bounds to find the foe exposed'.[133] The *calachur* was a sword of Middle Eastern and Turkish origin and it is difficult to determine whether the Portuguese observers were speaking of the same weapon or something similar to it.[134] The Dutch and the British never use the term, simply referring to swords or broadswords in the hands of the Sinhalese. It is also unlikely that Ribeiro who spent 18 years in Sri Lanka would have used the term if it was not current. In the *calachuru* we are probably looking at the origins of the 'Kastane sword', which is now commonly known as the typical Sinhala sword, with its lion-headed pommel and light, slightly curved blade.

The Kandyan spears are given various lengths by Europeans. Sa y Menezes refers to a short spear of only seven palms length[135] while Ribeiro mentions a spear that is 18 palms in length.[136] However, the latter also mentions the Kandyans throwing javelins at the Portuguese during the Battle of Randeniwela in 1630.[137] Possibly the Kandyans were using spears and lances of many sizes, some for throwing and others for thrusting or stabbing. The Dutch traveller Heydt speaks of pikes made of bamboos with their sharpened tips hardened by fire. Pikes are rarely heard of during the wars against the Dutch and the British in the eighteenth and nineteenth centuries, and then only as weapons captured from fleeing Kandyans rather than as weapons used in combat. The author of the '*Aanmerkingen*' considered them to be of little significance.[138]

When no weapon was available, the Kandyans resorted to that most primitive of weapons, the club. In 1762, a detachment of lascarins was massacred by a band of about 100 Kandyans, the majority of whom were armed with pikes and clubs.[139] In 1818, the British surgeon Kennedy is said to have been bashed to death by a club.[140]

The '*Aanmerkingen*' also mentions a weapon which it calls a 'fire arrow' but which resembles an Indian rocket in its appearance. This was an iron tube of about 6½ in length and about 2 inches in diameter having a hollow about half an inch across, filled with gunpowder and attached to a stick about 6 feet in length. However, unlike the Indian rocket, this weapon did not carry a blade but seems to have functioned as little more than a conveyor of fire, hence the term 'fire arrow'. Martin Wintergrest, a Swabian visitor to the island in 1712–16, mentions 'fire-tubes' which he describes as 'wooden tubes in which fireworks are let off, of which elephants are terribly afraid'.[141] Another traveller, the Dutchman J. Haafner who travelled to Colombo from Jaffna by foot, brought with him similar fireworks as a precaution against elephants.[142] The rockets or 'firearrows were only rarely used by Kandyans. About 10 or 12 of them were reported with a Kandyan force that engaged the Dutch at Gonawila in March 1764. The author of the '*Aanmerkingen*' dismissed them as harmless, saying that the Sinhalese did not know how to aim them in a true arc.[143] Interestingly, Major Medeler took 25 of them with him on his expedition, probably for signalling.[144]

There is little evidence of defensive equipment. The Sinhalese chronicle *Rajavaliya* speaks of targe bearers[145] in the Sitawaka and Kotte armies, possibly referring to men armed with bucklers. But the shield is hardly mentioned in the hands of Kandyan troops.

ARMING THE PEASANTRY

The previous sections have looked at the technology available in the Kandyan highlands and the weapons produced and acquired by the Kandyans. This section examines the means by which the peasantry came to be armed. According to Captain Arthur Johnstone, each Kandyan peasant soldier was given a musket by the chiefs while according to Davy, each peasant levy turned up with his own musket. Both these claims are too general to be accepted at face value. The truth probably lies somewhere in between. To a considerable extent the Kandyan peasant was expected to maintain himself in a state of armed readiness. As explained in the previous chapter, in the Sabaragamuwa province in early nineteenth century, the Hewawasam people were expected to maintain firearms, depending on the size of the land they held. This was probably the case in other parts of the Kandyan kingdom as well.[146] When the peasants were rallied to the beat of tom-toms during wartime, they were required to come with their arms. Thus, when the Kandyans arrived in Katuwana on their way to invade Matara in 1803 the people were ordered to assemble with swords and muskets.[147] In 1810 and 1812, when mobilization was taking place in some parts of the Kandyan kingdom, the British received reports of men being ordered to gather with their arms.[148]

The peasants no doubt relied on the village smiths to produce their weapons. Knox provided an interesting description of the process by which the Kandyan peasant dealt with his smith:

> The ordinary work they do for them [villagers] is mending their tools, for which every man pays to his smith a certain rate of Corn in Harvest time according to ancient custom. But if any hath work extraordinary as making new Tools or the like, besides the aforesaid Rate of Corn, he must pay him for it. In order to do this, they come in an humble manner to the smith with a present, being Rice, Hens, and other sorts of provisions, or a bottle of Rack, desiring him to appoint his time when they shall come to have their work done. Which when he hath appointed them, they come at the set time, and bring both Coals and iron with them.[149]

No doubt this was the usual process through which the Kandyan peasantry obtained their weapons of war. It is also likely that the weapons captured from the enemy in battle also found their way into the hands of the peasantry. It is interesting to hear the views of King Senarat (1604–30) in this regard. When negotiating the Kandyan–Portuguese treaty of 1617 he expressed willingness to return all the cannon and arms captured from the Portuguese with the addendum that 'the arms which the people of the country took from them may be recovered from them'.[150] Whether the arms were ever recovered from the 'people of the country' we are never told but it clearly shows that the peasantry could easily arm themselves with enemy weapons as well as weapons produced locally.

There is also some evidence to suggest that the Kandyan hierarchy made efforts to arm the peasants. We have already seen how in 1810 a Kandyan chief was grilling his people about guns given to them during the Dutch times. Around the same time there were also reports of guns having been sent to the provinces[151] while British spies also reported the production of iron implements and weapons, including guns, under the supervision of the Kandyan chiefs. On one instance, in November 1810, a spy reported having seen near Batugedera in the Sabaragamuwa province a row of ironsmiths' shops with 18 furnaces near the Dissawa's resthouse where agricultural implements like hoes and hand bills were being made, but no guns.[152] But in January the following year another spy reported that the smiths were also making guns, a thousand each of all implements and weapons to be sent to Kandy.[153] Efforts were also being made to keep track of weapons in peoples' hands.[154]

All this appears like an attempt by the Kandyan authorities to play an active role in the improvement of the military readiness of the peasantry. Similar efforts are also reported from earlier times. The seventeenth-century Sinhalese poem *Mandarampura Puvatha* speaks of king Vimala Dharma Surya I setting up about 170 iron foundries in his kingdom.[155] He is also said to have stored large quantities of weapons including guns, lead, and gunpowder in a large cave on top of a mountain.[156] This seems like a stupendous effort for a state with a highly decentralized administration. Besides Sinhalese poets singing the praises of their kings (like all such poets) were inclined to exaggerate the achievements of their heroes. But it is also not surprising if Vimala Dharma Surya took an active interest in arms production.

The king's reign was crowded with intense fighting with the Portuguese and the urgency for the production of weapons such as firearms to match their adversaries would have been great. The poet probably refers to the state's encouragement of widespread arms production in response to the increasing demands of war rather than establishing a centralized arms production programme. It was probably organized at the provincial level, very much like the process reported by British spies in the early nineteenth century. It was the most effective way in which the Kandyan hierarchy could promote arms production, given the decentralized structure of government and the productive resources available. Ironsmiths were worked in their village smithies and the Dissawas and other provincial chiefs who had command over the provincial and local labour resources could endeavour to bring them together on occasion to produce a considerable quantity of weapons and implements.

Such efforts would have certainly boosted the army's battle-readiness as much as it could be boosted with the technology available. Moreover, the initiative and sponsorship of chiefs was also perhaps the only way in which heavy weaponry like cannon and gingals could be produced. The ordinary peasant was in no position to maintain these weapons and the state had to take the responsibility of maintaining the heavy guns. It is interesting that Ehelepola was able to give details of the location of all the gingals and cannon in the Kandyan kingdom in 1814, which suggests that there was some sort of central monitoring of these weapons.[157]

Last but not least, the king also possessed a substantial armoury, at least in the early nineteenth century. At this time the king is reported to have been in possession of about 3,000 muskets among many other weapons. The firearms were under the supervision of a special official who was responsible for their maintenance.[158] However, it is not likely that these guns were meant to be distributed to the troops during war. Most certainly they formed part of the king's treasure, to be displayed on ceremonial occasions rather than as an arsenal from which arms could be distributed to the peasantry during an outbreak of war. Using arms from the royal armoury in actual combat ran the risk of losing them in the case of a reverse. Besides, there was also the security factor. A private arsenal of well-oiled guns when placed in trusted hands could be an insurance against rebellion. According to Knox, during the rebellion of 1666, it was the possession of a large number of 'good fowling-pieces' that prevented the rebels from catching up with the fleeing king.[159]

To sum up, the Kandyan soldiers were armed with a motley array of weapons ranging from the primitive to the 'modern'. Their firepower, however, was curtailed by the lack of good guns and the almost total absence of heavy artillery. There was little central organization of weapons production, with the peasants usually providing their own weapons. In the next chapter, we shall examine the strategies and tactics pursued by the Kandyans in confronting their European enemies with these weapons.

NOTES

1. Robert Knox, *An Historical Relation of the Island of Ceylon, Revised, Enlarged & Brought to the Verge of Publication as the Second Edition by Robert Knox together with his Autobiography and All the New Chapters, Paragraphs, Marginal Notes added by the Author in the Two Interleaved Copies of the Original Text of 1681*, Edited with Introduction and Notes by J.H.O. Paulusz, published as the *CHJ* Monographs series, vol. 14, Dehiwela, Sri Lanka: Tisara Publishers, 1989, 1st edn., 1681, pp. 249–50. Quote from p. 249.
2. See also John Davy, *An Account of the Interior of Ceylon and of its Inhabitants with Travels in that Island*, Dehiwela, Sri Lanka: Tisara Publishers, 1969, rpt. of 1821 edn. p. 272.
3. The eighteenth-century Dutch traveller Wolfgang Heydt noted: 'They copy in gold or silver everything set before them. For this they carry with them a small anvil, some files, 8 or 10 punches, a couple of hammers, a pair of pliers, and some clay for casting. . . . They bring also 3 or 4 crucibles, and a few graves'. *Heydt's Ceylon, being the relevant sections of the 'Allerneuster Geographisch und, Topographischer Schauplatz van Afrika und Ost-Indien etc., etc.,'* trs. and ed. Major Roland Raven-Hart, Colombo: Govt. Information Dept., 1952. Originally published in Willendorf, 1742, p. 113. Ananda K. Coomaraswamy, *Medieval Sinhalese Art*, New York: Pantheon Books, 1979; 1st pub. 1907, pp. 200–14.
4. 'The Dutch Embassy to Kandy in 1731–2: Diary of Wijesiriwardene Mahamudaliyar, otherwise called Lewis de Saram Mahamudaliyar', trs. from the Sinhalese by P.E. Pieris, *JRAS(CB)*, vol. 21, no. 62, 1909, pp. 210–11.

5. Bryce Ryan, *Sinhalese Village*, Coral Gables, Florida: University of Miami Press, 1958, pp. 29–30.
6. Davy, *An Account*, p. 13; Knox, *An Historical Relation*, pp. 272–3; Joao de Ribeiro, *The Historic Tragedy of the Island of Ceilao*, trs. P.E. Pieris, Colombo: Lake House, 1948, p. 28
7. Davy, *An Account*, pp. 195–6. See also Knox, *An Historical Relation*, pp. 273–4; Coomaraswamy, *Medieval*, pp. 190–2; *Granville Report on the Matara Disttrict, 1813*, Historical Manuscripts Commission of Ceylon, Bulletin no. 5, Colombo: Colombo Museum, 1952, p. 10. William Granville was a Collector of the Matara district in the early nineteenth century.
8. Coomaraswamy, *Medieval*, pp. 192–3.
9. Knox, *An Historical Relation*, p. 194.
10. *Granville Report*, pp. 10–11.
11. Coomaraswamy, *Medieval*, pp. 192–3. Acording to Granville, the people of Kirama sold iron in 'cakes of 9 or 10 lbs., dross and all', *Granville Report*, p. 10.
12. Ibid., p. 194.
13. Davy, *An Account*, p. 196.
14. The residents of Colombo are said to have informed their king: 'The report of their cannon is louder than thunder when it bursts upon the rock Yugandara. Their cannon balls fly many a gawwa and shatter fortresses of granite.' *Rajavaliya or a Historical Narrative of Sinhalese Kings from Vijaya to Vimala Dharma Surya II*, ed. B. Gunasekera, Colombo: Govt. Printers, 1954, rpt. 1900 edn., p. 63. Elsewhere, the chronicle says that when the Sinhalese came to attack Colombo in 1519 the Portuguese scared them away by firing a cannon which brought down the branch of a jack tree. Ibid., p. 64.
15. Fernao de Queyroz. *The Temporal and Spiritual Conquest of Ceylon*, trs. S.G. Perera, Colombo: Govt. Printers, 1930, p. 200.
16. 'The Portuguese in Ceylon in the First Half of the Sixteenth Century: Gaspar Correa's Account', trs. S.G. Perera, *CALR*, vol. 4, no. 6, Dec. 1935, pp. 269–70.
17. Iqtidar Alam Khan, 'Early Use of Cannon and Musket in India', *Journal of the Economic and Social History of the Orient*, vol. 24, no. 2, 1981, pp. 162–4.
18. In 1504, two Milanese deserters from the Portuguese helped the Keralites to construct several brass cannon. When the Samudri came to attack the Portuguese at Cochin later in the year he is said to have brought with him 382 pieces of cannon. Many of these must have been light pieces but it illustrates the use of cannon on the Kerala coast at the time. Frederick Charles Danvers, *The Portuguese in India, being a History of the Rise and Decline of their Eastern Empire*, 2 vols, London: Frank Cass, 1966, 1st pub. 1894, vol. l, pp. 104–6.

19. See John Vogt, 'Saint Barbara's Legion: Portuguese Artillery in the Struggle for Morocco 1415–1578', in *Military Affairs*, vol. 41 (Lexington, VA), 1977, p. 76. Queyroz speaks of the guns before Colombo firing wooden shafts, '10 palms in length with feathers of wild boar', Queyroz, *The Temporal and Spiritual Conquest*, p. 200.
20. In fact, Couto says that in one of the actions between the Portuguese and the Malabaris, the latter had fortified their positions on land with guns taken from their *paraos* (light coastal craft). Joao de Barros and Diogo do Couto, 'The History of Ceylon from the earliest times to A.D. 1600, trs. and ed. Donald Ferguson, *JRAS(CB)*, vol. 20, no. 60, 1908, p. 78.
21. Barros and Couto, 'History of Ceylon', pp. 104–5, Miguel Fereira to D. Joao IV, 26 November 1539, P.E. Pieris and M.A.H. Fitzler (eds), *Ceylon and Portugal Part 1: Kings and Christians 1539–1552, from the Original Documents at Lisbon*, Liepzig: Verlag der Asia Major, 1927, p. 40.
22. Dom Affonso de Noronha to D. Joao III, 1 January 1552, Pieris and Fitzler, *Ceylon and Portugal*, p. 268.
23. *Rajavaliya*, p. 82, speaks of the Sitawaka army under Mannapperuma discharging 900 gingals at a Portuguese force with devastating effect. Queyroz mentions the incident in a similar fashion but does not give numbers of gingals.
24. A Dutch visitor to Batticaloa in 1603 found the local ruler's men armed with firelocks and spears although he judged from the way they fired a salute that 'they did not yet know how to manage the muskets very well'. This may suggest that the use of firearms was a somewhat novel experience to the inhabitants on the east coast. 'Description of a History as Recorded by Johann Herman van Bree', in Donald Ferguson (ed.), 'Earliest Dutch Visits to Ceylon', *JRAS(CB)*, vol. 31, no. 81, 1928, p. 135.
25. Antonio Moniz Barretto to the governor, 10 October 1547. Pieris and Fitzler, *Ceylon and Portugal*, p. 202. 'Espingarda' was a term for early muskets.
26. Barretto to the Governor, 10 October 1547, Ibid., p. 202. Barretto mentions no fighting whatsoever on this retreat but Couto speaks of some heavy fighting, but even here the Kandyans are using only bows and arrows, not guns. Barros and Couto, 'History of Ceylon', p. 130.
27. According to Couto, the Kandyans 'did not wish to risk themselves, but from a distance, showered clouds of arrows upon our men of which almost all of them were hurt'. Ibid., p. 130.
28. Queyroz, *The Temporal and Spiritual Conquest,* p. 438.
29. '. . . when he [Dom Jorge] was now a league or a little more from the cidade [Kandy] the king of Candia's captains with the people of the country fell upon him and defeated him and killed about 200 of his men and wounded many and captured his arms and baggage . . .',

Dom Affonso de Noronha to Dom Joao III, 1 January 1551, Pireris and Fitzler, *Ceylon and Portugal,* p. 236.

30. Joao de Ribeiro, *The Historic Tragedy of the Island of Ceilao,* trs. P.E. Pieris, Colombo: Lake House, 1948, pp. 87–8.
31. Queyroz, *The Temporal and Spiritual Conquest,* pp. 546–7.
32. Ribeiro, *The Historic Tragedy,* p. 179. In the battle which ensued, the Portuguese are said to have captured 700 foot-muskets and 'innumerable espingards [muskets]'. Ibid., p. 182.
33. *The Expedition to Uva made in 1630 by Constantine de Sa de Noronha, Captain General of Ceylon, as narrated by a soldier who took part in the Expedition together with an Account of the Siege laid to Colombo by the King of Kandy written by Afonso Dias da Lomba,* trs. S.G. Perera, Colombo: Govt. Printers, 1930, pp. 27–8.
34. *'Aanmerkingen over den Oorlog met de Singaleesen',* Mackenzie Ms. 39, p.11.
35. During the rebellion, the British captured 91 gingals, 7 wall-pieces, 8001 muskets, seven pistols, 165 musket barrels, and 5 pistol barrels. Colvin R. de Silva, *Ceylon under the British Occupation, 1795–1833,* 2 vols, New Delhi: Navrang, 1995, 4th edn., 1st pub. 1941, vol. 1, p. 190.
36. See the guns depicted in P.E.P. Deraniyagala 'Sinhala Weapons and Armour', *JRAS(CB)*, vol. 35, no. 95, 1942, Pl. IV and D.H.D.H. de Silva, *A Catalogue of Antiquities and Other Cultural Objects from Sri Lanka (Ceylon) Abroad,* Colombo: Govt. Printers, 1975, p. 150.
37. Deraniyagala, 'Sinhala Weapons and Armour', p. 121.
38. Arthur Coke Burnell (trs. & ed.), *The Voyage of John Huyghen van Linschoten to the East Indies from the Old English Translation of 1598,* 2 vols, New York: Burt Franklin, 1963, vol. 1, p. 81; Albert Gray (ed. & trs.), *The Voyage of Francois Pyrard of Laval to the East Indies, the Maldives, the Moluccas and Brazil,* 2 vols in 3 parts, New York: Burt Franklin, 1963, vol. 2, part 1, p. 142.
39. *Rajasinha Hatana,* ed. Ellepola M.M. Somaratne, Kandy: T.B.S. Godamune and Sons, date unavailable, verse 382, p. 65.
40. M.D. Raghavan, *The Karava of Ceylon: Society and Culture*, Colombo: K.V.G. de Silva and Sons, 1961, pp. 16–24.
41. Davy, *An Account,* p. 197.
42. '*Aanmerkingen*', pp. 8–9.
43. *Heydt's Ceylon,* p. 113. This was echoed by Baldeaus: 'they work in gold, silver, ivory ebony and iron, and are very dexterous in the forging of arms, and artfully inlaying them with silver'. Philippus Baldaeus, *True and Exact Description of the Great Island of Ceylon,* trs. Pieter Brohier, published as *CHJ,* vol. 8, nos. 1–4, July 1958–April 1959, p. 384.
44. '*Aanmerkingen*', p. 9.

45. Noted Davy: 'To the natives, it may be worthwhile to collect scattered masses of iron ore, for their little furnaces; but unless an extensive bed or vein of ore be found, the attempt to establish a foundry would be idle in the extreme'. Davy, *An Account*, p. 13.
46. Ceylon Government Gazette, 21 November 1818, *CLR*, vol. 4, no. 1, August 1889, p. 4. This difficulty probably explains why two flintlocks, stolen from a Dutch party in 1742, were recovered without their locks. *Heydt's Ceylon*, p. 127.
47. Captain Arthur Johnstone, *Narrative of the Operations of a Detachment in an Expedition to Candy in the Island of Ceylon in the Year 1804 with Some Observations on the Previous Campaigns and on the Nature of Candyan Warfare &c, &c*, London, 1810, p. 5.
48. Minutes, 31 January 1763, SLNA 1/4864, p. 109.
49. Baldaeus, *True and Exact Description*, p. 26.
50. Queyroz, *The Temporal and Spiritual Conquest*, p. 187.
51. Ibid., p. 928.
52. Johnstone, *Narrative*, pp. 87–8. Numbers of these were recovered in subsequent actions. For instance, in an encounter with Kandyans before Gonawila in April 1764, the Dutch recovered 6 VOC muskets in good condition. Major Dufflo to Colombo, 9 April 1764, Letters from outstations to Colombo, 1764, SLNA 1/4898. When some Kandyans were taken prisoner in 1815 some of them were found to be carrying muskets taken from the British troops massacred in 1803. George Calladine, *The Diary of Colour Sergeant George Calladine*, ed. M.L. Ferrar, London: Eden Fisher & Co., 1922, p. 38.
53. P.E. Pieris, *Sinhale and the Patriots*, Delhi: Navrang, 1995, rpt. of 1950 edn., pp. 494–5, note 33.
54. John Whitchurch Bennett, *Ceylon and Her Capabilities: An Account of its Natural Resources, Indigenous Productions and Commercial Facilities*, London: William H. Allen, 1843, p. 417.
55. Johnstone, *Narrative*, p. 90.
56. *Diary of Mr. John D'oyly*, with introduction and notes by H.W. Codrington, Delhi: Navrang, 1995, 1st published as *JRAS(CB)*, vol. 25, no. 69, 1917, p. 19.
57. Johnstone, *Narrative*, p. 5.
58. '*Aanmerkingen*', p. 9.
59. Johnstone, *Narrative*, p. 90.
60. *Diary of Mr. John D'oyly*, p. 12.
61. Ensign Pendergast at Hambantota to Colombo, September 1803, SLNA 7/43, pp. 1118–19.
62. Pendergast to Colombo, 28 August 1803, SLNA 7/43, p. 1127.
63. R.L. Brohier, *The Golden Age of Military Adventure in Ceylon: An Account of the Uva Rebellion 1817–1818*, Colombo: Plate Ltd., 1933, p. 14.

64. Queyroz, *The Temporal and Spiritual Conquest*, p. 579.
65. C.R. De Silva, *The Fortuguese in Ceylon 1617–1638*, Colombo: H.W. Cave & Co., 1972, p. 119.
66. Ribeiro, *The Historic Tragedy*, p. 33
67. W.P. Coolhaas (ed.), *Generale Missiven van Gouverneurs-General en Raden aan Heren xvii Der Verenigde Oostindische Compagnie*, 9 vols., s'Gravenhage: Verkrijgbaar bij Martinus Nijhoff, 1971, vol. 4, p. 76.
68. Major Roland Raven-Hart (trs. and ed.), *The Dutch Wars with Kandy 1764–1766*, Ceylon Historical Manuscripts Commission Bulletin no. 6, Colombo: Government Publications Bureau, 1964, p. 99.
69. For the cannon captured in 1803, see SLNA 7/42, pp. 333–4. For 1815, see the report of Brooke Young, Colonel of the Royal Artillery, reproduced in P.E. Pieris, *Tri Sinhala: The Last Phase*, Delhi: Navrang, 1995, rpt. of 1950 edn., p. 495, n. 33.
70. Heydt was confident that the Dutch had little to fear from the Kandyans since the latter hád no heavy guns. 'I have never heard and far less seen, that they cast heavy guns either of iron or gun metal', he declared. *Heydt's Ceylon*, p. 17.
71. H.W. Codrington, 'The Kandyan Navandanno', *JRAS(CB)*, vol. 21, no. 62, 1909, p. 231.
72. '*Aanmerkingen*', pp. 5–6.
73. James Cordiner, *Description of Ceylon, containing an Account of the Country, Inhabitants, and Natural Productions with a Narrative of a Tour around the Island in 1800, the Compaign in Kandy in 1803 and a Journey to Ramisseram in 1804*, 2 vols., Delhi: Navrang, 1983, rpt. of 1807 edn., vol. 2. p. 246.
74. D.H.D.H. De Silva, *A Catalogue of Antiquities and Other Cultural Objects from Sri Lanka (Ceylon) Abroad*, Colombo: Govt. Printers, 1975. Tikiri Abeysinghe suggests that the Sinhalese word for cannon is derived from the Tamil term 'Kal-tupakki', meaning foot-gun, a direct translation of 'mosquetes de pee', the portuguese term for the gingal. T.B.H. Abeysinghe (trs. & ed.), *A Study of Portuguese Regimentos on Sri Lanka at the Goa Archives*, Colombo: Dept. of National Archives, 1974, p. 68, n. 47.
75. Deposition of Gerrit de Vos, 28 March 1761, Minutes, 30 March 1761, SLNA 1/747.
76. Cordiner, *Description*, vol. 2, pp. 234, 238.
77. For instance, see the list of weapons and stores captured by the British in 1803. Governor's Secret Diary February–April 1803, SLNA, 7/42, pp. 333–5. In September 1803, the British recovered several English 3 and 6 pounders and two 4.25 inch mortars from Kandyan forces operating around Hanwella, about 15 miles from Colombo. Cordiner, *Description*, vol. 2, pp. 234, 238.
78. Cordiner, *Description*, vol. 2, pp. 234, 238.

79. Pieris, *Dutch Power*, p. 58.
80. J.H.O. Paulusz, 'The Outbreak of the Kandyan–Dutch War of 1761 and the Great Rebellion: Secret Minutes of the Dutch Political Committee', *JRAS(CB)*, vol. 3, 1953, pp. 28–55, p. 45. Paulusz does not cite his original source.
81. The Dutch abandoned 18 guns to the Kandyans but spiked them before doing so. Minutes, 30 March 1761, SLNA 1/747.
82. Manuel Faria e Souza, *Portuguese Asia or the History of the Discovery and Conquest of India by the Portuguese*, trs. Capt. John Stevens, London, 1695, p. 400.
83. Cordiner, *Description*, 2, pp. 234, 238.
84. Ehelepola's deposition, Pieris, *Tri Sinhala*, appendix I, p. 187.
85. In September 1818, a British detachment in pursuit of Pilimatalawwe captured two light three pounders among other booty. Governor of Ceylon to the Secretary of State, 9 October 1818. SLNA, 5/9, pp. 514–15.
86. '*Aanmerkingen*', p. 5.
87. E. Reimers, 'Old Matara and the Rebellion of 1761', *JDBUC*, vol. 15, no. 7, January 1926, p. 90 and vol. 15, no. 2, October 1925, p. 62; Minutes, 3 March 1761, SLNA 1/747 and the report by Nicholas Kist of Fulda 2 February 1761, SLNA 1/747.
88. Letter from Matara 27 February 1761, SLNA 1/747.
89. 'We have now 6 fine guns, gunpowder and lead, also large balls and everything in abundance'. Greeving's diary, Vimalananda Tennekoon, *British Intrigues in the Kingdom of Kandy*, Colombo: Gunasena, 1973, p. 510.
90. For instance, the gingal depicted in the photograph appearing in M.S.C. de Silva's 'The Sinhalese Army', plate iv, shows a very crude weapon, little more than a short iron tube mounted on two wooden legs and a short equally crudely fashioned butt. The gun is said to be from the Medagoda Pattini Devala. Sometimes the Kandyans yielded some very curious pieces to their European adversaries. One gun captured by the British from the army that besieged Hambantota in August 1803 had a stock like in a musket but a barrel almost 6 feet long and as thick as that of a gingal and had a similar caliber. SLNA 7/43, p. 1127.
91. Ribeiro, *The Historic Tragedy*, p. 146. According to the WS a gingal ball weighed between four and eight ounces. Considering the possibility that the gingals had no fixed caliber, this is probably closer to the truth. According to Christopher Shweitzer, a German national who was in the Island in the 1680s, the gingal fired a ball the size of a nutmeg. *Germans in Dutch Ceylon, by Von der Behr (1668), Herport (1669) Schweitzer (1682) and Fryke (1692)*, Colombo: National Muséum, 1953, p. 47.
92. Ribeiro, *The Historic Tragedy*, p. 146.

93. '*Aanmerkingen*', pp. 4–5. According to Davy the long, slender butt end rested on the ground when firing. Davy, *An Account,* p. 96.
94. W. Zwier, *Het Verdraag van 1766 Tusschen de O.I. Compagnie en de Vorst Van Kandi,* Amsterdam: H.J. Paris, 1927, p. 36.
95. '*Aanmerkingen*', p. 5, Zwier, *Het Verdraag,* p. 36.
96. Ribeiro, *The Historic Tragedy,* p. 52.
97. Coolhaas, *Generale Missiven,* vol. 4, p. 77.
98. Zwier, *Het Verdraag,* p. 36.
99. Raven-Hart, *The Dutch Wars,* p. 144.
100. Diary of the 1764 Campaign, Raven-Hart, *The Dutch Wars,* p. 30.
101. SLNA 1/4944, pp. 32–3.
102. Thomas Ajax Anderson, *Journal of the Proceedings of the Trincomalee Detachment Commanded by Lieut. Colonel Barbut His Majesty's 73rd Regiment from their Leaving Trincomalee till their arrival at Kandy,* London, 1809, Appendix A, p. 278. Davy also describes the gingal as a 'very small piece of ordnance, light enough to be carried with ease by a single man and very well adapted for a desultory warfare amongst mountains'. Davy, *An Account,* p. 96, footnote.
103. Abeysinghe, *Portuguese Regimentos,* p. 68, note 47.
104. Queyroz, *The Temporal and Spiritual Conquest,* pp. 612–13. Queyroz even suggested demanding, among other things, 100 gingals and 1000 firelocks as tribute from Kandy if the Portuguese re-conquered the island. The tribute was to be reduced to only 20 gingals per year after the first year. Queyroz, *The Temporal and Spiritual Conquest,* p. 1151. According to Baldeaus, among the weapons captured by the Dutch from the Portuguese fort in Kalutara in 1655 were 5 cannon (5, 8 and 10 pounders) and 5 gingals and 1/3 barrels of gingal balls. The gingals no doubt complemented the cannon. Baldaeus, *True and Exact Description,* p. 134.
105. 'Van Imhoff's Tour of the Matara District [March 1737]' *CALR,* vol. 1, no. 2, February 1931, pp. 85–6.
106. Diary of the 1764 campaign, Raven-Hart, *The Dutch Wars,* p. 26.
107. Queyroz, *The Temporal and Spiritual Conquest,* p. 928.
108. The Sinhalese have been importing sulphur since the late sixteenth century. So did the Portuguese who established powder mill in Colombo in the 1620s. Pieris, *Sinhale,* pp. 264–5. In September 1818, the Kandyan rebels are said to have dug up a large quantity of sulphur in Diyatalawa. Report of Ganneywe Mohandiram, 4 September 1818, Vimalananda Tennekoon, *The Great Rebellion of 1818: The Story of the First War of Independence and Betrayal of the Nation,* Colombo: Gunasena, 1970, p. 281.
109. De Silva, *The Portuguese in Ceylon,* p. 135.
110. When the Portuguese Captain General Constantine de Saa set-up a gunpowder factory in Colombo in the 1620s he is said to have

obtained his saltpetre supplies from Madura. Queyroz, *The Temporal and Spiritual Conquest*, p. 740. Later, in 1634, the Portuguese government in Colombo concluded an agreement with the Nayak of Madura to exchange elephants caught in Sri Lanka for saltpetre. De Silva, *The Portuguese in Ceylon*, p. 143.

111. In his instructions to his successor in Sri Lanka, Azevedo speaks of the need to keep a close watch on the ports on the east coast of the island to prevent the importation of ammunition among other things from the opposite coast. Abeysinghe, *Portuguese Regimentos*, p. 50.
112. John Davy, *An Account*, p. 198.
113. Sulphur was not essential to making gunpowder even though the inclusion of sulphur increased the range dramatically. Gavin White, 'Firearms in Africa: An introduction', *Journal of African History*, vol. 12, no. 2, 1971, p. 174.
114. Davy, *An Account*, p. 199.
115. Ralph Pieris, *Sinhalese Social Organization: The Kandyan Period*, Colombo: Ceylon University Press, 1956, pp. 128–32.
116. Knox, *An Historical Relation*, p. 158. Knox presented the gunpowder to the Vanniyar whose territory he was crossing, noting that gunpowder was 'a thing somewhat scarce with them'.
117. Tennekoon, *The Great Rebellion*, p. 446.
118. *Ceylon Government Gazette*, Saturday 13 June 1818, *The Uva Rebellion*, p. 30 and Saturday 21 November 1818, Ibid., p. 5.
119. Letter from A. Kelly, Colombo Museum Microfilms, 6 c/20, reel 0043, pp. 20095–9.
120. Arthur C. Dep, 'Walapane Unnanse and the Walapane Rebellion 1842–1843', *JRAS(SLB)*, New Series, vol. 29, 1984, p. 60. The rebellion, ill conceived and ill-organized by a few Kandyan chiefs, never got off the ground.
121. Minutes, 20 January 1763, SLNA, 1/4864, p. 93. Dep, 'Walapane Unnanse', p. 60.
122. Report of Godamune Unnanse, *Diary of Mr. John D'oyly*, p. 12.
123. Pieris, *Sinhale and the Patriots*, p. 531, note 14.
124. Colombo to Batavia, 30 March 1766, Raven-Hart, *The Dutch Wars*, p. 154.
125. Colvin R. de Silva, *Ceylon*, vol. 1, p. 190.
126. Ribeiro, *The Historic Tragedy*, p. 182.
127. Joao Rodriguez de Sa y Menezes, 'The Rebellion of Ceylon and the Progress of its Conquest under the Government of Constantino de Sa y Noronha', trs. from the Spanish by H.H. St. George, *JRAS(CB)*, vol. 11, no. 41, 1890, p. 547.
128. Queyroz, *The Temporal and Spiritual Conquest*, p. 99.
129. Calladine, *Diary*, pp. 49–67.

130. For instance, the Dutch Governor Rycloff Van Goens wrote that the veddahs were 'brave fellows in the hunt and expert bowmen'. *Selections from the Dutch Records of the Government of Ceylon: Memoirs of Rykloff Van Goens 1663–1675,* trs. E. Reimers, Colombo: Govt Printers, 1932, p. 44.
131. Queyroz, *The Temporal and Spiritual Conquest,* p. 69.
132. Ribeiro, *The Historic Tragedy,* pp. 52–3.
133. Queyroz, *The Temporal and Spiritual Conquest,* p. 637. On 'calachurros' in the hands of the Sinhalese, see also de Menezes, 'The Rebellion of Ceylon', p. 575.
134. Jagadish Narayan Sarkar, *The Art of War in Medieval India,* Delhi: Munshiram Manoharlal, 1984, pp. 101, 119. According to Sarkar, the *calachur* was a long sword and seems to bear closer resemblance to the weapon described by Queyroz than that described by Ribeiro.
135. Sa y Menezes, 'Rebellion of Ceylon', p. 547. Menezes contrasts this with the pike in Europe which he says are 25 palms long.
136. Ribeiro, *The Historic Tragedy,* p. 146. Christopher Schweitzer who was in Sri Lanka from 1675 to 1682 also speaks of a half-pike in the hands of the Sinhalese. Raven-Hart, *Germans in Dutch Ceylon,* p. 47.
137. Ribeiro, *The Historic Tragedy,* p. 92.
138. '*Aanmerkingen*', p. 9.
139. SLNA 1/4940, p. 16.
140. Kennedy and his escort was ambushed on their way to join Lieutenant Colonel Hook in December 1817. The small party of about fifteen were waylaid by Kandyans armed with bows and guns. When the party tried to flee after expending their ammunition they were pursued and killed. One of the servants who escaped by hiding overheard the Kandyans bragging about killing Kennedy with a club. *Ceylon Government Gazette,* Saturday 20 December 1817, *Uva Rebellion,* p. 8.
141. Raven-Hart (trs. and ed.), *Travels in Ceylon 1700–1800,* Colombo: Associated Newspapers Ltd. 1963, p. 19.
142. J. Haafner, *Travels on Foot through the Island of Ceylon,* New Delhi: Asian Educational Services, 1995; 1st pub. 1821, p. 10.
143. '*Aanmerkingen*', p. 7.
144. Major Roland Raven-Hart (trs. and ed.), 'Major Medeler's Relief Expedition', *JRAS(CB),* New Series, vol. 5, 1957, p. 190.
145. *Rajavaliya,* pp. 75, 78, 80, 83.
146. Herbert Wright to Secretary, Kandyan Provinces, Ratnapura Cutcherry, 6 October, no. 10, vol. 551A, in Pieris, *Tri Sinhala,* Appendix R, p. 644.
147. Lewis Gibson to Colombo, 13 August 1803, SLNA, 7/43, p. 904.
148. *Diary of Mr. John D'oyly,* pp. 58–60.

149. Knox, *An Historical Relation*, pp. 204–5.
150. 'The First Treaty of Peace between the Portuguese and the King of Kandy, 1617', trs. S.G. Perera, *CLR*, vol. 3, no. 4, 1933, p. 161.
151. *Diary of Mr. John D'oyly*, p. 59.
152. Ibid., p. 36.
153. Ibid., p. 53.
154. For instance, in 18 Ratwatte Disawe was reported to be registering firearms in his province. Ibid., p. 106.
155. *Mandarampura Puvatha*, ed. Labugama Lanakananda, Colombo: Ministry of Cultural Affairs, 1996, verse 152, p. 20.
156. Ibid., verses 415–16, p. 56.
157. Ehelepola gave the location of 19 cannon and 87 gingals which he claimed was all that the Kingdom had. Pieris, *Tri Sinhala*, Appendix I, p. 167.
158. John D'oyly, *A Sketch of the Constitution of the Kandyan Kingdom*, ed. L.J.B. Turner, published as the *CHJ*, vol. 24, Dehiwela, Sri Lanka: Tisara Publishers, 1975, rpt. of 1929 edn., p. 207.
159 Knox, *An Historical Relation*, p. 180.

FOUR

The Struggle

Kandyan Strategy and Tactics

The two preceding chapters have looked at some key aspects of Kandyan military strength. We have seen that apart from a few hundred foreign soldiers, the vast majority of the Kandyan troops were part-time peasant soldiers mobilized during war and supported by a simple system of logistics. These peasant armies were not very large, an army exceeding 10,000 being a rarity. The peasant soldiers used a wide variety of weapons, including modern weapons like muskets and artillery. But good guns were lacking and there was almost no heavy artillery. The Kandyans had no presence whatsoever in the ocean.

By regional standards, this was not a powerful military force. In terms of numbers and armaments the Kandyan army would have compared favourably with a large Zamindari or poligar army on the neighbouring subcontinent. Like the Kandyans these local lineages also mustered large numbers of peasant soldiers rather indifferently armed with matchlocks and, occasionally, with a few pieces of artillery.[1] Despite similar peasant background, the Burmese army was a much larger and better equipped force than the Kandyan army, with the potential to field armies up to 50,000 strong with large trains of artillery and occasionally cavalry.[2] But like the Burmese army, the Kandyans were also drawn into a lengthy struggle with European forces whereas the peasant armies on the subcontinent were usually pitted against similarly armed and organized forces. And the Kandyan army with its motley array of primitive and modern weapons held out against Portuguese, Dutch, and British forces for over two centuries. How did they do it?

KANDYAN STRATEGY

Kandyan military strategy was aimed at meeting the challenge posed by the Europeans established in the coastal areas. This challenge was twofold: on the one hand, the Europeans threatened to subjugate Kandy by occupying or devastating it while on the other hand, there was the threat of being slowly strangled by growing European encirclement. Of these two challenges, European occupation of Kandyan highlands posed the graver and more palpable threat to Kandyan existence. The main elements of Kandyan strategy for meeting these challenges are outlined below before examining the tactics employed in pursuing these strategies.

What was the strategy adopted by the Kandyans against European invasions? Some European observers have suggested the existence of a uniform yet simple strategy. In his narrative of the expedition to Kandy in 1804, Captain Arthur Johnstone described Kandyan military strategy in the case of an invasion as one of avoiding confrontation with the invading force. Once the Europeans had entered Kandyan territory, the strategy shifted to trapping the Europeans within the mountains of the Kandyan heartland by cutting off its supply lines and blocking routes of egress. Then they waited for starvation and the insalubrious climate to take their toll on the trapped Europeans, and force them to retire, before making the final move: 'When encumbered by a long line of sick and wounded, exhausted by fatigue and want of provisions, and probably destitute of ammunition (which frequently happens from desertion of coolies), then it is and then only, that they attack him, exerting all their skill to harass and cut off his retreat.'[3]

Queyroz, writing more than a century earlier, seems to be speaking of a similar strategy when he describes Kandyans concentrating on avoiding open confrontations and making optimum use of irregular tactics, forcing the Europeans—in this case the Portuguese—to expose themselves to hunger and sickness. Then, when the Portuguese army retired with its sick and the wounded the Kandyans struck back, trying to cut-off the retreat and inflict maximum damage.[4]

According to these observations, the Kandyans were following a very clear, simple strategy that mirrors the classic strategy of partisan and guerrilla fighters of all times: avoiding superior force and concentrating on weakening the enemy until they are weak enough to be overwhelmed. However, even a general survey of Kandyan warfare over two centuries reveals that this was but a very simplistic view of Kandyan strategy against invasion. Actually, the Kandyans did not adopt a regular strategy to meet European invasions. It is true that the British expeditions in 1803 and 1804 met with only light resistance and that the Portuguese marches of 1630 and 1638 were virtually unopposed, the Kandyans abandoning their capital after decorating it like a 'heavenly city', according to a Sinhalese poet.[5] But on most occasions, the Kandyans did resist the invading armies. Pedro Lopez de Souza met with stiff resistance at Balana in 1594 and eight years later, Jeronimo de Azevedo's invading force was blocked at the same spot for several days by a stubborn Kandyan garrison.[6] In 1764 and 1765, the Kandyans attempted to resist the Dutch advance. In 1764, the Dutch advance guard was attacked just beyond Wisenawiya in the Seven Korales while the Dutch had to overcome two Kandyan attempts to stand and fight in 1765 before they entered Kandy.[7] Even in 1803 and 1804, there was resistance, albeit not as stiff as on previous occasions, against British invaders. In 1803, the Kandyans resisted at Girihagama while in 1804, Johnstone's march itself was hotly disputed by a battery from across the Mahaveli river.[8]

Sometimes, Kandyans also resorted to diversionary measures to keep European invasions off-balance. In 1603, during Azevedo's invasion, Vimala Dharma Surya sent a Kandyan force to attack Talampitiya in the Seven Korales.[9] In 1803, another such attempt was made when the Kandyans made a foray in force into the Four Korales. Both incursions were beaten back with ease but it did demonstrate the flexibility of Kandyan strategy.

On the other hand, Queyroz and Johnstone were quite right about one thing: there *was* a clear focus on destroying the enemy after they had entered Kandyan territory. The emphasis was on weakening them through numerous ways, which included guerrilla attacks on outposts and supply lines, and attempts to subvert non-European auxiliaries in the invading force. There was also a concentrated effort to cut-off the enemy on the retreat. The biggest Kandyan successes came against the retreating enemies. De Souza, De Sa, and De Mello were all defeated and their armies destroyed while on the retreat. Similar attempts were made against the Dutch army in 1765 and Johnstone's detachment in 1804. These, however, proved unsuccessful.[10]

However, the attempt to overwhelm the invaders was not necessarily only when they were on the retreat. In 1765, the Kandyans did attempt to overrun the main Dutch camp in Kandy, and in 1803 the British garrison was attacked in a clear attempt to crush it. The attempt in 1765 ended in failure. The assault in 1803 was beaten back but the Kandyans succeeded in encircling the garrison and forcing the British to surrender.[11]

Thus, it is not possible to draw a comprehensive picture of a general strategy employed by the Kandyans in opposing European invasions and raids. Invasions at different times produced different responses. The features that were common to all periods were the attempts to weaken the enemy within the highlands and the attempt to cut him off on the retreat.

However, as pointed out earlier, Kandyan strategy was not limited to countering invasions. Even if the Europeans did not invade Kandyan territory, their threat to Kandyan security and interests remained. The Kandyans were well aware of the need to destabilize or even wipe out European power in the lowlands in order to maintain their own security. What was the Kandyan approach to handling European power in the lowlands? One way of maintaining pressure on European territories has been already mentioned. This was to foment unrest amongst the inhabitants in those areas, which sometimes led to direct Kandyan intervention. But a more direct way of challenging European power was to make incursions into their territories in force or launch large-scale invasions. Defeat of invading European armies in the highlands presented the most favourable opportunity for descending on their possessions in the low country as happened in 1603, 1630, and 1803. On these occasions, taking advantage of the reverses suffered by the Europeans in the highlands, the Kandyans swept down on the European territories. The Kandyans also undertook raids into the low country on their own initiative, rather than as the follow-up of a successful defensive campaign. For instance, when the Portuguese were fortifying the eastern coast and threatening to seal Kandy off from the world in the 1620s the Kandyans launched raids into Jaffna peninsula and attempted to overthrow the Portuguese rule there with the help of the local population. Two attempts made in 1628 and 1629 resulted in failure with heavy losses to the Kandyans.[12] In 1761, the Kandyans again went on the offensive on their own initiative taking advantage of the rebellion in the low country and overran the south-west of the island while making threatening inroads into many other parts.

As explained earlier, the European forts in the interior were either abandoned or captured by the Kandyans during these onslaughts. Thus in 1630 the Kandyans first took over the Portuguese fort in Sabaragamuwa while and Kalutara were abandoned. Menikkadawara held on for nearly four months before finally succumbing.[13] The low country was overrun right up to the gates of Colombo, which was placed under siege. In 1761, a string of outposts in the interior in the south-west became the first target before the fort at Matara was besieged.[14]

Thus, it can be said that Kandyan strategy pursued two main objectives: the destruction of invading European armies and undermining and even destroying European power in the lowlands. The section below looks at the tactics employed by the Kandyans in pursuing their strategic objectives.

KANDYAN TACTICS

SUBVERSION OF AUXILIARIES

As noted earlier, once the European forces were inside Kandyan territory, attempts were made to weaken them. One favourite ploy was the subversion of the non-European auxiliaries that accompanied the European forces. Like all European armies that campaigned in Asia and Africa, the European forces in Sri Lanka also contained a large number of non-European troops. In fact, they formed the majority of the European armies that invaded Kandy. The Portuguese employed Sinhalese auxiliaries or lascarins. De Souza's army in 1594 had 15,000 lascarins[15] while De Sa took with him nearly 13,000 indigenous troops in 1630.[16] De Mello's army included 5,000 lascarins and also several hundred Canarese and Africans.[17] The Dutch and the British used Malay and Indian troops. The main Dutch force in 1765 comprised 900 Europeans, 800 Malays or 'Easterners', and about 100 sepoys[18] and the Dutch garrison in Kandy in March 1765 included about 550 Europeans and nearly 700 sepoys and Malays.[19] The British also made use of Sepoys and Malays. The majority of the troops left in Kandy in 1803 were Malays while every detachment and outpost had a proportion of Malay troops and sepoys.[20]

Of these, the troops most susceptible to subversion were the lascarins. All major Portuguese expeditions to Kandy suffered from the desertion of their lascarin forces, and at least on two occasions Kandyan involvement was detectable. For instance, during the expedition of 1594, the Portuguese discovered a letter which the Kandyan king Vimala Dharma Surya had written to the lascarin commander referring to an impending betrayal of the Portuguese army. As a consequence, the commander of the lascarins was murdered by the Portuguese and his troops deserted *en masse* to the Kandyan camp. It is not certain if there was a real conspiracy or if, as Portuguese historians point out, Vimala Dharma Surya allowed a letter referring to a non-existent conspiracy to fall into Portuguese hands in order to create divisions within the enemy camp.[21] In either case there is no doubt that the Kandyans played an active role in separating the lascarins from their masters.

A real conspiracy did come into play during the expedition of Constantine de Sa in 1630. According to a plan worked out between the Kandyans and the lascarin commanders the latter were to desert with their men during the campaign and seal the fate of the Portuguese expeditionary force. At the same time, the lascarins in Colombo were expected to rise and deliver the fort to the Kandyans. The first part of the plan worked perfectly; during the Portuguese retreat from Kandy, the majority of the lascarins decamped to the Kandyans.[22] De Sa's fighting retreat was cut-off at Randeniwela and the Captain General with a large number of Portuguese soldiers slain. However, the second part of the plan failed as the plot to deliver Colombo was discovered and foiled in time.[23]

Lascarin desertions took place during the expeditions of 1602 and 1638 but it is not certain whether the Kandyan intrigues played any part in precipitating these.[24] In the latter instance, some of the Canarese and Africans also deserted De Mello's army and, as pointed out earlier, later took service with the Kandyans.

During the wars with the Dutch and the British too, the

Kandyans focused heavily on subverting the Malays and sepoys. They succeeded in detaching a number of Malays from the British during the expeditions of 1803 and 1804.[25] As described earlier, the Kandyan attack on the British garrison stationed at the palace in 1803 was led by one such Malay named Sankilan.[26] The Kandyans used promises of good treatment and money to entice the Malays into deserting.[27] Usually, Malays already in Kandyan service were used to encourage desertion by those in European service. Thus, Sankilan, it was reported, offered Nouradhin, the commander of the British Malays, the income from 14 districts and better pay than under the British to lure him.[28] During the Kandyan offensive in August 1803, even the Malays in Mullaitivu were called on to join the Kandyan Malays who had surrounded them.[29] Material inducements were not the only incentives offered to leave the Europeans. In 1804, Arthur Johnstone found the Kandyans urging the Malays and sepoys in his army to desert as the only means of saving their lives.[30]

GUERRILLA WARFARE

Kandyans very rarely offered pitched battles to their European enemies. 'Very sensibly so', notes the author of the '*Aanmerkingen*', explaining that while the Kandyans were not trained for pitched battles, they had 'thousands of opportunities to damage and even defeat an enemy'.[31] Accordingly, like many other Asian, African, and American peoples faced with similar challenges, the Kandyans too opted for guerrilla warfare as their main combat tactic against their European adversaries.

In order to understand Kandyan guerrilla tactics we need to first consider the country in which the fighting took place and the place of Kandyan forces in it. Kandyan–European fighting took place in the central highlands as well as in the lowlands, and in both cases in country that was extremely rugged. The geographical and topographical setting in the highlands particularly favoured guerrilla fighting. Ringed by hills, Kandy was a natural fortress. Entry into the Kandyan heartland was possible only through a limited number of passes that served as the gateways to this fortress. Within the hills rugged hillsides overlooked narrow pathways and defiles, hemmed in by impenetrable jungle. Having spent 20 years within this mountain fastness, Knox was well qualified to describe its natural strength:

> The Kingdom of Conde Uda is strongly fortified by nature. For which way soever you enter into it, you must ascend vast and high mountains, and descend little or nothing. The wayes are many, but very narrow, so that but one can go abreast. The hills are covered with wood and great Rocks so that 'tis scarce possible to get up anywhere, but only in the paths.[32]

Others agreed. John Andrews, the British ambassador who visited Kandy in 1795 and 1796 noted that an army entering Kandy had to 'meet with various difficulties in the country itself', adding that the 'continued windings of the roads commanded almost every situation by impending hills would enable an inferior force of natives, possessed of moderate resolution and ability, to give very serious opposition to an enemy in every respect their superior'. He also noted the flimsiness of the bridges that spanned the many rivulets that flowed through the Kandyan territories, contrasting them with the sturdy constructions found in the Company's territories.[33]

Indeed, the greater part of the island was thickly forested, although the lowlands lacked the rugged terrain of the Kandyan highlands. Ribeiro, who spent almost as long as Knox in the low country, speaks of jungle too thick to see beyond a few paces.[34] Queyroz wryly pointed out that it was only in south-east Sri Lanka that an army could march in ranks because the country was open.[35] Even in parts of the country close to the European territories the terrain was so rugged that sometimes scaling ladders were required to negotiate it![36] This was a country for guerrilla warfare, not for pitched battles.

KANDYAN GUERRILLA TACTICS

Kandyan guerrilla tactics showed a keen appreciation of the geographical circumstances. They focused their main efforts on attacking the enemy on the narrow, winding tracks that criss-crossed the countryside. Very often, the Kandyans sought to throw more impediments in the way of the European armies. They blocked the paths by cutting down huge trees. According to Captain Johnstone, in places like narrow passes where they could not be avoided, felled trees presented 'a most serious obstacle to the march of troops; for cutting up and removing a large tree is not the business of a moment'.[37] Blocking the paths was particularly effective against a retreating foe who had little time to spare for clearing obstacles from their path. Felled trees served to impede the retreating armies of Pedro Lopes de Souza and Diogo de Mello in 1594 and 1638 respectively.[38]

The Kandyans also made use of field fortifications to impede the enemy's progress through the jungle. These batteries or breastworks were erected at strategic points that commanded pathways and river crossings. Sometimes a series of batteries were built one behind the other as the Dutch found on the road leading to the hill-fort at Galagedera in 1765.[39] Kandyan field fortificaions were built mostly of wood and earth[40] although stone was also occasionally used. The '*Aanmerkingen*' makes a distinction between a stockade and a battery, the former being 'merely a double-row of rammed-in stakes filled with fascines or earth and provided with loopholes' while a battery is described as a more substantial work built of either masonry, wood, or earth. They were about eight or ten feet tall and had two rows of loopholes, for gingals and muskets.[41] Sometimes cannon were also mounted on them. A Dutch route-clearing party moving from Galle to Matara in 1762 came across such a battery, a massive stone structure 255 long and nine feet high.[42] Another battery encountered by the British near the Korunda oya during operations against Kandyan rebels in 1818 consisted of a 'most substantial wall about 8 feet high and 6 feet thick . . . built of large flat stone with a ramp ascending behind to a stone banquet'.[43] One field entrenchment captured by the Dutch in the Matara district in November 1761 was even provided with a substantial underground bunker.[44]

The '*Aanmerkingen*' also describes a second kind of fieldwork called a stockade, built of trees rammed into the ground in two rows and tied together with cane. The space between the rows of trees was filled up with stones, earth, and wood. Inside were one or two platforms for the musketeers and the gingal bearers who fire through loopholes in the battery.[45] Sometimes, in order to prevent a quick capture, buffalo thorn was strewn around the stockades. Pits were also dug in paths leading to them and charred bamboo splinters 8–10 inches in length were placed in them.[46] In November 1633, the Kandyans are reported to have raised a large stockade in Ganetenna close to the Kandyan frontier 'surrounded by a ditch seventy feet broad and as many deep, the bottom of which was furnished with caltrops made of bamboo spikes and scorched nibao wood'.[47]

According to the '*Aanmerkingen*', the Kandyans placed outposts ahead of their batteries and main parties, with sentries placed on rocks or tall trees. As the enemy approached, they signalled the outposts who fired a few warning shots to alert the main body.[48]

Mention must also be made of the Kandyan forts. The Kandyans constructed several of these structures, usually at passes. These appear to have been enclosures built of stone. The famous Balana Pass was guarded by one for some time and was strong enough for the Portuguese to employ cannon to batter it down in 1603. The Portuguese were in possession of the pass from 1610 to 1617 and they too must have added to the fortifications.[49] The passes at Galagedera and Girihagama were also provided with forts. The Dutch in 1765 and the British in 1803 found both these to be constructed of hewn stone, with two large gateways in the front and rear and heavily defended by artillery.[50]

Though strongly built and well defended by nature, Kandyan fortifications were rarely defended with determination and were often abandoned at the first charge made by the enemy. Europeans often marvelled at the readiness of the Kandyans to abandon their strong batteries and forts. This was probably because, as the '*Aanmerkingen*' points out, the field fortifications were built more for the purpose of hindering an advance than stopping it.[51] But the fieldworks were often rebuilt as readily as they were abandoned. In 1762, the Dutch had a tough time destroying Kandyan batteries around Matara which seemed to spring up again, and on a bigger scale, as soon as they were demolished.[52] Often they carried away their dead and wounded.[53] Sometimes they even managed to save some of their cannon leaving the carriages behind.[54]

But the Kandyans did not limit their guerrilla activity to obstructing paths and assailing the enemy from the security of fortifications. They also moved freely through the forest looking for opportunities to ambush the enemy, hovering around the paths, waiting patiently 'in high and low places in the four divisions', as a Sinhala war poet put it.[55] They often broke up into several small groups and kept up a constant attack on the enemy from several sides, usually with their missile weapons. A British colour sergeant Calladine, describes how the Kandyans had divided themselves into a number of small bodies to constantly engage his detachment on one of its marches in 1817.[56] According to the '*Aanmerkingen*', the usual practice was to block the road and attack from the rear and flanks.[57] This was often the case against retreating enemy forces. As Ribeiro describes with regard to De Souza's retreat in 1594: 'despatching a small body to block the road by cutting down the trees in our rear and spreading his archers and musketeers through the wood, where they were hidden from our men they were exposed to their incessant fire without perceiving their assailants'.[58]

In 1630, De Sa's army was pursued by the Kandyans who constantly attacked it from the front and the flanks. According to Ribeiro, on De Mello's retreat eight years later, 'the enemy soon appeared on our flanks under cover of the forest and opened such a heavy fire, that few escaped being killed'.[59] Dutch detachment that was returning from Hanguranketa in 1765 suffered similarly its rearguard being heavily attacked and suffering considerably.[60] Rocky passes were often favoured for launching such heavy attacks—for obvious reasons. They could be effectively blocked while the surrounding heights provided launching pads for guerrilla attacks as many retreating European forces found to their dismay. When Major Medeler led his relief column back from the Kandyan highlands in 1765 he found the road through the Balana pass heavily blocked with felled trees while the Kandyans kept up a heavy fire from the surrounding heights and even rolled down heavy rocks on his struggling troops.[61] Almost four decades later, Captain Arthur Johnstone's detachment faced a similar challenge while descending the Trincomalee pass during their retreat. The British gained the bottom of the closely obstructed and heavily defended pass only after several hours of heavy fighting and considerable loss.[62]

Clearings in the jungle were also favoured for launching sustained attacks. Clearings exposed a considerable number of the enemy to clear view while still affording enough cover to the guerrillas. When the Dutch retired from Kandyan territory in 1764 they were heavily fired on while crossing a flat ground hemmed in by jungles and rocky heights.[63] Bombardier Alexander who was with Johnstone's detachment also speaks of a heavy attack while the little army was crossing a clearing.[64]

The Kandyans often targeted the baggage train, knowing very well that it represented the lifeline of the enemy. Porters and pack animals were attacked in an attempt to kill them and force them to flee. This was not a difficult task since the porters were utterly defenceless. Such attacks often met with success. In 1638, the Kandyans launched a heavy attack on the baggage train and cut it off from the main army. During Medeler's expedition, any porter that strayed from the lines could expect to be 'babarously handled'.[65] The porters became a focus of Kandyan attacks during the British occupation of Kandy in 1803. Before long, the British were treated to the sight of porters returning from their work outside the camp 'shockingly mangled'.[66] When the British detachment sent to apprehend the king in Hanguranketa returned, the Kandyans took particular care to target the porters, killing 19 of them and wounding many more.[67] As a consequence, the British lost the services of most of their porters soon due to desertion, 300 of them slipping away within days.[68] During Johnstone's retreat too, the Kandyans cut in amongst the coolies who panicked and abandoned two of the wounded soldiers to the Kandyans.[69]

Kandyan guerrillas usually employed their missile weapons—bows and arrows and firearms—in carrying out these attacks. Although gingals were frequently used, cannon remained firmly in the batteries and stockades owing to the difficulty of transporting them in the thick jungle and across broken ground. Usually, the enemy was subjected to irregular fire from the jungle, sometimes intense, sometimes desultory, little more than a few shots or arrows fired at the marching troops. Quite frequently, volley firing was also used: 'The Cingalese lie concealed till you come close upon them, then they give one regular fire and fly; this is the general case and I suppose I was almost six yards from their grass hoppers, the balls of which are about one inch thick in diameter, when they let them off.[70]

Knox also appears to be speaking of similar tactics in his description of Kandyan warfare.[71] As Ribeiro mentions in the case of De Souza's retreat, it was usually difficult for the Europeans to see their assailants during Kandyan guerrilla attacks. The only possible response was to fire blindly, which the Europeans often did. Queyroz speaks of one remarkable incident during Azevedo's retreat in 1603 when blind firing by the Portuguese resulted in the killing of a deer which was later found riddled with nine bullets.[72] On such instances, the only clue to the whereabouts of the Kandyans was provided by the puffs of smoke from their firearms.[73] Even that was not an option when the Europeans were assailed by arrows which left no tell-tale signs of their source. And to make matters more complicated for the Europeans, the Kandyans could always retreat from their hiding places in safety. As Johnstone explains, the paths up to the Kandyans' mountain perches were on the opposite side of the hill and they could easily melt into the jungle along these routes.[74] In 1803, British spies even reported seeing Kandyans cutting 'narrow paths to right and left through the jungle so that they may easily outflank an invading army'.[75]

But it was not only European detachments that came under attack from Kandyan guerrillas. Their outposts and camps also became targets. According to the '*Aanmerkingen*', the Kandyans were unlikely to attack an overnight camp but if the camp or outpost was of a more permanent nature they did everything possible to harass it. This was done by denuding the surrounding country of supplies and by setting up their own batteries and outposts around the European position. Thus established, they proceeded to launch desultory attacks on the European positions. During the British and Dutch occupations of Kandy in 1803 and 1765 their outposts were constantly fired on by Kandyans. At times this consisted of sustained firing but sometimes, some of these attacks amounted to little more than harassing sniping. The diary of the Dutch Governor Van Eck's refers to some such Kandyan snipers who 'showed themselves on the hills in small parties and now and then fired some shots on our people . . . and approached without fear to disturb our field station at Girihagama' in 1765.[76] Calladine speaks of a similar incident in 1818 when Kandyans lurking in the surrounding area occasionally fired arrows into their camps. On one occasion the attack was with fire arrows.[77]

GUERRILLA TACTICS AND OPEN CONFRONTATION

Kandyan guerrilla tactics were often aimed at harassing the enemy and steadily chipping away at their strength. In this sense, Kandyan tactics had parallels with the tactics employed by many Asian and, African peoples against European encroachment. The Kandyans' use of field fortifications in conjunction with hit and run attacks on camps and moving columns has close similarity to the approach of the Burmese to defending themselves from the British in the nineteenth century. The Burmese too built stockades at strategic points to intercept British columns and combined this positional warfare with mobile guerrilla tactics in tropical surroundings somewhat similar to the Kandyan environment.[78] However, the Burmese effort was on a bigger scale given the larger resource base of the Burmese army. Interestingly, in Malaya too, the British ran into a similar opposition from the Malays who erected fortifications along lines of communication and sniped at enemy columns from the safety of their stockades and the surrounding jungles.[79] They were tactics aimed at harassing and wearing down an enemy already inconvenienced by the rugged and inhospitable terrain.

But sometimes the Kandyans also tried to overwhelm their enemy. This was often attempted against retreating enemy forces, which they tried to cut up into smaller bodies and destroy. Sometimes the Kandyans met with success. Keeping a large army of several hundred together on the narrow, winding trails in the Kandyan highlands was difficult at the best of times and required a stupendous effort when conducting a running battle with the Kandyan guerrillas. In these circumstances, the possibility of the army being split up and defeated in detail was very real. This is exactly what happened to the armies led by De Souza and De Sa in 1594 and 1630 respectively. The advance, van and rear guards of De Souza's army were separated from each other and overwhelmed.[80] De Sa's rear guard was separated from the main body and almost annihilated. The main body itself was later surrounded and completely defeated.[81]

Isolated outposts and small detachments were also prime targets for efforts at annihilation. European attempts to dominate the interior presented plenty of opportunities for this as European armies often relied on outposts and small patrols to keep parts of the interior under control. During Pedro Lopes de Souza's expedition, a detachment of 150 Portuguese sent in search of provisions was attacked at a place called Hallololuwa and suffered heavy casualties.[82] The Dutch War of 1761–6 began with the annihilation of a Dutch detachment of 24 soldiers in Morawak Korale in the south-west in January 1761.[83] A few weeks later another, larger detachment was attacked and all the troops captured or killed while withdrawing from Tangalle. Individual stragglers stood no chance. Several soldiers that went missing during the Dutch and British occupations of Kandy in 1765 and 1803 were found killed, sometimes mutilated.[84]

The Europeans were very conscious of this danger. The instructions given by the outgoing Portuguese Captain General, Don Jeronimo de Azevedo, to his successor are very illuminating in this regard. He advised the new Captain General to maintain pressure on Kandy by raiding Kandyan territories regularly, then added this strong admonition:

> When you enter Kandy, never divide your troops for longer than one day, so that at night they all join you, and even this may be undertaken only when it is known that the enemy is not marching in a body and is scattered in flight at a distance from your force; when such is not the case, it is unwise to divide the troops or make long marches, and you should advance in such order that the advanced guard can hear the rearguard's fight, should there be any, because the lands of Kandy are very treacherous and their troops are very troublesome and know how to turn to advantage any opportunity that their good luck or our own carelessness might present to them. For this reason it is best that you move with such wariness as if each hour you were expecting to run into the enemy.[85]

The author of the '*Aanmerkingen*' makes a similar observation, pointing out that when marching in hostile country, 'the advance-guard must never be out of sight of the main body, or at least not out of hearing of its drums: in hilly country not over 50 yards, in open country 150'.[86] In 1803, we find General Hay Mcdowall issuing Colonel Baillie with instructions strikingly similar to those issued by Azevedo to his successor. Writing to him before the expedition to Hanguranketa, Mcdowall advised Baillie to make sure that detachments were not sent out more than ten or twelve miles or half a day's easy march from the main body. And that too, 'with the certainty of being able to reach you again the same night'.[87]

When Kandyans moved in to cut-off, surround, and annihilate a detachment or outpost the action often moved to a more open confrontation with the Kandyans coming out of concealment to engage the enemy at close range, even in hand to hand confrontation. This is what happened in 1594 and 1630, when the running battles culminated in a final battle when the Kandyans eventually succeeded in surrounding the survivors of the decimated enemy force. In 1594, after his vanguard and advance guard were defeated, De Souza fought on with his rear guard until it was surrounded and then 'fought with spears' until dark.[88] In 1630, De Sa's main body continued the retreat after the rear guard was cut-off in hand to hand fighting with spears and was forced to make a stand at Randeniwela in Wellawaya where the final battle lasted from 6 O'clock in the morning till 2 O'clock in the afternoon.[89] Here too fighting seems to have been at close range, if not always hand to hand, the Kandyans engaging and disengaging as circumstances dictated. Says Queyroz, 'the Kandyans played on them from afar with arrows and spears, and when our men tried to have recourse to their swords, they either shot them down before they were able to do so or fled from the field'.[90] According to Sa y Menezes, 'the barbarians came on like a pack of mad dogs, who, craving to bite like all who pass by them, whenever attacked run, but anon return and bark at a distance, importunate and furious until they their prey'.[91]

In 1638, however, there was not much of a running battle. According to Queyroz, the Kandyans did attack the Portuguese continuously until they reached the Mahaveli river. Here they were not allowed to draw water and were forced to spend the night in thirst. During the night, the king brought up his main force, which was probably still being collected the previous day, and attacked the enemy as they attempted to continue their retreat.[92] In this final engagement the Portuguese seem to have been attacked at close range by the Kandyans who 'charged down the slope, covering themselves behind trees'.[93] According to Queyroz, 'the Chingulays attacked them with such resolution and at such close quarters without minding the men they lost that there was not even space where to wield their arms'.[94] This was no doubt wilful exaggeration by the Jesuit but the point is well taken.

Attempts to overwhelm garrisons and outposts also produced close range open encounters. This was the case when the Dutch and British garrisons occupying the Kandy palace were attacked with force in 1765 and 1803 respectively. In the first instance, the Kandyans first attacked the outposts in order to draw out the troops from the garrison and then 'charged with terrible shouts down the hill behind the palace'.[95] Some tried to climb the wall while others attacked down the road. The attack was repulsed, albeit with considerable difficulty. In 1803, the British garrison at the same place was attacked in the early morning of 24 June by the Kandyans led by their Malay troops. In this instance, however, there was no diversion, the attack being a straight-forward attempt to overpower with numbers a garrison already heavily depleted by sickness and desertion. This attack also failed but the subsequent blockade of the garrison forced the British to surrender.

Sinhalese war poems provide graphic descriptions of some of the open confrontations between the Kandyan and European forces in their recounting of major battles. For instance the *Rajasinha Hatana* describing the Kandyan victory in 1638 speaks of the Sinhalese grabbing Portuguese firearms and bashing them with their butts, clubbing the Portuguese to death, cutting off heads with swords, laying *Kapiri* or African soldiers on the ground and kicking them in the guts.[96] Even more realistic is the behaviour of the victorious Sinhalese who are described as fighting among themselves for the spoils, dying in the stampede, looking on with pleasure, snatching necklaces, shooting (with arrows) enemies and removing weapons after checking if they are dead while some linger to cut-off heads and others carry away their loot.[97] The *Kustantinu Hatana* describes similar acts: cutting enemies to pieces, cutting off limbs, noses, and ears, some stabbing several people, others stabbing enemies with their lances and putting them to aside, some killing two or three enemies with one shot, sparing lives out of compassion and tying up captives.[98] The poets are no doubt giving generous play to their imagination and using their poetic licence to describe these events but in doing so they are probably describing what was a likely scenario in a contemporary battle. All the above-mentioned behaviour are consistent with soldiers engaged in an orgy of violence and plunder with early modern weapons and this, no doubt, is what happened when the Kandyans closed in to overwhelm their enemies.

After defeating the enemy, it was common practice to cut-off their heads and pile them in a heap as a sort of grisly war trophies. *Rajasinha Hatana* likens them to a heap of coconuts while the *Maha Hatana* compares them to a pile of king coconuts.[99] Individual soldiers were very keen to cut-off enemy heads—called *tharam*—in order to get rewards from the king. Interestingly, according to the *Kustantinu Hatana*, the Portuguese also acquired the habit of gathering enemy heads to celebrate victory.[100] There are also some interesting references in the war poems to prisoners being subjected to torture. The punishments are imaginative but not improbable. Enemy prisoners are described as being forced to eat mud, being split open, gored by buffaloes, bitten by dogs, buried up to the neck and burnt alive, and tied up and beaten up by children.[101]

However, it was not only against retreating or depleted forces that the Kandyans tried open confrontation. For instance, during the Dutch invasion in 1765, the First Adigar offered the Dutch battle at a place called Periwille. The Kandyans, estimated at about 4,000 or 5,000, took post on a slope covered with scrub jungle and with a paddy field in front and a river at the back and awaited the Dutch attack. As the Dutch attacked the Kandyans defended themselves with musketry and Gingal fire but were soon forced to retire with heavy losses. The Dutch suffered no casualties.[102] On another occasion, in 1764, Dufflo reported a battle he had with a large Kandyan force on the banks of the Kandapola oya. The Kandyans were drawn up in a regular order of battle with their right wing consisting of sepoys, Malays, and Sinhalese resting on a grove and their Europeans and another Sinhalese body on the right wing which extended into the jungle. The centre was composed of a large force with gingals and rockets. Dufflo's troops defeated the Kandyans after 'considerable resistance' with six killed and fifteen wounded.[103]

Thus, although guerrilla warfare was the chief tactic employed by Kandyans against the European forces, it was not the only type of fighting the Kandyans opted for. They also dared to take on their opponents in more open confrontation, sometimes with resounding success. However, it would be fair to say that guerrilla warfare was the norm.

The tactics described above were used mainly against enemy forces operating in Kandyan territory. As noted earlier, Kandyans also sought to take the battle to the Europeans and attack their territories. During such invasions the fortified posts maintained by Europeans often became the focus of the invading Kandyan armies. Sometimes, as in 1630, 1675, and 1761, they succeeded in capturing some of these posts. What were the tactics employed by them in these operations?

KANDYAN SIEGE WARFARE

Rarely did the Kandyans storm a fortified place. It is interesting that the term commonly used in Sinhala writing of the period to describe the capture of a fort is *aravanawa*, or 'forcing open'.[104] It is very rarely that a term like *bindinawa*—breakdown—is used. This probably implies that the Kandyans saw the capture of a fort in terms of forcing it open or, more to the point, of forcing its surrender rather than battering it down or storming it. The general Kandyan approach to capturing forts and outposts confirms this. The general practice seems to have been to surround it and invest it. Batteries were built at strategic places and the fort was fired at.

This is where the Kandyans' lack of heavy artillery had an effect. The gingal was good in the jungle but pathetically inadequate for threatening a fort. During Johnstone's expedition in 1804, the Kandyans tried vainly to demolish a wattle-and-daub hut occupied by the British with their gingals.[105] Often the only cannon available were a motley collection of light pieces. In 1603, the Portuguese stockade at Talampitiya was bombarded with an 'iron esphera of great length', two falcons, two demi-falcons, and two iron *caes* besides many *roqueyras* and *chicorros*.[106] These were all light guns. During the siege of Colombo in 1638, the Kandyans had to make do with the few cannons they had acquired from the Portuguese garrisons they had captured, while for the attack on Bibilegama in 1675 they could deploy only four light pieces. Against Katuwana in 1761, four 8 pounders were used.[107]

Perhaps the most impressive deployment of siege artillery was at Matara in 1761. Against this fort which was really an enclosure protected by a real rampart only on one side, the Kandyans deployed a number of guns, placed in five batteries. Some of the batteries were higher than the walls of the fort which enabled the Kandyans to view the interior of the fort. The heavy fire from the Dutch cannon made no impression on them. Within a few days the Kandyans moved their works closer to the walls in what appeared to be a preparation for an assault when the Dutch decided to abandon the fort. But even during this siege, there were no heavy guns. As noted earlier, the Dutch reported only balls of 4 and 6 pounds falling into the fort.[108] During the siege of the government House in Hambantota in August and September 1803, the Kandyans built 7 batteries around the building. The batteries were found to be proof against British musketry but again the Kandyans lacked the artillery. The batteries mounted only gingals.[109]

In spite of the lack of firepower the Kandyans frequently showed much ingenuity in the conduct of sieges. During the above-mentioned siege of Talampitiya, they covered their trenches with rope netting as protection against the bombs and fire-pots the Portuguese were hurling at them.[110] Before Bibilegama in 1675 they built fascines and piled them around the fort, pushing them closer every night in an apparent attempt to set fire to them. They also planted guns on a *Bo*-tree in the vicinity of the fort and fired into it. Guns were also aimed at a trench by means of which the Dutch obtained water from the nearby stream while fire arrows forced the besieged to pull down their thatched roofs, exposing themselves to the elements during the rainy season.[111] According to Queyroz, in 1630, the Kandyans constructed 'wooden engines' before Colombo and neutralized the Portuguese artillery to such an extent that the Portuguese had to sally out and destroy them.[112] In 1761, they approached the Negombo fort along a sophisticated trench system. After ejecting the Kandyans from them, the Dutch found some wicker-work mantelets 10–12 feet long and 3–4 feet tall. In approaching Dutch outposts in Kandy, the Kandyans made use of fascines made of straw which were tough enough to stop a musket bullet. The author of the '*Aanmerkingen*' thought they were stronger and longer lasting than those used by the Dutch.[113]

Nevertheless, on rare occasions there were attempts by Kandyans to storm European forts. In August 1675, they tried to take the Dutch fort of Bibilegama by storm while in 1803, the

Grand army of Kandy approached the British outpost of Hanwella with the apparent intention of overwhelming it by a frontal attack. The first occasion seems to have been particularly remarkable for the doggedness shown by Kandyans which is totally at variance with the usual Kandyan strategy of avoiding head-on clashes. If the Dutch soldiers are to be believed, the Kandyans attempted to penetrate the defences with scant regard to the heavy losses they suffered, sometimes stepping over their dead and wounded.[114] The attempt on Hanwella was more sedate, the Kandyan army approaching the post with artillery in front, in a massive show of strength.[115] Both attempts failed but as we have noted earlier, Bibilegama was eventually captured by the Kandyans.

On another occasion, during an attempt to take Balana in 1617, the Kandyans appear to have resorted to an interesting tactic. According to a Jesuit priest, the Kandyans approached the fort behind wooden mantelets which withstood the shot from Portuguese muskets and light artillery and proceeded to dislodge the stones in the wall with iron hooks. The king is said to have offered a reward for every stone thus removed.[116]

Trench systems and artillery were relatively modern ways of targeting fortifications. But the Kandyans also resorted to ancient military practices in attacking forts. This was reflected in the use of elephants. The elephant has been the battering ram and the tank of ancient and pre-modern warfare in the East. In their wars with the kings of Sitawaka, the Portuguese had to contend with elephants, 'terrible warfare of Ceylon', as Queyroz called them. They were used to great effect in a number of encounters, particularly in the Battle of Mulleriyawa in 1562. The sieges of Kotte and Colombo by Rajasinha I also saw the employment of large numbers of elephants. Kandyans, however, used elephants sparingly.[117] In 1603, the Portuguese fort at Talampitiya was repeatedly assaulted with elephants.[118] Senerath brought a number of elephants to the siege of Colombo. They participated in one general assault which was beaten back.[119] Apart from such limited use, elephants did not feature prominently in Kandyan warfare. They are totally absent from the wars against the Dutch and the British in the eighteenth and nineteenth centuries. The reasons are easy to understand. The Kandyan terrain and the type of warfare practised by the Kandyans did not allow the use of elephants, and even in the lowlands where their use may have been possible, the increasing use of artillery by the Europeans made it impossible to use elephants with any chance of success.

Kandyan attacks on forts seem to have caused very few casualties—no doubt a testimony to their lack of artillery. The impressive effort around Matara was quite fruitful in terms of enemy losses. The Matara Dissawa himself was killed while many others were wounded. The wall itself was considerably damaged, prompting the Dutch to place sandbags to prop it up.[120] But this was a rare occasion. Usually the losses were trifling. In 1630, the Portuguese suffered only a few dozen men killed and wounded while the garrison in Bibilegama suffered just a handful of casualties.[121] The attack on Hanwella in 1761 killed one and wounded another.[122] Very often, tiny European forces managed to hold out against large numbers of Kandyans from behind fortifications. The Government House in Hambantota was defended by 60 invalid Malays, while in August 1803, the small square fort at Chilaw was defended by two young civil servants and 60 sepoys against an army of 3000 Kandyans.[123]

But the Kandyans also succeeded in capturing some of the enemy's forts. This was due to a number of reasons. As already noted, in 1675 Bibilegama surrendered and Matara was evacuated due to the sheer pressure from the Kandyans while Hanwella surrendered in 1761 due to a lack of supplies. Katuwana surrendered apparently due to a combination of a lack of resolve on the part of the garrison and a belief in a promise of safe conduct given by the Kandyans. A note must also be made of those posts which were evacuated at the approach of the Kandyans. These were usually posts which were in the periphery of major fortifications. In 1630, the Portuguese evacuated a number of posts in the interior due to apprehensions for their safety after the defeat of the main Portuguese army at Randeniwela. Similarly, after the fall of Bibilegama in 1675, the Dutch pulled back all their posts in the surrounding region. In 1761 too, a number of posts in the deep south were evacuated. The British also evacuated Dambadeniya in the Seven Korales and Tangalle in the south in 1803.[124] These evacuations, though not the direct result of Kandyan assaults upon those posts, were nevertheless caused by a fear of such a development. They underlined a tacit recognition of a potential threat to isolated posts in the countryside once the countryside itself was lost to the Kandyans. Such a loss implied dire consequences for the posts themselves. Once the countryside passed under the Kandyans the possibility of the post being starved into submission was very real. Thus, the potential disaster which accompanied direct Kandyan investment was as instrumental in forcing the abandonment of European posts as were the consequences of a direct siege.

Such, then, were the tactics adopted by the Kandyans in fighting their European opponents in their own territories as well as outside the highlands. Their tactics were dominated by guerrilla fighting but at times they also dared to risk open confrontations. Their invasions and incursions into the lowlands pitted them against European fortifications that had to be besieged. In all this their tactics showed an admirable ability to use the terrain and their meagre resources to advantage.

KANDYAN TACTICAL STRENGTHS AND LIMITATIONS

As with all strategies and tactics, Kandyan strategy and tactics also had their strengths and weaknesses. The main strength of Kandyan warfare was that it exploited something over which the Kandyan peasant had command—the environment. The Kandyan peasant soldier was well acquainted with his country and even if he was fighting outside his home province the terrain was not 'foreign' to him. Climbing rugged hillsides and navigating across broken and wooded country was part of their life, and they could move cross-country without difficulty, a great asset in guerrilla fighting. Kandyan military organization also greatly favoured guerrilla warfare. They could operate in small bodies without suffering disruption to command and they carried little baggage. They could exist on a little rice and vegetables obtained from the forest. The second advantage was that very often they had command over the countryside which meant that they could leave their supplies in bases in the jungle and move about carrying only their arms and ammunition without fear of the enemy falling upon their supplies. Small bodies of loosely organized and lightly equipped men were well suited for fleeting actions in rugged terrain. Furthermore, guerrilla warfare did not require any special training or drill which the Kandyans lacked. What it needed was knowledge of the country and initiative on the part of the guerrillas. Small bodies of self-sustaining troops had much scope for using their own initiative and engaging and disengaging the enemy as circumstances dictated. It also enabled them to menace European territories on several fronts at once. Thus we find the Kandyans attacking Dutch possessions in the west, south, and the east. At the beginning of 1761, Kandyan troops engaged the Dutch on a very broad front from Puttalam to Matara.[125] Likewise, in August and September 1803, there were simultaneous operations in Matara, Hambantota, Ruwanwella, Halawata (Chilaw), and Mullaitivu. This was possible because of the decentralization of the military command which enabled the formation of numerous Kandyan armies organized on a regional basis.

The Kandyans were at their strongest when they were fighting in the Kandyan heartland against the invading European armies. Here they were fighting closer to home and not far from their supply bases. Therefore, the Kandyans could mobilize large armies for the defence of the hills. They were also fighting in familiar country that enabled them to move troops with ease from one theatre to another. However, problems could arise if the war turned out to be a long one. A long war was not very healthy for the peasant economy. This was aggravated by the disruption to the economic lifeline with the coast, the natural result of fighting a defensive war in the interior against a foe dominating the coastline.

When they moved out of the highlands closer to and across the frontiers these problems increased. The terrain still remained friendly for the most part but the problem of supply became more pronounced as they were fighting far from home and the base areas of supply. As a consequence, fielding large armies for long periods was a serious problem. This problem was compounded by the complete absence of a navy and the lack of heavy artillery. They made the task of quickly capturing European forts, especially their coastal strongholds, the mainstay of European power in the lowlands, impossible. It also made short wars difficult in strategic terms.

Despite all the advantages of the terrain, guerrilla tactics also suffered from a major problem. As explained earlier, Kandyan irregular, guerrilla actions were often fought at long range with the Kandyans taking cover behind natural features or defensive constructions. They ventured to fight close order battles only when they had surrounded the enemy with overwhelming numbers and were quite certain of victory. If the initial attempt to overwhelm the enemy failed, the action shifted back to long range. This attitude was maintained against forts as well, as is clearly shown from the reluctance to storm even the weakest forts.

The problem with this was that it allowed for little scope for inflicting heavy casualties often. The reluctance to engage the enemy at close range unless victory was assured also limited the opportunities for inflicting harm with the weapons at their disposal. From a distance, only missile weapons could be used and these lost much of their accuracy anywhere beyond point blank range. Furthermore, in guerrilla fighting, just as the foliage and rocks concealed the Kandyans from their enemies they also obstructed a clear view for him to shoot at. As we have seen, Kandyan guns were maintained in a very bad condition. In the case of bows and arrows, the problem was further complicated by the need to draw the bow string, not always possible in thick foliage. In these circumstances, even volley firing could have done little to improve the chances of hitting the target. Some sources, however, speak of impressive Kandyan marksmanship. Queyroz for instance speaks of the Sinhalese being capable of stupendous feats of marksmanship, such as sending as many as five bullets into the same spot in a target and putting out matches by night.[126] But Queyroz is either exaggerating or he is speaking of special cases because contemporary firearms were rarely blessed with such accuracy—even in the hands of gifted marksmen. Poorly maintained ordinary Kandyan guns could have achieved nothing of the sort. The Dutch Governor, Van Anglebeek, was closer to the truth than Queyroz when he wrote in 1764 that there was little reason to fear Kandyan guerrillas because they had few good guns and bad powder, and fired from among trees or from a distance.[127]

It is not surprising therefore to hear of Kandyan tactics producing few signal successes in the field. There were just three major victories in 1594, 1630, and 1638 and all against the Portuguese. All other victories were against small detachments and patrols. And these were few and far between. Usually the Europeans managed to beat off Kandyans or fight their way out of trouble only occasionally with substantial casualties.

Of course, we are depending on European sources for all this and it is easy to ascribe their observations to bias. As Tikiri Abeysinghe has pointed out with regard to Queyroz, the Portuguese casualties were often only a fraction of the casualties suffered by Kandyans and this was because Queyroz had his own agenda, namely to promote the idea that Sri Lanka could be won with a small number of Portuguese soldiers.[128] However, the interesting thing is that Queyroz was not the only Portuguese writer who wrote thus; Couto and Ribeiro also did the same.[129] Moreover, later Dutch and British writers also spoke of light European casualties, though not necessarily of massive Kandyan casualties. These accounts are more reliable on account of them being mostly official reports rather than the work of later narrators with axes to grind.

Therefore, despite the colourful language, I do not think there is any reason to seriously doubt the words of Portuguese chroniclers when it comes to the Portuguese suffering only a handful of casualties even after 'fierce battles' against seemingly overwhelming odds. What is to be doubted is not the number of casualties but the 'fierceness' of the battles, the size of the Kandyan armies, and the casualties the Kandyans are said to have suffered. Portuguese chroniclers give accounts of Kandyan casualties in hundreds and sometimes in thousands. This was highly unlikely, again due to the mode of fighting. Not willing to fight at close range and usually fighting from behind cover, the Kandyans lost few men from enemy action. Besides, as pointed out earlier, they also carried away their dead and wounded and would have left precious little on the battlefield for Portuguese chroniclers to have formed their opinions. Interestingly, Dutch and British observers say very little about Kandyan casualties, and when they are the numbers mentioned are quite digestible. The difference between their accounts and those of Portuguese writers lie in the casualty figures for the Kandyans, not for the European side, which suggests that the Portuguese propensity was to downplay their own losses by inflating the forces and the losses of their enemies and not necessarily by reducing their own body count.

However, high Kandyan casualties, though unlikely, were not impossible either. It was sometimes possible for the casualty ratio to be extremely lopsided, as for example, in the action before Hanwella where a massive Kandyan army was routed by a handful of British troops. After the battle the British counted 270 dead Kandyans on the battlefield.[130] Considering the Kandyan propensity for carrying their dead and wounded, it is safe to assume that the actual number of dead would have been twice as many. All this carnage cost the British only two wounded![131] The Kandyans had been surprised by a flank attack and fired on at point-blank range by artillery, and the ensuing panic turned a defeat into a massacre. Given the lack of discipline in the Kandyan armies, they had the potential to incur such disparate losses but never to the extent claimed by the Portuguese chroniclers.

KANDYAN OPTIONS: REBEL SUPPORT AND FOREIGN ASSISTANCE

What options did the Kandyans have for overcoming these limitations? To put it bluntly, very few. The weaknesses of the Kandyan strategy and tactics was an integral part of the Kandyan peasant–military system. The Kandyans could not fight long wars because the soldiers were peasants who could not be away from their fields for too long and the peasant economy was not strong enough to logistically sustain long campaigns. There was little scope for improving their armaments because purchasing or manufacturing superior weaponry was severely restrained by the economic and technological backwardness of the kingdom. As for tactics, guerrilla warfare was the only kind of fighting that could be practised in these circumstances.

It was difficult to find answers to these problems from within the network of indigenous political, military, and economic relationships. Where the problem of logistics outside the highlands was concerned, one option was to enlist the support of the low country population. This had the salutary effect of reducing the logistical burden of fighting outside the base areas as the sympathetic low countrymen could be used to do much of the fighting. This was possible when large segments of the low country population rose in revolt following a European defeat in

Kandy, as was the case in 1603, 1630, and 1803. In 1603, revolts jolted Portuguese power in the low country after Azevedo was forced to retreat and the Captain-General's headquarters in Malwana itself was sacked and his staff massacred.[132] Many of these revolts were the result of local leaders attempting to assert themselves when European authority seemed threatened. At other times, such as in 1761, Kandyan invasion was synchronized with a massive rebellion in the low country that had already been raging for months. On all these occasions, the Kandyan invaders received the active assistance of their low country brethren. In 1761, low country rebels were active in cutting off supplies and manning batteries before Matara.[133]

But this strategy also had its problems. Active participation was not readily forthcoming from everybody in the lowlands. Sometimes, as already seen, the Kandyans had to threaten some sections of the local population into joining. It was also possible for the Kandyans to prove harsher masters than the Europeans. In 1761, for instance, many people in the Matara Dissawany rejoined the Dutch fold when they realized that the Kandyan yoke was harder to bear than Dutch oppression.[134] According to the Sinhala chronicle *Rajavaliya*, in 1630 too, the Kandyan attempts on Colombo had to be abandoned due to 'the ill-disposition of low-country people'.[135]

The Kandyans also tried to change things in their tactical approach. For instance, as we have seen, they began drilling their men in European style. However, this apparently was not a very effective change. We have no evidence that they led to any remarkable change in the Kandyan approach to fighting. This was to be expected, as what the Kandyans needed was not piecemeal solutions but major reforms that changed the basis of military organization. And any major reform to the Kandyan military had to be in the form of a drastic change to the system itself. This, needless to say, was to expect too much from a pre-modern peasant political economy.

In these circumstances, the only salvation for the Kandyans had to come from outside, especially in the form of European help. Sri Lankan rulers have often been blamed for soliciting foreign assistance that eventually undermined their own interests, but it is testimony to the insight of the Kandyan rulers that they appreciated the importance of foreign help as the most effective way to overcome their weaknesses. A European ally could prevent the other Europeans on the island's coast from obtaining reinforcements from across the seas. They could also deploy substantial firepower, particularly artillery, against the European coastal strongholds that were hitherto impervious to Kandyan firepower. In return, the impoverished highland kingdom could offer trading concessions to the Europeans.

The first major attempt—and the only successful one—in this regard came with the alliance with the Dutch. As we have seen earlier, the Dutch signed an agreement with the Kandyans in 1638. According to this agreement, the Dutch moved against the coastal forts of the Portuguese while the Kandyans overran the interior. By 1658, the island was completely cleared of the Portuguese.

However, obtaining foreign help was also fraught with dangers. Following the ejection of the Portuguese, the Dutch allies turned into enemies with territorial ambitions and a threat to Kandyan economic interests rather than peaceful traders. But the Kandyans persisted with the search for foreign assistance as the only real option they had for overcoming their military weakness. However, all these later attempts to seek foreign aid ended in failure. The Kandyan–Dutch war in 1670–5 saw an attempt by the Kandyans to seek help from another European power, the French. In March 1670, the French commander, M. De la Haye, arrived from France with a naval squadron to establish a French commercial presence in the Indian Ocean. Trincomalee in the east coast of Sri Lanka was among the places selected for French settlements. In January 1672, De la Haye arrived in Kottiyar on the east coast of Sri Lanka and opened negotiations with the Kandyan king to obtain supplies. The king used the opportunity to press for French assistance against the Dutch, a request received with little enthusiasm by the French admiral. De la Haye did not wish to commit hostilities against the Dutch with whom France was not at war. But it did not take much for the Dutch to initiate hostilities. They closed in on the Frenchmen on the coast, already suffering from a lack of supplies, and taking advantage of the departure of the French fleet in search of provisions, captured their post. That put a prompt end to all Kandyan hopes of European assistance against the Dutch.[136]

Attempts to obtain foreign help against the Dutch in the eighteenth century also came to nothing. As noted earlier, an attempt to negotiate a military alliance with the British failed in 1762 due to the reluctance of the British to commit themselves to a war against the Netherlands. Then in 1776, the Kandyans again made an attempt to get French help by writing to the French in Pondicherry and offering the ports of Kottiyar and Batticaloa in return for help. The attempt was aborted by the outbreak of the American War of Independence which pitted France and the Netherlands against Britain.[137] When the British finally took over the Dutch possessions it was little more than a transaction between the two European nations. Kandy did offer some logistical support, sending provisions to the British troops that landed in Trincomalee but the brief war was far from a joint Kandyan–British effort. And then when the British clashed with Kandy, the option of foreign aid was almost totally closed. The British was the paramount and naval power in the region with no real challengers who could be canvassed as allies.

Thus, the option of foreign assistance, while attractive, was not always an easy one. If the establishment of the Dutch in Portuguese possessions on the coast showed the risks inherent in alliances with foreign powers, the failure of later attempts showed that it was also difficult for Kandyan strategic needs to always find common ground with the commercial and political interests of the European powers operating in the Indian Ocean region. The Dutch helped Kandy because they were already at war with the Portuguese over the control of the Indian Ocean trade. However, the failure of later Kandyan attempts to secure foreign help showed that the Europeans did not wish to initiate hostilities with each other on behalf of Kandy. When the British finally moved against the Dutch interests in Sri Lanka, they did not require Kandyan help. And when the Kandyans were left with the 'British problem' in the coast, the option of foreign aid was very much out of their reach.

The result of all this was that for much of its long struggle against the Europeans, Kandy was left to fight its enemies with the limited human and material resources at their disposal. How did they fare?

NOTES

1. On Zamindari and Poligar armies, see Irfan Habib, *The Agrarian System of Mughal India 1556–1707*, New York: Asia Publishing House, 1963, pp. 165–9 and Nicholas B. Dirks, *The Hollow Crown: The Ethnohistory of an Indian Kingdom*, Ann Arbor: University of Michigan Press, 1993, pp. 168–71.
2. For instance, in December 1824, during the First Burma War, the Burmese leader Maha Bandula attacked the British at Kemmendine with a force estimated at 50,000–60,000 including several hundred cavalry and a large train of artillery. Despatch from Brig. Gen. Sir Archibald Campbell to George Swinton, 8 December 1824, H.H. Wilson (ed.), *Documents illustrative of the Burmese War with an Introductory Sketch of the Events of the War*, Calcutta: Govt. Gazette Press, 1827, pp. 86–90.
3. Captain Arthur Johnstone, *Narrative of the Operations of a Detachment in an Expedition to Candy in the Island of Ceylon in the Year 1804 with Some Observations on the Previous Campaigns and on the Nature of Candyan Warfare &c &c*, London, 1810, pp. 6–7.
4. Fernao de Queyroz, *The Temporal and Spiritual Conquest of Ceylon*, trs. S.G. Perera, Colombo: Govt. Printers, 1930, pp. 1062–3.
5. Kirimetiyawe Metindu, *Maha Hatana*, ed. T.S. Hemakumar, Colombo: Samayawardene Printers, 1964, verses 50 and 87, pp. 9, 15.
6. Queyroz, *The Temporal and Spiritual Conquest*, pp. 480, 578.
7. On resistance to Dutch invasion, see the diary of the 1764 campaign in Major Roland Raven-Hart (trs. and ed.), *The Dutch Wars with Kandy 1764–1766*, pp. 37–8, Diary of the 1765 campaign, ibid., pp. 90 and 92.
8. On the resistance at Galagedera, see James Cordiner, *Description of Ceylon containing an Account of the Country, Inhabitants and Natural Productions with a Narrative of a Tour around the Island in 1800, the Campaign in Kandy in 1803 and a Journey to Rammisseram in 1804*, 2 vols., Delhi: Navrang, 1983, rpt. of 1807 edn, vol. 2, pp. 177–8. On resistance to Johnstone's advance, see Johnstone, *Narrative*, pp. 53–9.
9. Abeysinghe, *Portuguese Rule*, p. 47.
10. On attempts to destroy the Dutch on their retreat, see the Diary of the occupation of Kandy, SLNA 1/4944. On Johnstone's retreat, see Johnstone, *Narrative*.
11. On the attack on the Dutch garrison, see SLNA 1/4944, p. 26, '*Aanmerkingen over de Oorlog met de Singaleesen*', Mackenzie Ms. 39, pp. 20–1; On the attack on the British garrison, see the deposition of Ensign Barry's Malay sergeant 11 July 1803, SLNA 7/43, pp. 816–17, Corporal Barnsley's deposition, ibid., pp. 756–7, Diary of Greeving, VimalanandaTennekoon, *British Intrigues in the Kingdom of Kandy*, Colombo: Gunasena, 1973, pp. 503–5.

12. C.R. De Silva, *The Portuguese in Ceylon 1617–1638,* Colombo: H.W. Cave and Co., 1972, pp. 94–5, 97–8; Queyroz, *The Temporal and Spiritual Conquest*, pp. 654–6; Baldaeus, *True and Exact Description of the Great Island of Ceylon,* trs. Pieter Brohier, published as *CHJ*, vol. 8, nos. 1–4, July 1958–April 1959, pp. 85–6.
13. De Silva, *The Portuguese*, pp. 112–14.
14. E. Reimers, 'Old Matara and the Rebellion of 1760–61', *JDBU*, vol. 15, no. 2, Oct. 1925, pp. 59–63; J.H.O. Paulusz, 'The Outbreak of the Kandyan-Dutch War of 1761 and the Great Rebellion: Secret Minutes of the Dutch Political Committee', *JRAS(CB),* vol. 3, 1953, pp. 40–4.
15. Queyroz, *The Temporal and Spiritual Conquest*, p. 481.
16. Ibid., p. 770.
17. Ibid., p. 803. Ribeiro gives the number of lascarins as 28,000 which is a gross exaggeration. Joao de Ribeiro, *The Historic Tragedy of the Island of Ceilao,* trs. P.E. Pieris, Colombo: Lakehouse, 1948, p. 100.
18. Raven-Hart, *The Dutch Wars*, p. 21.
19. Ibid., p. 143.
20. The troops left in Kandy were: 700 Malays and 300 European troops. There were also over 150 gun lascars. Cordiner, *Description*, vol. 2, p. 197.
21. See Queyroz, *The Temporal and Spiritual Conquest*, pp. 486–7; Joao de Barros and Diogo do Couto, 'The History of Ceylon from the earliest times to A.D. 1600', trs. and ed. Donald Ferguson, *JRAS(CB),* vol. 20, no. 60, 1908, p. 402; Baldaeus, *True and Exact Description*, pp. 22, 24, and *Rajavaliya of a Historical Narrative of Sinhalese Kings from Vijaya to Vimala Dharma Surya II*, ed. B. Gunasekera, Colombo: Govt. Printers, 1954, rpt. of 1900 edn., p. 84.
22. *The Expedition to Uva made in 1630 by Constantine de Sa de Noronha, Captain General of Ceylon as narrated by a Soldier who took part in the Expedition with an Account of the Siege laid to Colombo by the King of Kandy written by Afonso Diasda Lomba,* trs. S.G. Perera, Colombo: Govt. Printers, 1930, p. 25, *Mandarampura Puvatha*, ed. Labugama Lanakananda, Colombo: Ministry of Cultural Affairs, 1996, verse 229, p. 29. Queyroz, *The Temporal and Spiritual Conquest*, pp. 770–5. As a result, de Sa had only about 500 lascarins left with him at the time of the final battle. Ribeiro puts this number at 150. Ribeiro, *The Historic Tragedy*, pp. 91–2.
23. De Silva, *The Portuguese in Ceylon*, pp. 112–13.
24. On the desertion of lascarins in 1603, see Queyroz, *The Temporal and Spiritual Conquest,* p. 580. Ribeiro says about the desertion of auxiliaries in 1638: 'They descended the mountain and halted alongside the river, leaving some men on the slopes to prevent the enemy cutting down the trees and blocking the road. These soon deserted to the king and

so did many who accompanied the general for they were all men of one tongue'. Ribeiro, *The Historic Tragedy,* p. 100.

25. Greeving's diary, Tennekoon, *British Intrigues*, p. 502; Cordiner, *Description*, vol. 2, pp. 203, 207.
26. Evidence given by Mahomed Gani, a Free Malay and late servant to Ensign Robert Barry of the Malay Corps in Ceylon. Tennekoon, *British Intrigues*, p. 355.
27. Major Davie to Colombo, 10 June 1803, SLNA 7/43, p. 686.
28. Ibid., SLNA 7/43, p. 691.
29. Captain Drieberg at Mullaitivu to Colombo, 23 August 1803, SLNA 7/43, p. 1084.
30. Johnstone, *Narrative*, p. 71.
31. '*Aanmerkingen over den Oorlog met de Singaleesen*', Mackenzie Ms. 39, p. 202.
32. Robert Knox, *An Historical Relation of the Island of Ceylon, Revised, Enlarged & Brought to the Verge of Publication as the Second Edition by Robert Knox together with his Autobiography and All the New Chapters, Paragraphs, Marginal Notes added by the Author in the Two Interleaved Copies of the Original Text of 1681,* Edited with Introduction and Notes by J.H.O Paulusz, published as the *CHJ* Monographs series, vol. 14, Dehiwela, Sri Lanka: Tisara Publishers, 1989, 1st edn. 1681, pp. 14–15.
33. 'Andrews' Embassies to Kandy in 1795 and 1796', ed. J.P. Lewis, *JRAS(CB)*, vol. 26, no. 70, 1917, p. 184.
34. Ribeiro, *The Historic Tragedy,* p. 31.
35. Queyroz, *The Temporal and Spiritual Conquest,* p. 65.
36. Cordiner, *Description*, vol. 2, p. 230.
37. Johnstone, *Narrative*, p. 6.
38. Ribeiro, *The Historic Tragedy*, pp. 87, 236. See also *Expedition to Uva,* p. 27 and Queyroz, *The Temporal and Spiritual Conquest,* p. 481.
39. 'Van Eck's diary of the 1765 expedition', *JRAS(CB)*, vol. 16, no. 50, 1899, p. 42.
40. An early nineteenth-century European observer described some of the batteries encountered on the route from Mannar to Anuradhapura as being made of 'three rows of stakes driven, at irregular distances, into the ground, the space between them being filled up with rubbish, wood, stones or anything which is at hand'. Cited in P.E. Pieris, *Sinhale and the Patriots,* Delhi: Navrang, 1995, rpt. of 1950 edn., p. 392.
41. '*Aanmerkingen*', p. 14.
42. J.H.O. Paulusz (ed.), *Secret Minutes of the Dutch Political Council 1762,* Colombo: Govt. Printers, 1954 p. 57.
43. *Ceylon Government Gazette,* Sat. 3 Jan. 1818, *The Uva Rebellion*, p. 9.
44. Entry, 3 November 1761, SLNA 1/4940, p. 29. According to a Dutch

officer, the bunker was 15 roods long, 10 or 11 roods broad, and 6 or 7 roods deep.

45. '*Aanmerkingen*', p. 15.
46. Ibid., p. 15.
47. *Expedition to Uva*, p. 83. According to S.G. Perera, the translator, H.W. Codrington interprets nibao as Nipa – kitul.
48. '*Aanmerkingen'*, p. 15.
49. Writing in the late nineteenth century, the former archaeological commissioner H.C.P. Bell describes the remains of Balana as two towers flanking a path and a stone wall 80 feet long and 11 feet tall. There were also two gates on the west and east. The four sides of the pass seem to have been enclosed by a wall built of stone and clay which lay in ruins. H.C.P. Bell, *Report on the Kegalle District of the Province of Sabaragamuwa, Archaeological Survey of Ceylon, Sessional Paper 19*, Colombo: Govt. Printers, 1892, p. 40.
50. Raven-Hart, *The Dutch Wars*, pp. 93–5. Also 'Van Eck's Diary of the Expedition in 1765', pp. 42–3.
51. '*Aanmerkingen*', p. 11.
52. Secret Minutes, 22 September 1762, Paulusz, *Secret Minutes*, p. 142.
53. Ensign Pendergast to Colombo, 28 Aug. 1803, SLNA 7/43 1128-9, 1765 diary, Raven-Hart, *The Dutch Wars*, pp. 88, 101; Wohlfahrts to Frankena, 10 May 1763, Letters received in Kandy 9 March–24 August 1765, SLNA 1/4943.
54. Minutes, 20 January 1763, SLNA 1/4864.
55. *Mandarampura Puvatha*, verse 228, p. 27.
56. George Calladine, *The Diary of Colour Sergeant Callodine,* ed., M.L. Ferrar, London: Eden Fisher & Co., 1922, pp. 49–50.
57. '*Aanmerkingen*', p. 23.
58. Ribeiro, *The Historic Tragedy*, pp. 87–8; Couto, writing of the Portuguese retreat in 150 says that when the king heard of the retreat of the Portuguese he came out with his whole army and 'followed after them by devious roads, and getting in front waited for them in these narrows where out men could not turn around, they continued shooting our people down with firelocks and arrows', Joao de Barros and Diogo do Couto, 'History of Ceylon from the Earliest Times to AD 1600', trs. and ed. Donald Ferguson, *JRAS(CB),* vol. 20, no. 60, 1908, p. 142.
59. Ribeiro, *The Historic Tragedy*, p. 101.
60. 'Van Eck's Diary of the 1765 Expedition', p. 46.
61. Major Rolond Raven-Hart (trs. and ed.), 'Major Medeler's Relief Expedition', *JRAS(CB),* New Series, vol. 5, 1957, p. 200. See also '*Aanmerkingen*', p. 107.
62. Johnstone, *Narrative*, p. 74.
63. Raven-Hart, *The Dutch Wars*, p. 42.

64. Alexander Alexander, *Life of Bombardier Alexander written by himself,* 2 vols, London: 1830, vol. 1, p. 160.
65. Raven-Hart, 'Major Medeler's Relief Expedition', p. 200.
66. Thomas Ajax Anderson, *Journal of the Proceedings of the Trincomalee Detachment Commanded by Lieut. Colonel Barbut His Majesty's 73rd Regiment from their Leaving Trincomalee till their Arrival at Kandy,* London, 1809, p. 176.
67. Cordiner, *Description*, vol. 2, p. 190.
68. Macdowal to Colombo, 18 March 1803. Governor's Secret Diary, Feb.–Apr. 1803, SLNA 7/42, p. 437.
69. Johnstone, *Narrative*, p. 75.
70. Quoted in Geoffrey Powell, *The Kandyan Wars: The British Army in Ceylon 1803–1818,* London: Leo Cooper, 1973, pp. 138–9.
71. 'Here they lye [sic] lurking, and plant their guns between the rocks and trees, with which they do great damage to their enemies before they are aware. Nor can they then suddenly rush in upon them, being so well guarded with bushes and rocks before them, thro which before their enemies can get, they fly carrying their great guns upon their shoulder and are gone into the woods, where it is impossible to find them, unless they come themselves to meet them after the former manner.' Knox, *An Historical Relation,* pp. 176–7.
72. Queyroz, *The Temporal and Spiritual Conquest*, p. 581.
73. Alexander, *Life*, p. 160.
74. Johnstone, *Narrative*, p. 6.
75. V.M. Methley, 'The Expedition of 1803' *Transactions of the Royal Asiatic Society 4th Series,* vol. 1, 1917, p. 102.
76. 'Van Eck's Diary of the 1765 Expedition', pp. 47–8.
77. Calladine, *Diary*, pp. 51, 66.
78. See the description of the Burma Wars in George Bruce, *The Burma Wars 1824–1886*, London: Hart-Davis, MacGibbon Ltd., 1973 and the despatches from British officers in the field in H.H. Wilson (ed.), *Documents illustrative of the Burmese War with an Introductory Sketch of the Events of the War*, Calcutta: Govt. Gazette Press, 1827.
79. See, for instance, the description of the Nanning War in the early 1830s in P.J. Begbie, *The Malayan Peninsula*, Kuala Lumpur: Oxford University Press, 1967, pp. 163–231.
80. Queyroz, *The Temporal and Spiritual Conquest*, p. 488.
81. Ibid., pp. 773–8; *Expedition to Uva*, pp. 25–31; Sa y Menezes, 'The Rebellion of Ceylon , pp. 599–604.
82. Queyroz, *The Temporal and Spiritual Conquest,* p. 487. According to Baldaeus, the Kandyans sent 50 of the survivors mutilated to the main body. Baldaeus, *True and Exact Description,* p. 26.
83. Deposition of Johannes Bys, Dutch Secret Minutes, 19 August 1761, SLNA 1/747.

84. Kandy diary, 6 June 1765, SLNA 1/4944, Cordiner, *Description,* vol. 2, p. 188.
85. T.B.H. Abeysinghe (trs. and ed.), *A Study of Portuguese Regimentos on Sri Lanka at the Goa Archives,* Colombo: Dept. of National Archives, p. 50.
86. '*Aanmerkingen*', p. 84.
87. Mcdowall's instructions to Colonel Baillie, 12 March 1803, SLNA 7/42, p. 514.
88. Queyroz, *The Temporal and Spiritual Conquest,* p. 480.
89. *Expedition to Uva,* p. 30. The author says that during the running battle leading up to the final confrontation at Randeniwela, the Kandyans 'came to exchange lead for lead and occasionally spear for spear', Ibid., p. 25. Those who survived from the rearguard carried severe spear or lance wounds. Ibid., pp. 27–8.
90. Queyroz, *The Temporal and Spiritual Conquest,* p. 777.
91. Sa y Menezes, 'Rebellion of Ceylon', p. 599.
92. Queyroz, *The Temporal and Spiritual Conquest,* p. 804.
93. Ribeiro, *The Historic Tragedy,* p. 236.
94. Queyroz, *The Temporal and Spiritual Conquest,* p. 805.
95. '*Aanmerkingen*', pp. 20–1.
96. *Rajasinha Hatana,* ed. Ellepola M.M. Somaratne, Kandy: T.B.S. Godamune and Sons, date unavailable, verse 384, p. 65, verse 386 p. 66, verse 392, p. 68.
97. Ibid., verse 387, p. 66 and verse 391, p. 67.
98. Alagiyavanna Mukaveti, *Kustantinu Hatana,* ed. Edwin Ranawake, Colombo: Gunasena, 1938, stanzas 158–9, pp. 102–3.
99. *Rajasinha Hatana,* stanza 400, p. 70, Kirimetiyawe Metindu, *Maha Hatana,* ed. T.S. Hemakumar, Colombo: Samaywardene Printers, 1964, verse 98, p. 17.
100. Mukaveti, *Kustantinu Hatana,* verses 158, p. 102.
101. *Mandarampura Puvatha,* verses 336–7, pp. 43–4.
102. Raven-Hart, *The Dutch Wars,* pp. 93–4.
103. Ibid., p. 74.
104. See, for instance, the land grants given to Kirielle Jayasundera Muhandiram, Yadhinne Wickremesinghe Mudiyanse, and Amitiyagoda Mudiyanse for their services during the capture of the Colombo fort in 1656 and Katuwana fort in 1761. Nanawimala, *Saparagamuwe Parani Liyavili,* pp. 51, 117, 124.
105. Johnstone, *Narrative,* p. 57.
106. Queyroz, *The Temporal and Spiritual Conquest,* p. 596.
107. Statement of Phillip Hartman, Minutes of 4 March 1761, SLNA 1/747. According to another Dutchman taken prisoner at Katuwana, the guns fired balls weighing only 4 pounds or less. This probably means that the Kandyans lacked balls of the proper calibre. Deposition of

Nicholas Kist of Fulda, E. Reimers, 'Old Matara and the Rebellion of 1760–61', *JDBUC*, vol. 15, no. 2, Oct. 1925, pp. 61–3.

108. Reimers, 'Old Matara and the Rebellion of 1760–61', *JDBUC*, vol. 15, no. 3, Jan. 1926, pp. 91–5.
109. Ensign Pendergast to Colombo, 25 Aug. 1803, SLNA 7/43, pp. 1122–5.
110. Queyroz, *The Temporal and Spiritual Conquest*, p. 598.
111. Knox, *An Historical Relation*, pp. 453–4. Knox probably obtained these details from the Dutch commanding officer Cornelius Blickant whom Knox met after he was taken prisoner by the Kandyans.
112. Queyroz, *The Temporal and Spiritual Conquest*, pp. 782–3. According to Afonso Dias da Lomba who was in Colombo during the siege, the Kandyans 'erected a structure of pallisades and rubble, that our artillery caused little damage to it. Whereby they approached the bastions of the king and of St. Joao, while a continuous and wild volley of balls did not cease to rain into our fortalice in a brisk round' Da Lomba's narrative in *Expedition to Uva*, p. 92.
113. '*Aanmerkingen*', p. 22.
114. W.P. Coolhaas, *Generale Missiven van Gouverneurs-General en Raden aan Heren xvii Der Verenigde Oostindische Compagnie*, 9 vols, S'Gravenhge: Verkrijgbaar bij Martiuus Nijhoff, 1971, vol. 4, p. 76.
115. Cordiner, *Description*, vol. 2, p. 226.
116. 'Historical Records of the Society of Jesus: "The Rebellion of Nikapetty: a report dated 15 October 1617, sent to Father Nuno Mascarenhas, Assistant to the General of the Society of Jesus by Manoel Ruiz s.j."', trs. S.G. Perera, *CALR*, vol. 2, no. 2, 1916, p. 135.
117. On the use of elephants at Mulleriyawa, see *Rajavaliya or a Historical Narrative of Sinhalese Kings from Vijaya to Vimala Dharma Surya II*, ed. B. Gunasekera, Colombo: Govt. Printers, 1945, rpt. of 1900 edn, p. 75, Barros and Couto, 'History of Ceylon', pp. 209–10, Elephants used against Kotte. Ibid., p. 220, against Colombo, ibid., p. 316.
118. Queyroz, *The Temporal and Spiritual Conquest*, pp. 597–8.
119. De Silva, *The Portuguese in Ceylon*, p. 120.
120. Letter from Matara 20 March 1761. Secret Minutes, 30 March 1761, Reimers, 'Old Matara and the Rebellion of 1761–2', *JDBUC*, vol. 15, no. 3, Jan. 1926, pp. 92–5.
121. De Silva, *The Portuguese in Ceylon*, p. 122, Coolhaas, *Generale Missiven*, vol. 4, p. 77.
122. Secret minutes of the Dutch political council, 6 April, 1761. SLNA 1/747
123. Powell, *The Kandyan Wars*, p. 141, Cordiner, *Description*, vol. 2, pp. 229–30.
124. Cordiner, *Description*, vol. 2, pp. 218–19 (Dambadeniya), p. 222 (Tangalle).

125. D.A. Kotelawela, 'The Dutch in Ceylon: 1743–1766', Ph.D. thesis, University of London, 1968, p. 222.
126. Queyroz, *The Temporal and Spiritual Conquest*, p. 99.
127. Diary of the 1764 campaign, Raven-Hart, *The Dutch Wars*, p. 42.
128. T.B.H. Abeysinghe, 'History as Polemics and Propaganda: An Examination of Fernao Queyroz' "History of Ceylon' ", *JRAS(SLB)*, vol. 25, 1980/81, pp. 42–4.
129. For instance, Couto speaks of the Portuguese killing 2000 Sitawaka troops in 1565 without losing a man and also of an encounter between the Portuguese and the Sitawaka troops before Colombo in 1587-8 where the Portuguese return to camp with the severed heads of some of their enemies and 'leaving the field strewn with dead bodies' all the while suffering only two lascarins 'slightly wounded'. Barros and Couto, 'History of Ceylon', pp. 239, 332. Ribeiro speaks of a battle in Wevuda in 1652 where the Portuguese kill 3,000 Kandyans while losing only 8 Portuguese and 5 lascarins killed. Again, in the following year, a Portuguese force of 220 Portuguese and 500 lascarins operating in Sabaragamuwa are attacked in the rear 'boldly and continuously' but only one Portuguese is killed during the whole retreat! Ribeiro, *The Historic Tragedy*, pp. 163, 168–9.
130. Cordiner, *Description*, vol. 2, p. 226.
131. Ibid., p. 234.
132. Queyroz, *The Temporal and Spiritual Conquest*, pp. 585–90.
133. Kotelawela, 'The Dutch in Ceylon', p. 229.
134. Ibid., p. 233.
135. *Rajavaliya*, p. 87.
136. Sinnappah Arasaratnam, *Dutch Power in Ceylōn*, Amsterdam: Djambotan, 1958; Lorna Srimathie Dewaraja, *Sri Lanka through French Eyes*, Colombo: Institute of Fundamental Studies, 1989, pp. 18–26.
137. V. Kanpathipillai, 'Dutch Rule in Maritime Ceylon 1766–1796', Ph.D. thesis, University of London, 1969, pp. 139–41; Dewaraja, *Sri Lanka through French Eyes*, pp. 43–5.

FIVE

The Toll

Warfare and the Fall of the Kandyan Kingdom

In the preceding chapters, we have looked at the military organization and resources of the Kandyan state and the military tactics employed by the Kandyans in fighting their European adversaries. In this chapter, we shall examine the potential Kandyan military power had for achieving the goals of fighting off European invasions and threatening European hold in the low country.

The foregoing sections have identified several problems with the Kandyan military organization and tactics. These were, namely, the difficulty of conducting prolonged campaigns, the deficiency in artillery, the absence of a navy, and the limitations of guerrilla and irregular warfare. The European forces operating in Sri Lanka also had their strengths and weaknesses. The potential for Kandyan success rested very much on how the strengths and weaknesses of the European forces measured up against Kandyan strengths and limitations.

EUROPEAN OPERATIONS IN SRI LANKA: STRENGTHS AND WEAKNESSES

European presence and military operations in Sri Lanka occupied two broad theatres: the coast and the interior. The Europeans felt most secure in their coastal strongholds due to the limitations of Kandyan military power against these places. The lack of artillery and the complete absence of a navy along with the logistical problems inherent in campaigning so far out of their heartland ensured that Kandyan arms could achieve little against the coastal forts and other fortified posts. On the other hand, the ability to reinforce these posts from the sea enabled the Europeans to continue resistance. But outside their coastal bases, a European army also had to deal with numerous challenges. Here, the Kandyans were stronger. They could concentrate larger numbers in familiar country where they could wage guerrilla warfare with confidence. The Europeans also had to contend with a number of logistical and tactical limitations. As we shall see, the success of European forces against the Kandyans depended largely on the ability of the Europeans to overcome these limitations.

TERRAIN AND WEATHER

As much as the Kandyans profited from their knowledge of and familiarity with the terrain, the Europeans suffered from a lack of it. The population was also unfriendly, either by choice or under duress. As a consequence, the movements of the Europeans in enemy territory were heavily curtailed and channelled into the existing network of footpaths, cross-country movement being risky considering their lack of knowledge of the country and the absence of friendly guidance from the people. This sometimes became very costly to European forces deep in Kandyan territory. During the retreat of De Souza's army, the advance guard lost its way and was separated from the rest of the army 'as they had no men of the country to guide them'.[1] But even the presence of guides was no guarantee against losing the way. During Johnstone's retreat, the guides often had to climb tall trees to figure out their location[2] in the jungle.

These circumstances ensured that European forces fighting in the interior moved in long, straggling lines of infantry along footpaths well known to the Kandyan guerrillas. As noted earlier, often the paths themselves had to be cleared on the march, a necessity which prompted one Portuguese writer to call war in Sri Lanka, 'the most laborious in the world'.[3] They also had to travel on foot, the ruggedness of the terrain ruling out the use of horses. This meant having to endure great physical hardships. Sa y Menezes gives a vivid description of the privations the Portuguese had to suffer in their campaigns in the highlands: 'They were scarcely able to defend themselves in the stagnant morasses and rivers over which they waded up to their necks with the greatest difficulty and fatigue; marching barefoot and almost naked, they came out with their feet torn and lacerated, bitten by leeches and other reptiles, which breed and swarm in these waters.'[4]

Leeches were particularly troublesome for Europeans. They swarmed over the ground in the wetter parts of the highlands and often took a heavy toll on the Europeans' feet. A British detachment suffered so much from leech-bites in 1818 that many developed festering wounds, one soldier's leg even being amputated.[5]

The weather was another impediment to the Europeans. The best time of the year to campaign in Kandyan territory was the first three or four months of the year and an army entering the highlands towards the latter part of the year had to face all the consequences of torrential rains. The experience of Major Medeler's relief column which marched on Kandy in September 1765 is a case in point. The column had to wade rivers swollen by heavy downpours while pack animals and porters slipped and fell with their loads in the mud,[6] creating immense problems for the march.

LOGISTICS

Campaigning in the inhospitable interior also gave rise to the problem of supplies. The Europeans could not rely on the generosity of the population or the bounty of the countryside and, therefore, all supplies had to be carried with them. These included the regular needs of an army, such as ammunition, as well as needs specific to a European army campaigning in the tropics. The European soldiers required either beef or fish as part of their diet in addition to rice. They also needed substantial amounts of arrack as a stimulant. They needed tents to sleep in and camp kettles to cook in. European officers in particular carried much baggage, and often took numerous items such as tables, chairs, and other things that provided a measure of comfort in the jungles. The fighting men could not afford to carry all this, not even their own food and ammunition. It was too much to carry in the first place and in hostile country where attacks were numerous and frequent, they had to be free of encumbrances to meet any emergency. The wounded also needed tending to. Last but not least, the need to stick to the narrow paths often required labour to clear them.

As a result, even small European detachments which expected to be away from their bases for several days carried a substantial baggage train with them. This was particularly the case with armies invading or retreating from Kandy. These consisted of porters, or coolies as they were often called, and pack animals to carry the burdens and pioneers to clear the roads, not to mention the many servants the European officers required. The '*Aanmerkingen*' reckoned that a European captain needed 12 porters while captains of the Malay troops needed two each. Artillery also required much labour—60 porters according to the writer.[7] Thus, about half the 7,000 men in the Dutch army that invaded Kandy in 1765 were coolies and camp followers,[8] and Medeler's relief expedition of about 1,200 was accompanied by about 1,000 coolies and over 350 pack animals.[9] Even a small detachment of 20–30 men required a substantial contingent of servants. Surgeon Kennedy's party of less than 20 people had a number of servants and pioneers accompanying it.[10]

The baggage posed several problems for the Europeans. As noted earlier, a long baggage train was an ideal target for Kandyan guerillas. The threat to the baggage train caused the porters to desert while also making it difficult to recruit fresh baggage carriers. In 1764, the Dutch went so far as to import porters from Batavia and India. This too was not a satisfactory solution as they could never recruit enough men to satisfy the demands. A large number of porters also perished during the voyage to Sri Lanka.[11] As a result, the Dutch had to struggle throughout the war in 1761–6 in the absence of sufficient baggage carriers.

MANPOWER

A major problem in campaigning in the interior was the availability of forces. Dominating the interior of the island required larger forces than were needed to defend the coastal strongholds and although the command of the ocean enabled European powers to induct troops into the island without fear of Kandyan interception, finding enough soldiers to induct in this way was a problem. It affected the three European powers in different ways. The Portuguese were particularly pressed for manpower. The main military strength of the Portuguese in Sri Lanka—as in all parts of their far-flung empire—lay in a small core of Portuguese soldiers. According to Antonio Boccarro, the number of Portuguese in Sri Lanka in the seventeenth century never exceeded 1,500.[12] The majority of them were soldiers while the rest were married settlers or casados. Not all these were necessarily full-blooded Europeans; as A.R. Disney points out, the term 'soldado' was often used loosely in Asia for soldiers sent from Europe as well as unmarried settlers and Lusitanized Eurasians.[13] In Sri Lanka, the number of soldiers barely reached a thousand—it reached its peak before the Portuguese invasion of Kandy in 1603 when Azevedo was in command of about 800 Portuguese soldiers.[14]

The number of married settlers was not very large either. Colonizing the Portuguese territories in Sri Lanka with Portuguese casados was an idea mooted during the years following Azevedo's disastrous attempt on Kandy in 1603. But despite offers of attractive land grants to those who wished to settle, their numbers never exceeded more than a few hundred.[15] It seems that many preferred to settle in the more salubrious and economically prosperous Brazil than in India, let alone Sri Lanka.[16] By the 1620s, hopes of augmenting Portuguese forces in Sri Lanka with married settlers had faded.[17] According to Boccaro, no more than 350 lived in Colombo in 1634.[18] The military value of the few who settled in Sri Lanka was also limited. They were not expected to fight unless their homes were threatened. Their main contribution in war seems to have been in performing garrison duty. Some of them also accompanied the soldados on campaigns but this number was always small.[19]

This was not peculiar to the Portuguese in Sri Lanka; as C.R. Boxer points out, there were never more than 10,000 Portuguese in the East.[20] There were a number of reasons for this chronic dearth of Portuguese personnel. Foremost were the lack of recruits and an abundance of stations. Portugal was not blessed with a large population and finding enough men to satisfy all the manpower needs of the empire was always difficult. In the East, chronic death and desertion took a heavy toll on those who survived a precarious sea voyage. According to an Augustinian priest, about 25,000 Portuguese soldiers died within the walls of the Royal hospital in Goa in the sixteenth and seventeenth centuries.[21] Furthermore, in the first half of the seventeenth century when the Portuguese clashed with Kandy, greater part of the meagre manpower resources had to be diverted to trouble spots elsewhere, to areas considered more important. The rise of the state of Acheh in Indonesia and the entry of the Dutch and the English into the Indian Ocean trade contributed heavily to this situation, as they threatened vital Portuguese interests in South and South-East Asia.

In these circumstances the Portugese in Sri Lanka could not expect anymore than a trickle of reinforcements from Goa, the Portuguese headquarters in Asia whence the Portuguese in Sri Lanka received their men and material. Even this trickle could completely dry up depending on the situation elsewhere in the empire. For instance, from 1605 to 1609, the Portuguese in Sri Lanka received no more than 50 recruits, the result of heavy troop commitments in Malacca.[22] When De Sa marched on Uva in 1630 his army was made up of any Portuguese who could be found, 'the old and the youngsters, about 200, almost incapable of bearing arms, as it ever happened in similar straits'.[23] When the Kandyans besieged Colombo in the same year, the Portuguese authorities in Goa and other parts of India were able to be more generous, but over a considerable period of time, the Portuguese in Colombo receiving about 800 soldiers[24] during the eight months following de Sa's defeat. The supply of Portuguese troops could also be affected by the vulnerability of their lifeline with India to enemy interception. Although the Kandyans had no naval power they could ally themselves with a power that possessed warships. This is what they did in 1638 when they signed a treaty with the Dutch. As a consequence, the Dutch blockaded Goa and the supply of Portuguese troops was severely affected.[25]

The lack of Portuguese troops made the Portuguese rely very heavily on their lascarins. But this option was not without its problems either. While the number of lascarins fluctuated, at their strongest they did not amount to more than a few thousand in all. Towards the end of the Portuguese rule their numbers had fallen to little less than 5,000.[26] Only a part of them were in the field during most of the campaigns in the lowlands. But an even greater concern was their loyalty. As we have seen, they were very susceptible to be subverted by the Kandyans. Their desertion during important campaigns left the small core of Portuguese and loyal lascarins exposed.

The unreliability of lascarins made the Portuguese look for other sources of manpower. In the 1630s, an attempt was made to bolster the Portuguese troops with Africans and Canarese but these could not be supplied in large numbers. According to some Sinhala sources, Asian and African troops seem to have been a part of the Portuguese forces in Sri Lanka from the early seventeenth century. The *Kustantinu Hatana,* for instance, speaks of Chinese, Persian, Telugu, Kannada, African, Arab, and Abyssinian soldiers in Constantine de Sa's army in 1619.[27] While this is probably an exaggeration it underlines the element of multi-ethnicity in the army even at that time. However, Asian and African troops became prominent only in the 1630s after the desertion of lascarins contributed to the defeat of de Sa's expeditionary force. To overcome similar problems in the future, African and Canarese troops were employed.[28] These, however, could not be obtained in large numbers and, as seen earlier, many of them also found service with the Kandyans.[29]

The Dutch had a somewhat similar problem with obtaining European troops. The VOC's army was made up of any European that could be found, resulting in a multi-ethnic force of Germans, English, Scots, and Irish besides Dutch.[30] As Kotelawela has shown, the Dutch struggled with fitting out a large fleet to take the fight to the Kandyans in 1761–2. Due to this they were very reluctant to launch an invasion of Kandyan lands and it was the British embassy to Kandy in 1762 that tipped the balance in favour of an expedition with the available resources.[31] However, their manpower problems were not as acute as the problem faced by the Portuguese. During the Kandyan–Dutch War of 1761–6 the Dutch soldiers in Sri Lanka never fell below 3,000 which was a much larger European army than the Portuguese could ever muster against Kandy.[32] By 1765, the Dutch were also getting more European troops following the conclusion of the Seven Years' War in Europe.[33]

The shortfall in European troops was met by recruiting non-Europeans. The Dutch too had little confidence in the lascarins, more because of their perceived inefficiency than due to unreliability. The Dutch governor Laurens Pyl (1680–92) considered the local levies 'poltroons' who could be depended on only as long as European troops were on the field.[34] This was a view echoed by others, a Dutch governor of Jaffna dismissing them as 'entirely wanting in courage'.[35] But the Dutch had a viable alternative source of non-European troops in their Malays or 'easterners', as explained earlier. During the war of 1761–6 there were several thousand of them in various Dutch garrisons.[36] There were also sepoys but their numbers were not large before the war in 1761–6. After the failure of the campaign in 1764 a considerable number of them were raised on the Coromandel coast and brought over to Sri Lanka.[37] In November 1764, Colombo wrote to Holland that sepoy recruitment in the Coromandel had been so satisfactory as to enable the Dutch to take the field again early next year.[38] By mid-April 1765, the number of sepoys in Sri Lanka had risen to 3,418 sepoys, up from 1,242 a year ago.[39]

The British had the least problems with regard to manpower resources. The British fought their wars against Kandy at a time when their power was at its zenith on the neighbouring subcontinent. There they had a massive army of sepoys which numbered well over 100,000 by the early nineteenth century.[40] They were supported by a smaller number of European troops. Following the departure of the Dutch they also obtained the services of their Malays. In the early nineteenth century they also employed several hundred Africans who soon exceeded the number of Malays.[41]

The sepoys and the Malays of the Dutch and the British were much less amenable to desertion than the lascarins. There were few desertions during the Dutch wars in 1763–6 and even though some Malays deserted in 1803, many chose to remain with the British. The British force that surrendered in 1803 included 250 Malays out of an original force of 700 but only a portion of the rest had deserted, the rest having died of sickness.[42] Moreover, some of the Malays who deserted later crossed over during the Kandyan army's unsuccessful attempt on Hanwella.[43] Such loyalty was a luxury which the Portuguese could not expect from their lascarins.

All this meant that the reliable portions of the Dutch and British armies in Sri Lanka were much larger than that which the Portuguese had at its service. The Dutch and the British could call upon several thousand European and Asiatic troops the great majority of whom were reliable in a crisis while the Portuguese could depend mainly on just a few hundred European troops in a crisis. This meant not only a stronger force to take into the Kandyan heartland but also more reliable troops to garrison the outposts with.

Thus, the European powers that fought Kandy faced different levels of difficulty in securing large, reliable armies against Kandy. But the problem with manpower was not only about finding enough troops to fight, it was also about keeping them healthy.

DISEASE AND MORTALITY

Mortality from disease was a perennial problem for the Europeans in the tropics. As noted earlier, the death rate from disease of the Portuguese in Goa was stupendous. In Sri Lanka, mortality from disease was particularly associated with campaigning in the interior, especially the Kandyan highlands. Nights in Kandy could be very cold and wet, enough to penetrate the triple covering of a European field tent.[44] The wet weather and the swampy ground provided ideal conditions for mosquitoes to thrive. This was the perfect setting for the spread of disease, especially fevers which showed symptoms akin to that of yellow fever—'excessive depression of spirits and strength, weakness, anxiety and oppression'.[45]

The spread of disease was also encouraged by a lack of food. Campaigning in the interior also created problems of supplies. This was especially the case if the Europeans were planning on occupying the interior rather than merely marching through it on campaigns of pacification. Maintaining supply lines through hostile territory was a very daunting task, especially given the threat to porters, while obtaining supplies from an unfriendly countryside was equally difficult. As a consequence, the occupying European forces often suffered severely from food shortages. The rice supplies of the Dutch steadily dwindled in 1765 as foraging parties could find little in the abandoned Kandyan villages while the supply lines with the low country were steadily disrupted.[46] The lack of meat was particularly troublesome for the European troops in 1765 and 1803, with the

Kandyans having taken particular care to hide or scare off the cattle in the countryside.[47]

The lack of food caused general physical weakness which made troops vulnerable to disease. The lack of fresh food in particular paved the way for beri-beri. The British, in 1803, suffered particularly severely from this disease which caused general physical debility and lethargy.[48] All this was compounded by the rigorous campaigning. Marching and fighting up and down the rugged slopes sapped the strength of many troops, particularly those Europeans who were not used to heavy physical exertion in a tropical climate. As pointed out by the compiler of the Medical report for April 1803, sickness was mainly caused by the 'excessive fatigue and labour which the men sustained in the service of foraging, during the hottest part of the day, from which they sometimes returned drenched with rain'.[49] A good example of the effects of over-exertion on European health is provided by the aftermath of the capture of the Kandyan outpost at Girihagama in 1803. When the British took Girihagama fort at the beginning of the campaign in 1803 only two European soldiers were wounded in the assault. But the strain of assaulting the precipitous height in the extreme heat of the day was enough to exhaust the men of the H.M. 51st regiment who were total strangers to the climate and made them prime targets for the bouts of fever that followed the occupation of Kandy.[50] A similar fate befell the survivors of Captain Johnstone's little army in 1804. Almost every man that escaped to the east coast entered the hospital upon their arrival in Trincomalee.[51]

Sickness took a heavy toll in European lives. According to Queyroz, a Portuguese force raiding Kandyan lands in 1639 lost nearly 300 men from the pestilential disease of beri-beri and many of them 'so rapidly that they did not even have time to make their confession'.[52] The Jesuit was probably overplaying the numbers but the point cannot be missed. The Dutch too suffered from sickness during their occupation of Kandy in 1765. By late August 1765, the army was so ravaged by sickness, particularly by beri-beri, that the number of guards had to be reduced.[53] Sickness was also rampant among the British in the interior. During the occupation of Kandy in 1803, European soldiers were dying of sickness at the rate of six per day. On

10 June, the British commander Major Davy wrote that the 19th Regiment was so wracked by sickness that it had not been able to provide a single man for duty for the preceding three weeks.[54] Very few of the hospitalized men in Johnstone's detachment survived. Campaigning against the rebels in 1817–18 was equally fatal to the British soldier. According to British medical officers, during the rebellion in 1818 disease carried away about one-fifth of the total British force in Sri Lanka, many of whom saw service in the rugged interior.[55] In 1818, the death rate of H.M. 19th Foot was 114 out of a 1,000 while that of H.M. 73rd Foot was of shocking proportions—412 out of 1,000![56]

Thus, European armies fighting in the interior had to contend not only with problems of manpower but also with the challenge of keeping their men healthy. It was also about the ability to meet the unique challenges posed by Kandyan guerrilla warfare.

TECHNOLOGY AND TACTICS

One of the major tactical problems faced by European armies in fighting in the interior of the island, namely having to expose themselves along narrow paths to an invisible enemy, has been already touched upon. This presented a tactical challenge for a European army, as fighting in long straggling lines in broken ground made a mockery of contemporary European tactics and firepower. Here we need to digress a fraction in order to examine European tactical developments. As noted earlier, since the early sixteenth century, European warfare had come to be gradually dominated by infantry using firearms and field artillery. The cavalry ceased to be the main arm but continued to function as an important tactical arm often delivering the final blow to a faltering enemy. However, the dominance of firepower was established only gradually. This was largely due to technological factors. Until the late seventeenth century, European military firearms were operated by the matchlock mechanism which consisted of a slow-burning matchcord pressing on a pan of priming powder at the press of the trigger. Matchlocks were cumbersome weapons to load and therefore the musketeer had to be supported by pikemen while reloading. Therefore, in European battlefields in the seventeenth century, the infantry came to be formed in tight blocks of pikemen and musketeers.[57]

At the beginning of the eighteenth century, European armies continued to be dominated by infantry with cavalry playing a supporting role. But infantry firepower underwent major changes as a result of a number of technical innovations. By the late seventeenth century, the flintlock musket had come into general use among the European infantry and this increased the reliability of the musket. The flintlock with its use of a piece of pyrite rather than a glowing match to ignite the priming powder overcame all the problems associated with wet weather and glowing matches, and also made the musket less cumbersome to carry. Furthermore, the invention of the iron ramrod and the paper cartridge made reloading easier, and increased the rate of fire of the musket. Finally, the invention of the bayonet made the musketeer self-sufficient in both offensive and offensive means. As a result, pikemen gradually disappeared from European battlefields and by the first few decades of eighteenth century, all European infantrymen came to be armed with muskets.

While they enhanced the firepower of the infantryman the above-mentioned technical innovations did not make the flintlock musket of the eighteenth century any more accurate than its seventeenth-century predecessor. It was still too optimistic to expect a musket to hit a man at a range of about 100 yards. But the increased rate of fire and the greater reliability were crucial improvements. Also of great significance were the improvements in artillery. Infantry firepower was considerably augmented by the addition of field artillery to infantry units. Although field artillery had been used in European battlefields since the early sixteenth century it was not until the late-seventeenth century that they became a regular accessory to infantry units. During the Thirty Years' War, the Swedish king, Gustavus Adolphus, had used light artillery pieces to his regiments but it took a few more decades for the adoption of light artillery as a part of the infantry became a common practice. By mid-eighteenth century, mobile field artillery had replaced the cumbersome pieces that impeded the armies of the previous century, enabling cannon to move with the infantry.[58]

These innovations gave a regiment of eighteenth-century European infantry a firepower which was the equivalent of what several European regiments could muster in the previous century. To make the best use of this enhanced firepower, the infantry was deployed in linear formation to present a long front of fire to the enemy. To combat cavalry, they were deployed in square formation with artillery support. But at the same time, the inaccuracy of the firearms meant that fire had to be delivered at very close—almost point blank—range. To face this daunting task and to deploy into firing formation, the infantry had to be intensely drilled and disciplined. Parade ground drill came into its own, placing great emphasis on automation-like responses. As a consequence, eighteenth-century European battles became primarily contests between lines of infantry trading fire at close range. But this did not make the cavalry redundant. As suggested by the square formation, the cavalry still retained a place of importance in spite of the dominance of the infantry arm. But by the early eighteenth century, its role was largely one of attacking infantry already shaken by the firefight and of cutting up already broken infantry.[59]

But what was good for Europe was not so good for the thickly wooded and rugged regions of Asia, Africa, and the Americas. It was no different in Sri Lanka. European style of fighting in tightly controlled formations was not a type of warfare to be employed in the Kandyan highlands—or anywhere in the interior of Sri Lanka, for that matter. Only infantry could be used in the rugged and thickly forested interior. Horses could barely negotiate the narrow and rocky paths, let alone be deployed in formation. It was also not very favourable to artillery—for the same reason. As for the infantry, the terrain allowed no scope for even a semblance of European-style tactical formation and even if they somehow managed to present a disciplined fire, Kandyan guerrilla tactics often denied the European infantrymen a target to fire at.

Significantly, the three European powers that clashed with Kandy had differing potential for coping with the challenge of Kandyan terrain and tactics. Where tactics were concerned, the Portuguese were the least affected by the difficulty to employ European tactical formations, but they were affected nevertheless. The Portuguese armies in the East were but a poor reflection of contemporary European armies. They often preferred the impetuous charge to the disciplined use of firepower and fought very much like the Scottish highlanders, using firearms for an initial discharge before falling upon the enemy.[60] As the narratives of Couto, Queyroz, and Ribeiro clearly show, the Portuguese in Sri Lanka had a very similar approach to fighting.[61] They preferred the headlong charge to drawing up in formation. Still, the terrain and the Kandyan preference for guerrilla tactics frustrated this type of approach too because they denied the Portuguese a target to charge at and clear ground to dash across.

Technology was not of any help either. Contemporary military technology did not confer any significant advantage on the Portuguese. According to Queyroz, neither the Portuguese nor their local enemies were able to carry artillery in a country which only had narrow paths.[62] But the evidence in Queyroz's work itself shows that the Portuguese did sometimes carry cannon with them. In 160 Azevedo battered Balana fort with a three pieces of artillery. Decades earlier in 1546, Antonio Moniz Barretto also took some artillery with him to Kandy. We do not know what kind of artillery they were, but only that they were abandoned by the retreating Portuguese and later returned over by the Kandyans.[63] However, there is no evidence of the Portuguese using cannon in the field in the interior. But there was more to this than geography and topography. As explained above, it was not until the mid-seventeenth century that light field artillery came to feature in European battles. But even in the early-eighteenth century they remained heavy and cumbersome, certainly in no state to be used in the rugged and densely wooded terrain of Sri Lanka. If they were to be used at all, they had to be used in sieges as Azevedo did in 1603. Siege operations entailed firing from entrenched positions at fixed targets rather than at moving and often concealed targets, most probably after being suddenly brought to a halt by an ambush. In the first type of action weight and mobility was not of great consequence but in the second type of action, which as we have seen, was what Europeans could often expect, the heavy and clumsy artillery of the era were of little use. Even in sieges, the Portuguese had to be content with light pieces.[64]

The adoption of the gingal by the Portuguese was a clear attempt to overcome the impracticability of artillery but, as we have seen, the gingal was a poor substitute for a cannon. Moreover, although the gingal was much easier to deploy in rugged terrain than cannon, its real potential lay in the facility with which it could be used from under cover and not against an often invisible opponent.

As a result, the Portuguese had to depend heavily on the firepower of their hand-held firearms. This did not confer any significant advantage to the Portuguese. Technologically, the Portuguese and Kandyan firearms were probably on par. The arquebus, which the Portuguese used, was an elementary firearm in itself with its simple matchlock mechanism as were the contemporary Kandyan firearms. If the Portuguese held an advantage over the Kandyans in their firearms it was probably in the maintenance of their weapons. But even this advantage could be undermined by other factors like the terrain, the demands of guerrilla warfare, and weather. Not only did the terrain impede firing in formation but the fact that guns had to be often fired while on the run made reloading even more difficult. As noted earlier, the matchlock arquebuses were rather cumbersome guns that had as an essential accessory a slow burning match that added to the clumsiness of the weapon. Loading and firing the matchlock was a very complex operation that took 20–30 seconds under most favourable conditions.[65] This became an even more complicated process when fighting Kandyan guerillas in rugged country. There was also the threat of running out of ammunition firing blindly at concealed enemies! During De Souza's retreat the vanguard of his army ran out of ammunition before the final confrontation with the Kandyans. This was no doubt partly due to excessive firing at an enemy who was often either invisible or out of range. Last but not least there was the weather. Wet weather was the enemy of the slow burning match as De Sa found to his dismay in 1630. A downpour put out the matches of his retreating army, making the Portuguese firearms only a little potent than clubs.[66]

Furthermore, only a portion of the Portuguese armies was armed with any firearms. Pikes or spears in the hands of Portuguese soldiers are often mentioned. According to Queyroz, in 1594 Balana was captured after an intense battle fought with spears[67] while the rearguard of De Sa's retreating army is also said to have fought with spears after a shower dampened the matches in their firearms.[68] Ribeiro even speaks of a battle between the Portuguese and the Kandyans at Tihariya in 1652 which was fought entirely 'at the point of the spear and the sword'.[69] The lascarins too were similarly armed. The troop contributions required from the landholders in Portuguese territories in the lowlands consisted of arquebusiers and pikemen.[70] These troops were mainly lascarins.

The use of the pike in the Sri Lankan context is interesting. As noted above, in contemporary Europe pikemen were used to guard the musketeers from cavalry while reloading. In Sri Lanka there was no threat of cavalry but the pike seemed to have persisted in spite of this. This was no doubt because of the persistence of the arquebus's limitations in the Kandyan terrain and against Kandyan tactics. Pikes in these circumstances functioned as more than an accessory to the arquebus. It was a major weapon which could be needed any moment as the firearms had such limited use. Little wonder then that De Sa's rearguard appears to have had spears with them when their firearms were rendered useless. On the other hand, the Portuguese inclination to seek close combat also induced them to carry weapons of hand to hand combat.

The pikes may have compensated for the limitations of firepower but they also had the consequence of putting the available firearms under a lot of strain. They had to be used excessively to make the maximum use of the limited firepower available. When used against an enemy like the Kandyan guerrillas who strove to keep out of the way or at a distance, this could have very serious consequences. The exhaustion of the ammunition in De Souza's vanguard may have also been partly due to the heavy dependence on a small number of firearms during a lengthy running battle.

With the Dutch and the British things were somewhat different. The Dutch and British armies that clashed with the Kandyans in the late eighteenth and early nineteenth centuries were perhaps more hampered by the difficulty to draw up in formation than the Portuguese. This was because these armies conformed more closely to contemporary European drill and discipline than did the Portuguese armies in the seventeenth century. True, the Dutch armies which bore the brunt of the Kandyan invasion in 1763 were not shining examples of contemporary European armies with their strict discipline and organization. As the outgoing governor, Schroeder, pointed out, they were badly trained and disciplined and were in much the same state as raw recruits in Europe were where these aspects of service were concerned.[71] However, the troops which arrived to reinforce the VOC's forces in 1762 brought with them higher standards of training and discipline which gave the Dutch forces on the island a more 'European' appearance. The British forces that operated in Sri Lanka included both regiments of the British regular army—one of the best disciplined European armies of the time—and sepoy units of the East India Company (EIC) as well as Malays and Africans. The non-European troops were under varying degrees of discipline. The Malays in Dutch service were first organized under their own chiefs with little attempt at providing training or up to date weapons. In the eighteenth century, efforts were made to integrate these soldiers into the VOC's regular army with regular organizational structure but these were rudimentary measures.[72] Still, they were an improvement on the lascarin forces. When first formed in the mid-eighteenth century, the British sepoys were given only a basic training and were organized into semi-regular units. But this changed markedly as the British military commitment in India increased. By the early nineteenth century the sepoys were organized into regular units like all European armies and trained and armed in the same fashion as the European troops in the EIC's employ.[73] The British introduced higher standards of training and organization into their Malays and Africans.

But even though the terrain undermined the tactical value of training and discipline of these troops, discipline helped the European forces in another sense: they produced unit cohesion and loyalty. This was most crucial in the case of the non-European troops. As explained earlier, these troops showed remarkable loyalty to their European masters. The British Malays and lascars went to the extent of rejoining them in the heat of battle. The regular organization and discipline played an important role in achieving this.

But as with the Portuguese in the seventeenth century, firepower remained the most significant factor with the Dutch and the British forces. The eighteenth and nineteenth-century European forces had a decided advantage over the Kandyans in their firearms. In the case of the infantry the flintlock 'fusil' used by the Dutch and the 'Brown Bess' carried by the British were far superior to the badly maintained muskets of all sorts used by the Kandyans. These weapons were used by both European and non-European troops in their armies. This is not to say that these firearms were without their problems. The flintlock was also somewhat vulnerable to wet weather; it was not always possible to protect the priming pan from rain and drizzle and constant exposure to damp weather also rusted the locks. Thus, in 1764 we hear of a rainstorm rendering useless the muskets of a Dutch detachment withdrawing from Ruwanwella while in 1818 a British detachment operating in Uva found that only one in ten of their muskets fired due to wet weather.[74] But there is no gainsaying that in terms of the rate of fire and reliability, the flintlock was far superior to the matchlock, even in the rugged guerrilla country of the highlands. It was also easier to reload than the arquebus, even under conditions of guerrilla warfare.

But the biggest advantage possessed by the Dutch and the British in the eighteenth and nineteenth centuries was in artillery. The Dutch and the British in Sri Lanka benefited greatly from the contemporary availability of light field guns and mortars which could be used even in the rugged interior of Sri Lanka. The Dutch carried several light field pieces and mortars during their expeditions in 1764–6 while the British also followed suit.[75] It was still difficult to drag even the lightest piece up the rugged slopes, but it was much easier than carrying a seventeenth-century light cannon. The light mortars of the period were particularly useful in that they took very little space and could be easily manhandled by two people, enabling them to be used in the rugged and wooded terrain without much trouble. The British were partial to the coehorn mortar which was a particularly small and light weapon, with a base a little over two feet long and a fraction over a foot broad.[76] It could be easily carried by two persons, not a very difficult task even in the Kandyan highlands.

THE BALANCE OF MILITARY POWER

KANDY *VS.* THE PORTUGUESE

The constraints on Kandyan and European forces heavily contributed to the balance of military power between the Kandyans and Europeans at different times. As noted earlier, the biggest Kandyan victories came against the Portuguese in the

Kandyan highlands. This was because the Kandyans could concentrate large forces against the enemy in the highlands and the Portuguese forces in Sri Lanka were less capable of preventing the Kandyans from obtaining a tactical superiority over them.

The Kandyan victories at Danture, Randeniwela, and Gannoruwa were achieved within days of mobilization which enabled the Kandyans to bring against the enemy a large, fresh army not suffering from any logistical problems or weariness. While the Kandyans had large fresh armies the Portuguese were struggling to keep their armies together. Mass desertions of auxiliaries in the highlands left only a few hundred Portuguese soldiers and lascarins to fight against the full might of the Kandyan army augmented by the deserted auxiliaries. In 1594, the desertion of lascarins had reduced the Portuguese force to around 400 troops. In 1630, the loss of the lascarin force cut the Portuguese force down to less than 500 with an equal number of lascarins. At Gannoruwa in 1638, about 700 Portuguese and perhaps a slightly larger force of auxiliaries fought the last battle. While their numbers were thus reduced the desertion of auxiliaries augmented the Kandyan forces, further increasing the disparity in numbers.

In this state, the Portuguese had very limited potential for staving off defeat or heavy losses. A force of only a few hundred, that too only partially armed with unreliable firearms, had limited effectiveness against the full strength of the Kandyan army fighting on home soil. As noted earlier, the arquebus was not greatly superior to the Kandyan guns and only a portion of the Portuguse armies carried them. On at least two occasions—at Danture and Randeniwela—the technical and tactical limitations of the arquebusier was aptly demonstrated to the detriment of the Portuguese. At Randeniwela, a rainstorm extinguished the matchcords. At Danture in 1594, the main body of the Portuguese army fought on until the ammunition was exhausted. This was no doubt partially the result of losing some of the ammunition due to the loss of the baggage but as explained earlier, it was also probably due the overuse of the small number of available arquebuses.

The most important result of all this was that the Kandyans' morale was boosted and made them confident of victory. As a consequence, the Portuguese were forced to struggle against a large and buoyant Kandyan army with their limited tactical means. At the best of times, the muskets and arquebuses used by individuals strung up along winding paths were not very effective against enemies hiding behind trees and bushes. They could not inflict heavy casualties on the guerrillas, and in fact, made them vulnerable to the Kandyans especially during long retreats. The limited firepower also made it difficult for the Portuguese to prevent the Kandyans from closing in, especially when the latter were brimming with confidence. As we have seen at Randeniwela and Danture, the firepower was almost totally extinguished. But even if the guns were operable they could achieve little against a rampant enemy in overwhelming strength. At Mulleriyawa in 1562, the Sitawaka troops clearly showed this by closing in with the Portuguese before they could reload, forcing the Portuguese to use their firearms as clubs.[77] The Portuguese in the seventeenth century were no better armed than the Portuguese army defeated at Mulleriyawa and faced a similar fate if surrounded by overwhelming numbers. Their propensity for hand-to-hand fighting could not be of great help in these circumstances. A Jesuit priest describes how, during a battle with the rebel Nikapitiye in 1617, a number of Portuguese soldiers broke ranks to charge at a numerically vastly superior enemy only to get killed to a man.[78] Likewise, even if they gave full expression to their dauntless fighting spirit, it was only a matter of time before they were overwhelmed in hand-to-hand confrontation if the enemy was in overwhelming strength. This is what happened to the armies led by De Souza, De Sa, and De Mello.

Thus, the tactical and organizational state of the Portuguese armies in Sri Lanka had few answers to the challenges posed by the Kandyans, especially in the highlands. However, it was a quite different scenario in the low country, closer to the Portuguese bases where larger forces could not be mustered with ease. Few battles in the lowlands ended with clear victories for the Kandyans. When they confronted small Portuguese forces they did manage to inflict considerable casualties in several battles fought in the lowlands although they never managed to secure singular successes as they did in the hills. For instance in 1652, in a battle which took place just six leagues from Colombo, a Portuguese force of 40 Portuguese and 1500 lascarins lost

19 Portuguese and 132 lascarins killed in a battle fought 'at the point of the spear and the sword',[79] while in 1654 a force of 250 Portuguese and 800 lascarins was attacked at Alawwa in the Seven Korales and forced to retreat to Colombo.[80] But generally, the threat of being defeated was not very great in the low country. Even in the highlands, it is important to remember that there were many occasions when Kandyan tactics failed against the Portuguese. A number of Portuguese raids into Kandy returned without suffering defeat or unbearably heavy losses and in the lowlands the Kandyans often had to withdraw after brief skirmishes. But the difference was that in the hills the possibility of suffering defeat was very real.

What was the overall impact of this on the ability of the Portuguese to dominate the interior? As noted earlier in Chapter 1, the Portuguese did succeed in creating havoc in Kandyan lands with their constant raids. The Kandyans were forced to abandon their villages, the king himself fleeing to the refuge of the forests.[81] The Portuguese ravages also placed the Kandyan peasant economy and the military system based on that economy under severe strain. Not only were fields destroyed and livestock killed but the constant warfare also kept the peasantry out of their fields for long periods, severely undermining the productivity of the land. However, there was a limit to what the Portuguese could achieve. The overall vulnerability of their troops in the field meant that the Portuguese had to use troops in large forces—small detachments were more vulnerable to be cut-off or suffer heavy casualties. This placed heavy constraints on the reliable manpower base of the Portuguese, already limited by the unavoidability of large numbers of recruits and the ravages of disease. This in turn limited their ability to dominate the interior. When the Portuguese raided and devastated Kandyan land in the early seventeenth century they had to use the greater part of their strength in one main army. For instance, the raid in 1611 included 700 Portuguese and 6,000 lascarins.[82] According to Azevedo, his raids were carried out with the 'entire body' of troops available to him.[83] Another raid launched by De Sa in 1628 included 500 Portuguese soldiers.[84] Even in areas closer to their bases, the Portuguese could not risk using small forces. This weakness was clearly exposed when the Portuguese had to fight on two or more fronts. A good example is the problem they faced in 1617 during Nikapitiye's revolt. Before the revolt broke out, the Portuguese had been systematically devastating Kandy and putting the Kandyans under severe strain. The revolt, however, forced them to fight on two fronts which was impossible given their limitations in resources and tactical capacity to fight under local conditions. A similar thing happened in 1655 when Gaspar Figueyra's field army's heroics against the Kandyans was cut short by the need to fall back on Colombo to save the fort from the Dutch.[85]

The need to move in large armies limited the area that can be destroyed, as one single unit—albeit a large one—could not be expected to cover a great area, especially during the few months chosen by the Portuguese to raid Kandy. This was not all. The vulnerability of the troops in the field and the need to use large forces also contributed to the vulnerability of Portuguese forts and outposts. As noted earlier, the Portuguese often had to denude their garrisons to strengthen their armies in the field. This is what happened in 1594, 1603, 1630, and 1638. In 1603, Ruwanwella was defended by only a factor while Sitawaka had only 5 Portuguese, 2 native Christians, and a priest, and the post at Rakgahawatta had only one Captain, two soldiers, and three or four young slaves.[86] When De Sa was defeated in 1630, Malwana had only 17 Portuguese while the forts at Sabaragamuwa and Menikkadawara were slightly better manned, having 50 and 70 Portuguese, respectively.[87]

Therefore, even though the Portuguese were able to exert considerable pressure on the Kandyans in the interior, what they could achieve was limited by their concerns for security. They also had to take serious risks to do it. The seriousness of this risk was clearly underlined when the Kandyans succeeded in defeating the main Portuguese army in the field. With the destruction of the main army, Portuguese power in the interior swiftly contracted, their weak outposts falling to the rampant Kandyans and low country rebels. This is what happened in 1594, 1603, and 1630. When the field army was defeated or badly mauled, the garrisons in the interior and outlying areas had to be withdrawn or were captured. And, occasionally, as it happened in 1630, the tables could be so turned that the Portuguese presence on the island had to depend entirely on their ability to command the sea. The defeat of De Sa threatened the Portuguese power in Sri Lanka so seriously because it destroyed the main Portuguese army on the island and swept away all the lightly defended Portuguese posts in the interior. Only Colombo and Galle remained in the area exposed to the Kandyans and these survived only because of the ability to get help from abroad.

From the Kandyan perspective, the Portuguese attempts to conquer and ravage their lands was a terrible experience. But the fact that the havoc committed by the enemy was limited by his vulnerability also enabled them to survive complete subjugation. Indeed, it is fair to say that the tactical vulnerability of the Portuguese forces and their lack of manpower also afforded the Kandyans the scope to wrest the strategic advantage from the Portuguese on occasions. A defeat of the main Portuguese army could rapidly clear the interior of any Portuguese presence and confine European power to their coastal strongholds where logistical problems and the lack of Kandyan artillery and naval power saved them from complete destruction.

Given this balance of power, the Kandyans' ability to obtain foreign assistance to control the sea while in possession of the interior could be decisive. The use of foreign assistance depended on its availability as well as its effectiveness. The Dutch were readily available as a major rival to the Portuguese and possessed a powerful navy. In the event, the Dutch took on the Portuguese on the coast while the Kandyans attacked the Portuguese possessions in the interior. The Portuguese withdrew their forces to the coast to fight the Dutch and the Kandyans became masters of the interior. Even though this withdrawal was not forced by Kandyan military success as in 1630, it exposed the Portuguese weakness of not being able to fend off the Kandyans with a small force while defending the coast. With their lifeline with India threatened, the Portuguese chose to direct all their resources to safeguard the coastal strongholds and the Kandyans overran all their possessions in the interior. This brought the situation to what it was in late 1630 when the Portuguese were bottled up in Colombo with the Kandyans controlling the interior. The difference in 1656 was that they now had little hope of succour from the sea.

KANDY VS. THE DUTCH AND THE BRITISH

Unlike the Portuguese before them, the Dutch and the British in the second half of the eighteenth and early nineteenth centuries had greater tactical potential for dominating the interior. Their cannon and mortars could march with them—albeit with some difficulty—and their fire could reach the Kandyans in their mountain fastnesses and stockades. And their firearms could lay down heavier and more frequent volleys than the Portuguese arquebuses.

This enhanced firepower placed in the hands of a detachment of 100–200 European/Malay/sepoy troops with a small mortar a firepower which was unavailable to a seventeenth-century Portuguese force that was ten times that number. The availability of light artillery and mortars, in particular, meant the negation of many of the advantages which the Kandyans had enjoyed in their wars against the Portuguese. The presence of field artillery enabled the Europeans to tackle the Kandyans from a distance, even in their commanding heights. The light mortars, in particular, were very useful in this regard. Not only could they hit the enemy from afar but their high trajectory of fire could also reach the Kandyans taking refuge behind natural features or fortifications and their explosive shells could rip through thick foliage.[88] The diarist of the 1765 campaign noted with satisfaction how the mortars could keep the enemy at a 'greater distance than could be done by musket fire'.[89] Nearly four decades later in 1803, Herbert Beaver echoed this view, declaring confidently that whenever he discovered the precise location of an enemy force he was 'sure to rout them out with a few shells' from their coehorns.[90] When that was the case at a distance, any attempt to overwhelm a European force supported by artillery with massed attacks was bound to prove disastrous. This is clearly shown by the attempt to assault the British garrison in the Kandyan palace in 1803. A single grapeshot put an end to the ambitious attempt, killing 24 Kandyans on the spot.[91]

Even without mortars or cannon, at close range, a small force of Reopens and sepoys with their flintlocks had the potential to keep the Kandyan guerrillas at a safe distance due to their high rate of fire. And it was often such detachments that struggled with the Kandyans to dominate the interior in 1762–6, 1803–5, and 1817–18. For instance, in March 1803, Captain Herbert

Beaver cleared the Four Korales of Kandyan intruders with only 30 men while in February 1818, Major Delattre marched with a detachment of just over a hundred men from Trincomalee to Kurunegala.[92] Many similar examples can be provided. Only on three occasions were the Kandyans successful in destroying a detachment during the three wars of 1761–6, 1803–4, and 1817–18. In December 1761 at Morawak Korale, a 24-man detachment was surrounded and annihilated while a larger force of about 150 was killed or captured shortly after. In December 1817, a detachment of about 15 men was wiped out at Tibbotugoda in the Uva province.[93] And interestingly, only on two occasions did the Kandyans attempt hand-to-hand or even close range engagement—against the Dutch and the British garrisons in Kandy in 1765 and 1803 which were beaten back. On all other occasions, the usual option was to play it safe and engage even tiny enemy detachments from a safe distance, even when operating deep within the Kandyan heartland where large forces could be concentrated. This was in sharp contrast to the Kandyan practice against the Portuguese in the seventeenth century when they had the confidence to engage even large enemy forces in close range and even hand-to-hand combat, especially in the highlands where they had the advantage of home terrain and numbers.

No doubt the Kandyan preference to keep at a safe distance during these wars owed a lot to the enhanced firepower of the European forces they encountered. Even without artillery a small detachment of Europeans and Malays or sepoys could project a firepower that would have been the envy of larger seventeenth-century Portuguese forces. But it is also very likely that the relationship between this enhanced firepower and Kandyan reluctance to offer battle at close range was not always based on realities on the ground. It must be noted that besides having no artillery, many of the detachments that the Kandyans refused to engage with resolution did not have the numbers to produce a heavy fire from the muskets. Many of the British detachments that traversed the countryside in 1817–18 did not number more than two or three dozen men, let alone carry artillery. But still, the Kandyans showed great reluctance to engage them at close range. Two examples will suffice to illustrate this. The first is the above-mentioned destruction of a British detachment of 18 men in December 1818. The detachment was surrounded by a large number of Kandyans who avoided coming into close range until the troops exhausted their ammunition.[94] When the guns fell silent, the rebels rushed in and finished off the troops. The other instance is the ambushing of a detachment of 18 men marching from Passara to Badulla in June 1818. The ambush killed two men and while five of the survivors guarded the bodies the rest fought their way to Badulla to bring reinforcements. After the initial ambush no other casualties were suffered because the Kandyans remained at a safe distance from the British and fired at them without effect. It is very likely that a single rush could have finished the affair but this was not considered an option.[95] The Kandyans would have needed little persuasion to rush a Portuguese force twice that size in the seventeenth century.

Almost all encounters between the Kandyans and British detachments in 1803–4 and 1817–18 reflected this reluctance to engage even tiny British detachments closely. I believe that this respect for even minuscule British forces that had little real potential for withstanding a strong attack by even a Kandyan force of 200–300 had much to do with the respect the Kandyans had come to feel for the power of contemporary European arms in general rather than for that particular force. Even small British detachments projected the power of contemporary European arms which was often clearly demonstrated when fairly large detachments took the field with their mortars and cannon. It probably explains the ease with which the British pushed the Kandyans back in 1803 and the Dutch to a lesser degree in 1762.

In all this, the non-European troops also played a crucial role. The Malays, in particular, were considered good jungle fighters, used to the climate and skilled in moving swiftly and stealthily through the jungle. It made the Kandyans feel less secure in their hideouts and further persuaded them to keep their distance.[96] But the biggest contribution of the Malay and sepoy troops was their loyalty. As explained earlier, they showed a remarkable loyalty to their European masters. This was very crucial as these troops made up at least half of the small detachments that were employed against the Kandyans. Their desertion had the potential to make the small detachments even more vulnerable than they usually were. Even in the case of the larger European detachments, desertion would have had dangerous consequences. For instance, had the Malays and sepoys deserted in large numbers in 1765 and 1803–4 it would have certainly spelled greater difficulties for the Dutch and the British. Furthermore, the desertion of Malays and sepoys would have also boosted Kandyan firepower by delivering to them more guns in a better state of repair than the firearms ordinarily used by the Kandyans. It would have also delivered to them troops who had greater confidence in fighting the European forces.

However, all this does not mean that the Dutch and the British had an easy time against the Kandyans. The Dutch and the British invasions of Kandy did run into serious difficulties against Kandyan resistance but the potential of this resistance lay more in its ability to grind down occupying European forces than in defeating them in the field. Even if they could not inflict heavy casualties, Kandyan tactics succeeded in making life so difficult for the invading/occupying forces as to make them abandon their goal. The Dutch were very clear as to why they quit Kandy in 1765:

> Frankena reported: of our losses on patrols and the little they brought in; the daily increasing sickness and weakness. . . . There was paddy for 3 days only; by sending out foraging patrols we might be able to hold out a little longer but by risking many casualties. Furthermore, the rains were beginning, and the weakness of the troops was daily increasing, so that with longer delay the impassable roads could bring us a miserable end. Therefore it was unanimously agreed that both for our own preservation and for the greater service of the Company to abandon Kandia. . . .[97]

The grim picture is very clear. The Dutch were facing a number of problems: casualties, lack of supplies, and weakness of their troops. The above entry does not mention the ever-present fear of desertion by the sepoys and Malays in the face of hardship which is expressed in a previous entry.[98] According to a plea for help sent to Colombo in June 1765, the Dutch situation had begun to get desperate very early. The message, written in Latin in case it was captured, mentions the Dutch having expended all powder and shot 'owing to the daily attacks by the enemy'.[99] The stocks of munitions may not have been as completely exhausted as the message makes out because the Dutch continued to fight Kandyans long after this, but the desperateness of the situation cannot be clearer. The Dutch had clearly come to the end of their tether without being defeated in battle, without even suffering the destruction of a single patrol or outpost.

The British faced a similar situation in 1803. Their patrols and outposts were never overwhelmed but often attacked, suffering slight but mounting casualties. The communications with their bases in the lowlands was almost completely cut and supplies were running low. As noted earlier, there was a shortage of food, especially meat, and sickness, particularly beri-beri, was rampant.[100] Mounting pressure, including a heavy attack on the garrison finally forced the British too to evacuate Kandy. On the way they were surrounded and forced to give up their weapons and then massacred. It was just such a fate, rather than military defeat, which Captain Johnstone was hoping to avoid when he decided to make a run for it after realizing that his detachment was all alone in Kandy.

The difficulty in maintaining communications in the face of Kandyan guerrilla threats also frequently forced the Dutch and the British to abandon their outposts in the interior. This was sometimes in anticipation of difficulties rather than as a result of difficulties experienced, as was the case in 1761 and 1803 when first the Dutch and then the British abandoned some of their posts in the interior. But it showed an appreciation of the problems associated with having to maintain outposts in hostile, not fully 'pacified' country. On the other hand, in 1817–18, the British abandoned a number of their posts in Uva and Matale due to the sheer inability to maintain them.[101] Had not the Three Korales remained loyal to the British the rest of the Kandyan territories too could have been lost.

It can be said that on all these occasions the Kandyans succeeded in ejecting the European invaders out of Kandyan territory and areas that were previously controlled by Europeans by making life difficult for them. While it is possible to put the abandoning of Kandy in 1765 and 1803 and of various smaller outposts to sickness and lack of food rather than military pressure, in the final analysis all these conditions were created by Kandyan resistance in the countryside. An army of occupation with the goodwill of the population and not having to dodge bullets and arrows at every outing would have suffered very few of these inconveniences. Occupying Kandy while the countryside remained hostile meant having to fight to obtain food, and to maintain lines of communication open. A hostile countryside could make the terrain itself appear threatening and aggressive, as described by Bombardier Alexander in his narrative of Johnstone's retreat:

> How different did this rich and fertile country appear in the advance from what it now did in the retreat? In the one, the high and craggy rocks, the stately palm, and coconut trees, the lofty timbers and rich fields of rice, were all objects of admiration; now that every tree or rock concealed a lurking foe, they were objects of distrust. In many places the roads were so narrow, the army had no other way to march than in Indian file, that is rank entire. They had wound along these roads, in the advance, with pleasure and admiration, flushed with the hopes of victory and success; now they were sources of their greatest uneasiness.[102]

Thus, the strength of Kandyan guerrilla warfare lay not simply in its ability to kill enemies with bullets and arrows but also in its potential for turning the environment itself into a challenge. As noted earlier in the case of the attack on Girihagama, the rigours of overcoming even a fairly ineffectual resistance in rugged terrain could be detrimental to European health. One British writer went so far as to claim that disease among British troops in 1817–18 was largely due to 'fatigues and privations' associated with the rigours of their operations than due to any particular insalubriousness of the climate.[103] In the case of the Dutch and the British, this kind of challenge seems to have been a greater threat than the direct challenge of arrows and bullets. But it was a threat nevertheless and an effective one at that.

THE SHIFTING BALANCE OF POWER

As we have seen above, despite their greater potential for resisting Kandyan warfare the Dutch and British forces had their own problems with Kandyan guerrillas who gradually ground them down with harassing action. However, the losses for the Kandyans were also severe. The wars of 1761–6, 1803–5, and 1817–18 caused much devastation in Kandyan territories and areas in the lowlands that threw in their lot with Kandyans. We have numerous reports of the hardship caused by this devastation. The Dutch ravages in 1764 and 1765 reduced many parts of Kandyan territory, especially the provinces of the Four and Seven Korales into wastelands, their fruit trees cut down and their fields destroyed.[104] Agriculture was at a standstill while the supply of salt and dried fish was badly disrupted.[105] In 1804, the Four Korales suffered again, British spies reporting that the people in the area were unable to sow their fields and were deficient of salt. The lack of salt, in particular, was the result of the economic blockade of Kandyan territories. In late 1804 and early 1805, it was reported that getting even a handful of rice was difficult for the Kandyan people and the people in the Seven Korales were reported to be migrating *en masse* into the less troubled Magul Korale in the region of Puttalam.[106] The frontier area of Hanwella and Avissawella was turned into a deserted, desolate land.[107] The British ravages of 1817-18 were truly devastating, preventing the cultivation of fields for two seasons, forcing the peasantry to sustain themselves on whatever grain they had hidden away.[108] The Kandyans were—again—said to be suffering woefully from a lack of salt.[109] The effects of the ravages could be still seen two years later in 1820, when Dr John Davy passed through 'its cottages in ruins, its fields lying waste, its cattle destroyed and its population fled'.[110] The total Kandyan losses in the rebellion have been estimated at around 10,000–15,000 dead, a massive loss to a small population.[111]

It is difficult to say if this damage was greater than what the Portuguese caused in the early seventeenth century. The lack of information makes it difficult to determine this but it is conceivable that the damage was more substantial. The Dutch and the British, especially the latter, were strategically and tactically better equipped to hurt Kandy more than did the Portuguese. The havoc wreaked by the Portuguese in Kandyan lands was limited by the need to use large forces. The Dutch and the British, on the contrary, could use much smaller detachments of troops to ravage the countryside with little fear of being overwhelmed. For example, in September 1764, a small force of only 400 men moved into Hapitigam Korale, which had rebelled in 1761, and, after massacring all those who made resistance and in prisoning the women and children, proceeded to kill or drive off the cattle and destroy the crops. The detachment continued to ravage the Korale and the nearby Hina Korale for more than a week, destroying huge quantities of rice and burning houses without suffering any loss.[112] The British did this even more effectively, using even smaller detachments. For instance, in early

December 1803, Sabaragamuwa province was ravaged by a small detachment of less than 200 men led by Captain Moubray, 'destroying all the houses, stores and gardens in the rich province'. Only a few days later another detachment of similar strength commanded by Captain Robert Blackall invaded the Seven Korales, destroying 93 villages and 80,000 parrahs of rice in 7 days.[113] The detachments that traversed the Kandyan country in 1817–18 were even smaller but no less brutal. They also ravaged the Kandyan heartland, not its periphery.

As a consequence of using smaller detachments simultaneously in different parts of enemy territory, the Dutch and the British could devastate and dominate a larger area than did the Portuguese. Their biggest enemy in this sort of war was disease, even though this threat was heavily aggravated by Kandyan resistance. Although the loss from disease was high it was compensated for by the possibility of using small forces. The availability of greater manpower resources also helped to replenish the losses from disease. The British were particularly well-placed in this respect with their huge army in neighbouring India.

Furthermore, the Dutch and the British could also defend their own possessions with greater ease than the Portuguese and minimize the damage which the Kandyans could inflict. Small forces could push the Kandyans out quickly and establish control. It was a force of 202 Europeans and 300 Malays that cleared the road from Galle to Matara in 1762. As noted earlier, the Kandyan incursion into the Four Korales in March 1803 was repulsed by less than 30 European troops and sepoys[114] while in September 1803, the British retook Hanwella with about 100 men and cleared the surrounding area—where a large body of Kandyans were concentrated—with tiny detachments made from this body.[115] In sharp contrast, when the Kandyans invaded the lowlands after De Sa's defeat in 1630, the Portuguese did not venture to clear the area around Colombo until they could put in the field an army of about 4000 European, African, Canarese troops and lascarins in January 1632.[116]

Therefore, it is fair to say that in terms of the potential risks and advantages, the balance of military power had shifted clearly in the Europeans' favour towards the second half of the eighteenth century. The Kandyans stood to lose more than they gained in a prolonged confrontation with the Europeans. Whereas in the seventeenth century the defeat of a large Portuguese army and putting the Portuguese under severe pressure was a real possibility, it was becoming increasingly difficult with the Dutch and the British. The losses the Kandyans stood to suffer in return were also potentially greater than what they suffered from the Portuguese.

Given this balance of power on land, only an outside power could change the equation in favour of the Kandyans. But as we have seen in the previous chapter, by the early nineteenth century, even this option was gradually closing for the Kandyans. When the Kandyans battled the Dutch the availability of potential powerful foreign allies was not a problem as the British were well placed in neighbouring India to offer assistance. But persuading the British to fight the Dutch on behalf of the Kandyans was a different matter. As a consequence, Kandyan attempts to obtain British help against the Dutch failed and the British takeover of Dutch possessions was not a case of British military assistance to Kandy but rather, a transaction between the British and Dutch authorities as a result of European political developments. In the nineteenth century, the option of foreign help was completely sealed. The British were clearly the paramount power in India and also in the Indian Ocean and there was no other power which could challenge it. On sea as on land, by early nineteenth century, the Europeans had gained a firm grip on Kandy.

WAR AND THE FALL OF KANDY

Thus, by early nineteenth century, Kandyan resistance had gradually lost its effectiveness against European military forces, shifting the balance firmly in favour of the Europeans. This was largely due to the European's ability to overcome Kandyan strengths and the limitations inherent in Kandyan military power. This growing effeteness of Kandyan resistance poses interesting questions about the survival of Kandy. Was European conquest of Kandy becoming inevitable by the early nineteenth century? Had the remarkable resistance of Kandy run its course?

Some historians ascribe the demise of Kandyan independence to treachery rather than military defeat. Lorna Dewaraja writes:

'A century of war was followed by a century of peace and when Kandy fell in 1815 it was not by conquest but as liberators, claiming to deliver Kandyans from the tyranny of their own king and it must be remembered that not a single British soldier died or was wounded in the act of deliverance.'[117]

Such claims, though evidently inspired by a streak of patriotism, are also based on irrefutable fact. As explained in Chapter 1, Kandy was delivered to the British on a platter in 1815. Even when the British had to fight to keep Kandy in 1817–18, collaboration played a crucial role in keeping the supply lines open and saving the British from a humiliating evacuation. Had it not been for the collaboration of Molligoda, who kept the lines of communication between Kandy and Colombo open through the strategically important three and four Korales, Kandy would have been able to eject the British and revert to independence. But the question is, for how long?

The 'Kandy was never conquered by the force of arms' thesis, while being true in a narrow sense, gives Kandy a false sense of invincibility. The fact is that Kandy's fall was imminent by the beginning of the nineteenth century because, as we have seen, Kandy's invincibility was becoming more a result of a rugged and inhospitable terrain and climate than the prowess of Kandyan arms. The British were in a good position in terms of resources and tactical capability to deal with these problems and also inflict severe damage on the Kandyan economy. A rebellious Three and Four Korales would have forced a British evacuation in 1818 but it would have been only temporary. The British would have certainly launched a fresh attempt to take Kandy, reinforced by their massive army in India. It would have been costly for the British but the cost would have been unbearable to the Kandyans who were already suffering severely from the devastation of their lands. Even if no fresh invasion was launched, it would have been very difficult for Kandy to recover from the losses of 1817–18.

Therefore, it is fair to say that despite its proud record of resistance, Kandy was doomed as an independent kingdom by the beginning of the nineteenth-century. The odds stacked against Kandyan survival by the beginning of the nineteenth century suggest that it was a matter of time before they became insurmountable. Completely cut-off from the outside world and with meagre resources of its own, Kandyan survival would have become increasingly a test of endurance between European armies and the Kandyan peasantry, rather than the outcome of military conflict. It was a struggle which the Europeans, with their more efficient weapons and greater resources, were bound to win.

NOTES

1. Fernao de Queyroz, *The Temporal and Spiritual Conquest of Ceylon*, trs. S.G. Perera, Colombo: Govt. Printers, 1930, p. 488.
2. Alexander Alexander, *Life of Bombardier, Alexander written by himself*, 2 vols, London, 1830, vol. 1, p. 162.
3. Joao Rodriguez De Sa y Menezes, 'The Rebellion of Ceylon and the Progress of its Conquest under the Government of Constantino de Sa y Noronha', trs. H.H. St. George, *JRAS(CB)*, vol. 11, no. 41, 1890, p. 118.
4. Ibid., p. 574.
5. George Calladine, *The Diary of Colour Sergeant George Calladine*, ed. M.L. Ferrar, London: Eden Fisher & Co., 1922, p. 58. Also James Cordiner, *Description*, vol. 2, pp. 254–5.
6. Major Roland Raven–Hart (trs. and ed.), 'Major Medeler's Relief Expedition', *JRAS(CB)*, New Series, vol. 5, 1957, p. 195 and Appendix VI, p. 259.
7. '*Aanmerkingen over de Oorlog met de Singaleesen*', Mackenzie Ms. 39, p. 45.
8. Major Roland Raven-Hart (trs. and ed.), *The Dutch Wars with Kandy 1764–1766*, Ceylon Historical Manuscripts Commission Bulletin no. 6, Colombo: Government Publications Bureau, 1964, p. 93.
9. Medeler calculations for labour requirements give a good idea of the needs of a European detachment of considerable size. He calculated that altogether 1000 coolies and 450 pack animals will be needed and the coolies were to be divided as follows: 224 for ammunition, 140 for 1400 cans of arrack, 8 for 450 grenades, 40 for cooking gear, and 195 for officers' baggage, Medeler's included. Raven-Hart, 'Major Medeler's Relief Expedition', p. 259.
10. For instance, a detachment of about 20 people that accompanied surgeon Kennedy in 1818 had almost an equal number of servants. *Ceylon Government Gazette*, 20 December 1817, *The Uva Rebellion: Extracts from the Ceylon Government Gazette, 1817–18*, Colombo: 1888, p. 8.
11. Raven-Hart, *The Dutch Wars*, p. 59.

12. 'Description of Ceylon by Antonio Bocarro', trs. and ed. T.B.H. Abeysinghe, *JRAS(SLB)*, New Series, vol. 39, 1995, p. 17.
13. A.R. Disney, *The Twilight of the Pepper Empire: Portuguese Trade in Southwest India in the Early Seventeenth Century*, Cambridge, Massachussetts: Harvard University Press, 1978, p. 19.
14. T.B.H. Abeysinghe, *Portuguese Rule in Ceylon 1594–1612*, Colombo: Lake House, 1966, p. 43.
15. Ibid., pp. 59–60.
16. C.R. Boxer, 'War and Trade in the Indian Ocean and the South China Seas 1600–1650', *The Great Circle, the Journal of the Australian Association for Maritime History*, vol. 1, no. 2, 1979, p. 7.
17. C.R. De Silva, *The Portuguese in Ceylon 1617–1638*, Colombo: H.W. Cave and Co., 1972, p. 83.
18. 'Description of Ceylon by Antonio Bocarro', p. 19.
19. De Silva, *The Portuguese in Ceylon*, p. 187.
20. Boxer, 'War and Trade', p. 7.
21. Disney, *The Twilight*, p. 21. According to Disney, there was also a high rate of desertion. Many joined religious orders or the armies of native rulers. In 1627, about 5000 Portuguese served under various native rulers in India. Ibid., p. 21; C.R. Boxer, *The Portuguese Seaborne Empire*, London: Hutchinson, 1969, pp. 131–2.
22. Abeysingne, *Portuguese Rule*, p. 64.
23. Queyroz, *The Temporal and Spiritual Conquest*, p. 771.
24. De Silva, *The Portuguese in Ceylon*, pp. 122–7.
25. K.W. Goonewardene, *The Foundation of Dutch Power in Ceylon 1638–1658*, Amsterdam: Djambatan, 1958, p. 168, n. 68.
26. Queyroz, *The Temporal and Spiritual Conquest*, p. 33.
27. Alagiyavanna Mukaveti, *Kustantinu Hatana*, ed. Edwin Ranawake, Colombo: Gunasena, 1938, verse 96, p. 65.
28. De Silva, *The Portuguese in Ceylon*, p. 129.
29. *Rajasinha Hatana* mentions Africans, *Kannanda*, *Paravara*, and *Javaka* troops in De Mello's army in 1638. *Rajasinha Hatana*, ed. Ellepola M.M. Somaratne, Kandy: T.B.S. Godamune and Sons, date unavailable, verses 232, 385 and 386, pp. 38 and 66.
30. C.R. Boxer, *The Dutch Seaborne Empire*, London: Hutchinson, 1965, p. 80.
31. D.A. Kotelawela, 'The Dutch in Ceylon: 1743–1766', Ph.D. thesis, University of London, 1968, p. 233.
32. See, for instance, the troop strengths for 1764 and 1765 given in Raven-Hart, *The Dutch Wars*, pp. 56, 60 and 134.
33. Kotelawela, 'The Dutch in Ceylon' p. 233, Raven-Hart, *The Dutch Wars*, p. 49.
34. W. van Damast Limberger, 'A Short History of the Principal Events that Occurred in the Island of Ceylon, Since the Arrival of the First

Netherlanders in the Year 1602, and Afterwards, from the Establishment of the "Honourable Company" in the Same Island till the Year 1757', ed. P.A. Leupe, trs. F.H. de Vos, *JRAS(CB)*, vol. 11, no. 38, 1889, p. 75.

35. The remarks of Hendrik Zwardecroon, Commander of Jaffna, 1697–1700. *Memoir of Hendrick Zwardercroon, Commandeur of Jaffnapatam*, trs. Sophia Pieters, Colombo: Govt. Printers, 1911, p. 28.
36. For instance, in May 1764 there were 2458 Easterners in Dutch garrisons. Raven-Hart, *The Dutch Wars*, p. 56. By the end of the year, these numbers had risen to 3082. Ibid., p. 60.
37. Colombo to Nagapattanam, 17 November 1764, SLNA 1/4924.
38. Colombo to Holland, 13 November 1764, SLNA 1/4876.
39. Raven-Hart, *The Dutch Wars*, pp. 134, p. 56.
40. Raymond Callahan, *The East India Company and Army Reform*, Cambridge, Massachusetts: Harvard University Press, 1972, p. 6.
41. In 1808, there were about 800 Africans but only about 600 Malays in British service in Sri Lanka. B.A. Husainmiya, *Orang Regimen: The Malays of the Ceylon Rifle Regiment*, Bangi, Malaysia: Penerbit University Kebangsaan Malayasia, 1990, p. 79.
42. The complete British force that surrendered comprised 34 European officers and soldiers, 250 Malays, and 140 gun lascars. Cordiner, *Description*, vol. 2, p. 210.
43. Ibid., p. 234. Altogether, 26 Malays and 150 Bengal and Madras gun lascars rejoined the British at Hanwella.
44. Hugh Boyd, the British ambassador to Kandy in 1782 bemusedly described his experience of having to eat his dinner in a 'cold bath'. A. Lennox Mills, *The Advent of the British to Ceylon*, London: Frank Cass, 1964, pp. 4–5.
45. V.M. Methley, 'The Expedition of 1803', Transactions of the Royal Asiatic Society 4th Series, vol. 1, 1917, p. 108. For a detailed view of the sickness which affected the British during the campaign in 1803, see 'The Medical Report in April 1803' in Cordiner, *Description*, vol. 2, pp. 262–86.
46. Kandy Diary, entries for 3, 16, and 28 August 1765, p. 35, 16 August and 28 August, SLNA 1/4944, pp. 35, 40, 46.
47. By early April 1803, beef of only a very low grade was available in Kandy and by 1 May 1803, only six bullocks were left to feed a force of several hundred Europeans and Malays. Thomas Ajax Anderson, *Journal of the Proceedings of the Trincomalee Detachment Commanded by the Lieut. Colonel Barbut His Majesty's 73rd Regiment from their Leaving Trincomalee till their Arrival at Kandy*, London, 1809, pp. 181–2.
48. Ibid., pp. 181–2.
49. Cordiner, *Description*, vol. 2, p. 280.
50. Methley, *The Expedition of 1803*, p. 104.
51. Henry Marshall, *Ceylon: A General Description of the Island and of its*

Inhabitants, Dehiwela, Sri Lanka: Tisara Publishers, 1982; 1st pub. 1846, p. 190. One mid-nineteenth-century British writer went so far as to say that it was the 'fatigues and privations' of the service that exposed the British to disease in 1817–18. John Whitchurch Bennett, *Ceylon and her Capabilities: An Account of its Natural Resources, Indigenous Productions and Commercial Facilities,* London: William H. Allen, 1843, p. 421.

52. Queyroz, *The Temporal and Spiritual Conquest,* p. 817. Ribeiro identified beri-beri as one of the major health problems of the Portuguese in Sri Lanka. Joao de Ribeiro, *The Historic Tragedy of the Island of Ceilao,* trs. P.E. Pieris, Colombo: Lake House, 1948, p. 62. Sa y Menezes claims that many Portuguese died from the cold alone, which probably refers to sickness contracted as a consequence of exposure to inclement weather among other things. De Menezes, 'The Rebellion of Ceylon', p. 575.
53. Kandy Diary, 23 August 1765, SLNA, 1/4944, p. 43.
54. Major Davy to Colombo, 10 June 1803, SLNA 7/43, p. 685.
55. Bennett, *Ceylon and her Capabilities,* p. 424.
56. Geoffrey Powell, *The Kandyan Wars: The British Army in Ceylon 1803–1818,* London: Leo Cooper, 1973, p. 251.
57. Fritz Redlich, *The German Military Enterpriser and his Workforce: A European Economic and Social History,* Wiesbaden: Steiner, 1964, p. 124. This tactic was perfected by the Spanish during the sixteenth century. Their squares of firearms and pikes, called *tercios,* had 3,000 men who were divided into twelve companies, ten of pikemen and the rest musketeers and arquebusiers. Bert S. Hall, *Weapons and Warfare in Renaissance Europe: Gunpowder, Technology and Tactics,* Baltimore: Johns Hopkins University Press, 1997, p. 178.
58. B.P. Hughes, *Open Fire: Artillery Tactics from Marlborough to Wellington,* Chichester, Sussex: A. Bird publications, 1983, p. 12.
59. On drill and military manoeuvres in the eighteenth century, see Christopher Duffy, *The Military Experience in the Age of Reason,* London: Routledge and Kegan Paul, 1987, pp. 198–204.
60. According to C.R Boxer, the Portuguese leaders fought like medieval champions at the head of their men. Boxer, *The Portuguese Seaborne Empire,* pp. 299–300. Also Geoffrey Parker, *The Military Revolution: Military Innovation and the Rise of the West 1500–1800,* Cambridge and New York, Cambridge University Press, 1998, p. 131.
61. For instance, according to Queyroz, the Portuguese attacked the Kandyan troops that surrounded the Balana fort 'so suddenly and with such impetuosity and determination that [t]he[y] put him to flight, first with musketry and then with spears and swords'. Queyroz, *The Temporal and Spiritual Conquest,* p. 614. Also see Sousa, *Portuguese India,* p. 232.
62. Queyroz, *The Temporal and Spiritual Conquest,* p. 99.

63. Joao de Barros and Diogo do Couto, 'The History of Ceylon from the earliest times to A.D. 1600', trs. and ed. Donald Ferguson *JRAS(CB),* vol. 20, no. 60, 1908, p. 131.
64. According to Queyroz, the Portuguese employed the light cannon called falcons against Gannetenna in 1603 'as kinds of cannon were not easy to use in those lands'. Queyroz, *The Temporal and Spiritual Conquest,* p. 552.
65. Bert S. Hall, *Weapons and Warfare in Renaissance Europe: Gunpowder, Technology and Tactics,* Baltimore: Johns Hoppins University Press, 1977, p. 149.
66. Queyroz, *The Temporal and Spiritual Conquest,* p. 777.
67. Ibid., p. 481.
68. *The Expedition to Uva made in 1630 by Constantine de Sa de Noronha, Captain General of Ceylon, as narrated by a Soldier who took part in the Expedition together with an Account of the Siege laid to Colombo by the King of Kandy written by Afonso Dias da Lomba,* trs. S.G. Perera, Colombo: State Printing Corp., 1946, pp. 27–8.
69. Ribeiro, *The Historic Tragedy,* p. 165.
70. Abeysinghe, *Portuguese Rule,* pp. 123–5.
71. *Selections from the Dutch Records of the Government of Ceylon: Memoirs of Jan Schreuder,* trs. E. Reimers, Colombo: State Printing Corp., 1946, pp. 22–3.
72. Jaap de Moor, 'The Recruitment of Indonesian Soldiers for the Dutch Colonial Army, *c.* 1700–1950', in David Killingray and David Omissi (eds), *Guardians of Empire: The Armed Forces of the Colonial Powers c. 1700–1964,* Manchester: Manchester University Press, 1999, pp. 55–6.
73. See the treatment of this subject in C. Wickremesekera, *The Best Black Troops in the World: British Perceptions and the Making of the Sepoy 1746–1805,* Delhi: Manohar, 2002, pp. 109–24.
74. '*Aanmerkingen*', p. 17, note; Calladine, *Diary,* pp. 58–9.
75. In 1764, the Dutch carried several 1-pounders and hand mortars besides a number of gingals. Diary of the 1764 campaign, Raven-Hart, *The Dutch Wars,* p. 27. In the 1765 campaign, they used 10 metal 1- and 2-pounders and six 4-inch mortars. Council Minute, 20 October 1764, Raven-Hart, Ibid., p. 52. Medeler's relief expedition also took two metal 1-pounders and 5 metal mortars. Raven-Hart, 'Major Medelers' Expedition', p. 190. The British took with them 6 brass 6-pounders, a 5.5-inch mortar, and three coehorn mortars. Powell, *The Kandyan Wars,* p. 72. Johnstone took with him one 1-pounder and one coehorn mortar. Ibid., p. 159.
76. Brigadier O.F.G. Hogg, *Artillery: Its Origin, Heyday and Decline,* London: C. Hurst & Company, 1970, pp. 64–5.
77. *Rajavaliya or a Historical Narrative of Sinhalese Kings from Vijaya to Vimala Dharma Surya II,* ed. B. Gunasekera, Colombo: Govt. Printers, 1954, rpt. of 1900 edn., p. 75.

78. 'Historical Records of the Society of Jesus: "The Rebellion of Nikapatty, a Report dated 15th Oct. 1617, sent to Father Nuno Mascarenhas, Assistant to the General of the Society of Jesus by Manoel Ruiz s.j." ', trs. S.G. Perera, *CALR*, vol. 2, no. 2, 1916, pp. 130–6.
79. Ribeiro, *The Historic Tragedy*, p. 165.
80. Queyroz, *The Temporal and Spiritual Conquest*, p. 925.
81. 'Jesuits of Ceylon in the 16th and 17th Centuries', trs. S.G. Perera, *CALR*, vol. 2, no. 1, July 1916, p. 11; Abeysinghe, *Portuguese Rule,* pp. 67–8.
82. Queyroz, *The Temporal and Spiritual Conquest,* p. 612.
83. T.B.H. Abeysinghe (ed.), *A Study of Portuguese Regimentos on Sri Lanka at the Goa Archives,* Colombo: Dept. of National Archives, 1974, p. 49.
84. Ribeiro, *The Historic Tragedy,* p. 86.
85. Ibid., p. 187.
86. Queyroz, *The Temporal and Spiritual Conquest,* pp. 588–9.
87. De Silva, *The Portuguese in Ceylon,* pp. 112–13.
88. See, for instance, the letter from Kinbergen at Negombo to Colombo, 2 April 1764. Letters from outstations to Colombo 1764, SLNA 1/4898. Also '*Aanmerkingen*', p. 25 and p. 37. The author recommended the use of hand mortars that could be fitted to muskets.
89. Diary of the 1765 campaign, Raven-Hart, *The Dutch Wars,* p. 101.
90. Cited in Powell, *The Kandyan Wars,* p. 139. This was something which happened quite frequently. For example, when the British invasion force from Trincomalee on the East Coast apporoached the Mahaveli river that bounded Kandyan territory, the opposite bank was seen to be crowded with armed Kandyans. Narrates a British soldier: 'We instantly threw a shell among hem, on which they set up a shout and fired a volley at us wihout the least execution, but on our giving them a few more shells they ran off as usual'. Anderson, *Journal,* p. 169.
91. Greeving's diary, Vimalananda Tennekoon, *British Intrigues in the Kingdom of Kandy,* Colombo: Gunasena, 1973, p. 504.
92. R.L. Brohier, *The Golden Age of Military Adventure in Ceylon: An Account of the Uva Rebellion 1817–1818,* Colombo: Plate Ltd., 1933, pp. 4–7.
93. This was the detachment which accompanied Surgeon Kennedy. Ceylon Government Gazette, 20 December 1817, *Uva Rebellion,* p. 8.
94. Governor to Secy. of State, 28 Decmber 1817, SLNA 5/9, pp. 312–13, *Colombo Gazetteer,* 20 Dec. 1817, *Uva Rebellion,* p. 8.
95. *Ceylon Government Gazette,* Saturday 4 July 1818, *Uva Rebellion,* p. 33.
96. Raven-Hart, 'Major Medeler's Relief Expedition', pp. 200 and 203.
97. Dutch Council of War, Kandy, 28 August 1765, SLNA 1/4944, p. 45.
98. '. . . since there was nothing apart from paddy available for food, and if it lacked, the desertion of the Malays and Sipahis was to be feared

especially as many had wives and children with them'. Dutch Council of War, Kandy 30 June 1765, SLNA 1/4944, p. 30.

99. S.G. Perera (trs.), 'Ceylon Documents at the Hague: A Latin S.O.S. from Kandy, 1765', *CLR*, vol. 3, no. 2, February 1932, p. 96.
100. Major Davy to Huskisson, 17 June 1803. Anderson, *Journal*, p. 188.
101. Colvin R. De Silva, *Ceylon under the British Occupation 1795–1833*, 2 vols., New Delhi: Navrang, 1995, 4th edn., 1st pub. 1941, vol. 1, p. 187.
102. Alexander, *Life*, vol. 1, p. 155.
103. Bennett, *Ceylon and her Capabilities*, footnote, p. 424.
104. A captured Kandyan woman told the Dutch in June 1765 that the people of the two afore-mentioned Korales had complained to the king about the hardships they were facing. SLNA 1/4944, pp. 14–15.
105. V. Kanpathipillai, 'Dutch Rule in Maritime Ceylon 1766–1796', Ph.D. thesis, University of London, 1969, p. 88.
106. The deposition of Talagama Unnanse, SLNA 7/44, pp. 156–61; deposition of Pannala Unnanse, 1 December 1804, Tennekoon, *British Intrigues*, p. 457; Deposition of Kar Bocus, a Malay priest, March 1805, ibid., pp. 478–9.
107. John Davy, *An Account of the Interior of Ceylon and of its Inhabitants with Travels in that Island*, Dehiwela, Sri Lanka: Tisara Publishers, 1969, rpt. of 1821 edn., p. 262.
108. Brohier, *The Golden Age*, p. 34.
109. Colvin R. De Silva, *Ceylon*, vol. 1, p. 190.
110. Davy, *An Account*, p. 302.
111. Bennett, *Ceylon and her Capabilities*, p. 421.
112. Raven-Hart, *Dutch Wars*, pp. 57 and 76.
113. Powell, *Kandyan Wars*, p. 145; Cordiner, *Description*, vol. 2, pp. 256-7.
114. V.M. Methley (ed.), 'Letters of Captain Herbert Beaver (H.M. 19th Regiment), March–April 1803', *CALR*, vol. 4, no. 2, Oct. 1918, p. 67.
115. Cordiner, *Description*, vol. 2, pp. 225–7.
116. De Silva, *The Portuguese in Ceylon*, p. 133.
117. Lorna Srimathie Dewaraja, *The Kandyan Kingdom of Ceylon 1707–1760*, Colombo: Lake House, 1972, p. 5.

SIX

Conclusion
The Kandyan Wars and European Military Dominance

What the Kandyan–European struggles from the seventeenth to the nineteenth centuries showed was the limitations faced by contemporary European armies in combating an indigenous army in South Asia supported by a subsistence economy and fighting in a rugged and inhospitable climate. This was not much different from the challenge faced by many European armies in other parts of Asia and Africa. Like many other armies in peasant and tribal societies, the Kandyan army fought in loosely organized and highly mobile units depending on a flimsy logistical base. They made optimum use of their knowledge of and the advantages offered by the rugged terrain. For European armies, hard-pressed for manpower, unused to fighting irregular actions in mountainous and inhospitable country, and dependent on larger logistical requirements, this was a serious challenge.

But Kandyan resistance also showed—as in the case of many similar societies that resisted European encroachment—that the capacity of a peasant society to resist European military power had its own limitations. If the Europeans were able to overcome or negotiate the challenges posed by Kandyan resistance they could hope to turn the tables on the Kandyans. This is what the Dutch and the British were able to do in the late eighteenth and early nineteenth centuries. On the one hand, they were able to withstand Kandyan guerrilla attacks and limit their losses mainly to that caused by sickness while on the other hand, they were able to replenish their losses without great difficulty. While checking the challenges of guerrilla warfare, the Dutch and the British also had the potential to place the Kandyan peasant economy under severe strain through total warfare. It was a struggle which the Kandyans, with their limited resources, were bound to lose, even though collaboration played its part in helping the British conquer and consolidate their power over the highland kingdom.

The interesting thing about the success and failure of Kandyan resistance was that they were related to developments outside Kandyan control. The improved muskets and light artillery that did so much to thwart the Kandyan guerrillas had originated in Europe in the course of developments in European warfare. Their impact on wars with Kandyan guerrillas was a reflection of the increasing ability of contemporary European armies in general to combat the type of challenges posed by Kandyan warfare. In contrast, in the sixteenth and seventeenth centuries, European military technology had little or no advantage over the Kandyan tactics, making the task of the Portuguese more difficult. Similarly, the Dutch and the British were also in command of greater manpower resources than the Portuguese in the sixteenth and seventeenth centuries, as a result of their position as colonial powers in Asia. The British, in particular, had mastery over the neighbouring Indian subcontinent and an army of over 100,000 soldiers when they clashed with Kandy.

The Kandyans had little control over these developments which had the potential to place them under increasing pressure. They also had limited capacity for overcoming the challenges posed by the increasing effectiveness of European arms and European regional power. The material and institutional resources of the kingdom were sufficient to hold out against a poor European power like the Portuguese without a significant technological advantage and a smaller resource base, but they were not quite adequate to withstand the struggle against colonial powers with greater potentials. The only conceivable option was to seek foreign assistance that would confer on the Kandyans all the advantages they lacked in their struggles against the Europeans. But this option too was not a viable alternative in the early nineteenth century.

Thus, by the early nineteenth century, the military power of the peasant kingdom in the highlands began to steadily lose its sting against the power of its European enemies, and with little hope of redeeming the situation. This, historians well-versed in similar struggles will tell us, was the fate of all peasant societies in Asia, Africa, and the Americas daring to resist the power of more dynamic European societies during the era of European expansion; that Kandy was simply bowing to the inevitable. There is little in the survival and fall of Kandy to contradict that view. But there is also little doubt that Kandyan resistance is the best example of this historical phenomenon in the South Asian region. This significance derives mainly from the historical circumstance of Kandy having to struggle against European expansion long enough to demonstrate the potential Kandyan society had for resisting European military power in different stages of progress. As such, it is a brilliant example of the changing balance of power between Asian and European military power at a level hitherto unexplored by historians.

Bibliography

PRIMARY SOURCES: UNPUBLISHED

Sri Lanka National Archives (SLNA)

DUTCH RECORDS

Diary of the Dutch Occupation of Kandy, 1765, SLNA 1/4944.
Diary of the events in Matara, February 1762–August 1764, 1/4940.
Letters from outstations to Colombo, 1764, 1/4898.
Letters received in Kandy, 9 March–24 August 1765, 1/4943.
Minutes of the Secret War Committee of the Dutch Political Council, 1761, 1/747.
Minutes of the Secret War Committee of the Dutch Political Council, 1763, 1/4864.

BRITISH RECORDS

Governor's Despatches to Secretary of State, 28 March–23 December 1803, 5/9.
Governor's Secret Diary, February–April 1803, 7/42.
Governor's Secret Diary, January–December 1804, 7/44.
Governor's Military Secret Diary, May–December 1803, 7/43.

NATIONAL MUSEUM COLOMBO

Ingrisi Hatana, Palm Leaf Ms.1859, K.11.
Letter from A. Kelly, Microfilm 6 c/20, reel 0043.
London, Oriental and India Office Collections (*OIOC*)
'*Aanmerkingen over de Oorlog met de Singaleesen*', London, Oriental and India Office Collection, Mackenzie Ms. 39.

PRIMARY SOURCES: PUBLISHED

Abeysinghe, T.B.H. (trs. and ed.), *A Study of Portuguese Regimentos on Sri Lanka at the Goa Archives*, Colombo: Dept. of National Archives, 1974.

Alexander, Alexander, *Life of Bombardier Alexander written by himself,* 2 vols, London: 1830, vol. 1.

Anderson, Thomas Ajax, *Journal of the Proceedings of the Trincomalee Detachment Commanded by Lieut. Colonel Barbut His Majesty's 73rd Regiment from their Leaving Trincomalee till their Arrival at Kandy,* London, 1809.

'Andrews' Embassies to Kandy in 1795 and 1796', ed. J.P. Lewis, *JRAS(CB),* vol. 26, no. 70, 1917, pp. 49–100, 115–51, 172–229; vol. 26, no. 71, 1918, pp. 6–31.

Baldeaus, Philippus, *True and Exact Description of the Great Island of Ceylon,* trs. Pieter Brohier, published as *CHJ,* vol. 8, nos. 1–4, July 1958–April 1959.

Barros, Joao de and Diogo do Couto, 'The History of Ceylon from the earliest Times to A.D. 1600', trs. and ed. Donald Ferguson, *JRAS(CB),* vol. 20, no. 60, 1908.

Burnell, Arthur Coke (trs. and ed.), *The Voyage of John Huyghen van Linschoten to the East Indies from the Old English Translation of 1598,* 2 vols, New York: Burt Franklin, 1963, vol. 1.

Calladine, George, *The Diary of Colour Sergeant George Calladine,* ed. M.L. Ferrar, London: Eden Fisher & Co., 1922.

Coolhaas, W.P. (ed.), *Generale Missiven van Gouverneurs-General en Raden aan Heren xvii Der Verenigde Oostindische Compagnie,* 9 vols, S'Gravenhage: Verkrijgbaar bij Martinus Nijhoff, 1971, vol. 4.

Cordiner, James, *Description of Ceylon containing an Account of the Country, Inhabitants and Natural Productions with a Narrative of a Tour around the Island in 1800, the Campaign in Kandy in 1803 and a Journey to Ramisseram in 1804,* 2 vols., Delhi: Navrang, 1983, rpt. of 1807 edn., vol. 2.

Culavamsa, being the more recent part of the Mahavamsa, trs. into German by Wilhelm Geiger, trs. from German into English by C. Mabel Rickmers, London: Pali Text Society, 1973.

Davy, John, *An Account of the Interior of Ceylon and of its Inhabitants with Travels in that Island,* Dehiwela, Sri Lanka: Tisara Publishers, 1969, rpt. of 1821 edn.

De Sa y Menezes, Joao Rodriguez, 'The Rebellion of Ceylon and the Progress of its Conquest under the Government of Constantino de Sa y Noronha', trs. H.H. St. George, *JRAS(CB),* vol. 11, no. 41, 1890, pp. 427–608.

'Description of Ceylon by Antonio Bocarro', trs. and ed. T.B.H. Abeysinghe, *JRAS(SLB),* New Series, vol. 39, 1995.

Diary of Mr. John D'oyly, with introduction and notes by H.W. Codrington, Delhi: Navrang, 1995, 1st published as *JRAS(CB),* vol. 25, no. 69, 1917.

D'oyly, Sir John, *A Sketch of the Constitution of the Kandyan Kingdom,* ed.

L.J.B. Turner, published as the *CHJ,* vol. 24, Dehiwela, Sri Lanka: Tisara Publishers, 1975; rpt. of 1929 edn.

Ferguson, Donald (ed.), 'The Earliest Dutch Visits to Ceylon', *JRAS(CB),* vol. 30, no. 80, 1927, pp. 361–409; vol. 31, no. 81, 1928, pp. 102–79.

Granville Report on the Matara District, 1813, Historical Manuscripts Commission of Ceylon, Bulletin no. 5, Colombo: Colombo Museum, 1952.

Gray, Albert (ed. and trs.), *The Voyage of Francois Pyrard of Laval to the East Indies, the Maldives, the Moluccas and Brazil,* 2 vols in 3 parts, New York: Burt Franklin, 1963, vol. 2, part 1.

Haafner, J., *Travels on Foot through the Island of Ceylon,* New Delhi: Asian Educational Services, 1995; 1st pub. 1821.

Heydt's Ceylon being the relevant sections of the 'Allerneuster Geographisch und Topographischer Schauplatz van Afrika und Ost-Indien etc., etc.', trs. and ed. Major Roland Raven-Hart, Colombo: Govt. Information Dept., 1952. Originally published in Willendorf, 1742.

'Historical Records of the Society of Jesus: "The Rebellion of Nikapetty, a Report dated 15th Oct. 1617, sent to Father Nuno Mascarenhas, Assistant to the General of the Society of Jesus by Manoel Ruiz s.j."', trs. S.G. Perera, *CALR,* vol. 2, no. 2, 1916, pp. 130–6.

'Jesuits of Ceylon in the 16th and 17th centuries', trs. S.G. Perera, *CALR,* vol. 2, no. 1, July 1916, pp. 1–24.

Johnstone, Captian Arthur, *Narrative of the Operations of a Detachment in an Expedition to Candy in the Island of Ceylon in the Year 1804 with Some Observations on the Previous Campaigns and on the Nature of Candyan Warfare &c &c,* London, 1810.

Kirimetiyawe, Mentindu, *Maha Hatana,* ed. T.S. Hemakumar, Colombo: Samayawardene Printers, 1964.

Knox, Robert, *An Historical Relation of the Island of Ceylon, Revised, Enlarged & Brought to the Verge of Publication as the Second Edition by Robert Knox together with his Autobiography and All the New Chapters, Paragraphs, Marginal Notes added by the Author in the two Interleaved Copies of the Original Text of 1681,* Edited with Introduction and Notes by J.H.O. Paulusz, published as the *CHJ* Monographs series, vol. 14, Dehiwela, Sri Lanka: Tisara Publishers, 1989, 1st edn. 1681.

Limberger, W. van Damast, 'A Short History of the Principal Events that Occurred in the Island of Ceylon, Since the Arrival of the First Netherlanders in the Year 1602, and Afterwards, from the Establishment of the "Honourable Company" in the Same Island till the Year 1757', ed. P.A. Leupe, trs. F.H. de Vos, *JRAS(CB),* vol. 11, no. 38, 1889, pp. 1–150.

Madarampura Puvatha, ed. Labugama Lanakananda, Colombo: Ministry of Cultural Affairs, 1996.

Memoir of Hendrik Zwardercroon, Commandeur of Jaffnapatam, trs. Sophia Pieters, Colombo: Govt. Printers, 1911.

Methley, V.M. (ed.), 'The letters of Captain Herbert Beaver (H.M. 19th Regiment), March–April 1803', *CALR*, vol. 4, no. 2, Oct. 1918, pp. 65–75.

Mukaveti, Alagiyavanna, *Kustantinu Hatana*, ed. Edwin Ranawake, Colombo: Gunasena, 1938.

Munro, Innes, *A Narrative of the Military Operations on the Coromandel Coast against the Combined Forces of the French, Dutch and Hyder Ali Cawn, from the Year 1780 to the Peace in 1784*, London, 1789.

Paulusz, J.H.O. (ed.), *Secret Minutes of the Dutch Political Council 1762*, Colombo: Govt. Printers, 1954.

Pieris, P.E. (ed.), *Prince Vijayapala of Ceylon 1634–1654, from the Original Documents in Lisbon*, Colombo: C.A.C. Ltd., 1927.

Pieris, P.E. and M.A.H. Fitzler (eds), *Ceylon and Portugal Part 1:Kings and Christians 1539–1552, from the Original Documents at Lisbon*, Liepzig: Verlag der Asia Major, 1927.

Queyroz, Fernao de, *The Temporal and Spiritual Conquest of Ceylon*, trs. S.G. Perera, Colombo: Govt. Printers, 1930.

Rajasinha Hatana, ed. Ellepola M.M. Somaratne, Kandy: T.B.S. Godamune and Sons, date unavailable.

'Rajasinha, his Military and other Resources', Report by Dissava Tenekoon in 1676', ed. J.H.O. Pauluzs, *JRAS(CB)*, New Series, vol. 5, 1957, pp. 160–72.

Rajavaliya or a Historical Narrative of Sinhalese Kings from Vijaya to Vimala Dharma Surya II, ed. B. Gunasekera, Colombo: Govt. Printers, 1954, rpt. of 1900 edn.

Raven-Hart, Major Roland (trs. and ed.), *The Dutch Wars with Kandy 1764–1766*, Ceylon Historical Manuscripts Commission Bulletin no. 6, Colombo: Government Publications Bureau, 1964.

_____(trs. and ed.), *Germans in Dutch Ceylon, by Von der Behr (1668), Harport (1669), Schweitzer (1682) and Fryke (1692)*, Colombo: National Museum, 1953.

_____ (trs. and ed.), 'Major Medeler's Relief Expedition', *JRAS(CB)*, New Series, vol. 5, 1957, pp. 183–275.

_____ (trs. and ed.), *Travels in Ceylon 1700–1800*, Colombo: Associated Newspapers Ltd., 1963.

Reimers, E., 'Old Matara and the Rebellion of 1760-61', *JDBUC*, vol. 15, no. 1, July 1925, pp. 7–14; vol. 15, no. 2, Oct. 1925, pp. 59–64; vol. 15, no. 3, Jan. 1926, pp. 88–95.

Ribeiro, Joao de, *The Historic Tragedy of the Island of Ceilao*, trs. P.E. Pieris, Colombo: Lake House, 1948.

Sangermano, Vincenzo, *The Burmese Empire a Hundred Years Ago*, with an introduction and notes by John Jarine, Bangkok: White Orchid Press, 1995, fifth edn., 1st pub. 1833.

Selections from the Dutch Records of the Government of Ceylon: Memoirs of Jan Schreuder, trs. E. Reimers, Colombo: State Printing Corp., 1946.

Selections from the Dutch Records of the Government of Ceylon: Memoirs of Rykloff Van Goens 1663–1675, trs. E. Reimers, Colombo: Govt. Printers, 1932.

Schurhammer, Revd. G.S., *Ceylon des Konigs Bhuvanakabahu*, Liepzig: Verla de Asia Major, 1928.

Souza, Manuel Faria e, *Portuguese Asia or the History of the Discovery and Conquest of India by the Portuguese*, trs. Capt. John Stevens, London, 1695.

Tennekoon, Vimalananda, *The Great Rebellion of 1818: The Story of the First War of Independence and Betrayal of the Nation*, Colombo: Gunesena, 1970.

_____, *British Intrigues in the Kingdom of Kandy*, Colombo: Gunesena, 1973.

'The Dutch Embassy to Kandy in 1731–2: Diary of Wijesiriwardene Mahamudaliyar, otherwise called Lewis de Saram Mahamudaliyar', trs. from the Sinhalese by P.E. Pieris, *JRAS(CB)*, vol. 21, no. 62, 1909, pp. 187–220.

The Expedition to Uva made in 1630 by Constantine de Sa de Noronha, Captain General of Ceylon, as narrated by a Soldier who took part in the Expedition together with an Account of the Siege laid to Colombo by the King of Kandy written by Afonso Dias da Lomba, trs. S.G. Perera, Colombo: Govt. Printers, 1930.

'The Fall of Ehelepola Maha Nilame. Documents Relating to the Insurrection', *CLR*, vol. 4, no. 10, April 1936, pp. 458–74; vol. 4, no. 11, May 1936, pp. 497–517.

'The First Treaty of Peace between the Portuguese and the King of Kandy 1617', trs. S.G. Perera, *CLR*, vol. 3, no. 4, 1933, pp. 155–66.

'The Portuguese in Ceylon in the First Half of the Sixteenth Century: Gaspar Correa's Account', trs. S.G. Perera, *CALR*, vol. 4, no. 6, December 1935, pp. 265–73.

The Uva Rebellion: Extracts from the Ceylon Government Gazette, 1817–18, Colombo: A.M. & J. Ferguson, 1888.

'Van Eck's, Diary of the 1765 Expedition', *JRAS(CB)*, vol. 16, no. 50, 1899, pp. 36–70.

Wilson, H.H. (ed.), *Documents illustrative of the Burmese War with an Introductory Sketch of the Events of the War*, Calcutta: Govt. Gazette Press, 1827.

SECONDARY SOURCES

Abeysinghe, P.M.P., *Udarata Vitti*, Colombo: Dept. of Cultural Affairs, 1998; 1st pub. 1960.

Abeysinghe, T.B.H., *Portuguese Rule in Ceylon 1594–1612*, Colombo: Lake House, 1966.

_____, *Jaffna under the Portuguese*, Colombo: Lake House, 1986.

Abeywardene, H.A.P. (ed.), *Kadaimpoth Vimarshanaya*, Colombo: Dept. of Cultural Affairs, 1978.

Arasaratnam, Sinnappah, *Dutch Power in Ceylon*, Amsterdam: Djambatan, 1958.

Axelson, Eric, *The Portuguese in South East Africa 1488–1600*, Johannesburg: C. Struick, 1973.

Bell, H.C.P., *Report on the Kegalle District of the Province of Sabaragamuwa, Archaeological Survey of Ceylon, Sessional Paper 19*, Colombo: Govt. Printers, 1892.

Bennett, John Whitchurch, *Ceylon and her Capabilities: An Account of its Natural Resources, Indigenous Productions and Commercial Facilities*, London: William H. Allen, 1843.

Birmingham, David, *Trade and Conflict in Angola*, Oxford: Clarendon, 1966.

Bertolacci, A., *A View of the Agricultural, Commercial and Financial Interests of Ceylon*, London, 1817.

Black, Jeremy, *European Warfare 1660–1815*, London: UCL Press, 1994.

_____, *Warfare in the Eighteenth Century*, London: Cassel, 1999.

_____, *War and the World: Military Power and the Fate of the Continents 1450–2000*, New Haven and London: Yale University Press, 1998.

Boxer, C.R., *The Dutch Seaborne Empire*, London: Hutchinson, 1965.

_____, *The Portuguese Seaborne Empire*, London: Hutchinson, 1969.

Brohier, R.L., *The Golden Age of Military Adventure in Ceylon: An Account of the Uva Rebellion 1817–1818*, Colombo: Plate Ltd., 1933.

Bruce, George, *Six Battles for India: The Anglo-Sikh Wars 1845–6, 1848–9*, London: Arthur Baker Ltd., 1969.

_____, *The Burma Wars 1824–1886*, London: Hart-Davis, MacGibbon Ltd., 1973.

Begbie, P.J., *The Malayan Peninsula*, Kuala Lumpur: Oxford University Press, 1967.

Callahan, Raymond, *The East India Company and Army Reform*, Cambridge, Massachusetts: Harvard University Press, 1972.

Campbell, James, *Excursions, Adventures and Field Sports in Ceylon: Its Commercial and Military Importance and Numerous Advantages to the British Emigrant*, London: T&W. Boone, 1843.

Coomaraswamy, Ananda K., *Medieval Sinhalese Art*, New York: Pantheon Books, 1979, 1st pub. 1907.

Danvers, Frederick Charles, *The Portuguese in India, being a History of the Rise and Decline of their Indian Empire*, 2 vols, London: Frank Cass, 1894, vol. 1.

De Silva, Colvin R., *The Portuguese in Ceylon 1617–1638*, Colombo: H.W. Cave & Co., 1972.

_____, *Sri Lanka: A History*, Delhi: Vikas Publishing House, 1987.

_____, *Ceylon under the British Occupation 1795–1833,* 2 vols, New Delhi: Navrang, 1995; 4th edn., 1st pub. 1941, vol. 1.

De Silva, D.H.D.H., *A Catalogue of Antiquities and Other Cultural Objects from Sri Lanka (Ceylon) Abroad,* Colombo: Govt. Printers, 1975.

De Silva, K.H., *Sinhala Hatan Kavi,* Colombo: Sri Lanka Publishers, 1964.

De Silva, K.M., *History of Sri Lanka,* London: C. Hurst & Co., 1981.

Dewaraja, Lorna Srimathie, *The Kandyan Kingdom of Ceylon 1707–1760,* Colombo: Lake House, 1972.

_____, *Sri Lanka through French Eyes,* Colombo: Institute of Fundamental Studies, 1989.

Dhammananda, Ven. Namulle, *Madyama Lanka Puravrta,* Colombo: Gunasena, 1970.

Dirks, Nicholas B., *The Hollow Crown: The Ethnohistory of an Indian Kingdom,* Ann Arbor: University of Michigan Press, 1993.

Disney, A.R., *The Twilight of the Pepper Empire: Portuguese Trade in Southwest India in the Early Seventeenth Century,* Cambridge, Massachussetts: Harvard University Press, 1978.

Duffy, Christopher, *The Military Experience in the Age of Reason,* London: Routledge and Kegan Paul, 1987.

Gamage, G.S., *Mahanuwara Rajya Arakshaka Kramopaya,* Colombo: S. Godage and Sons, 1997.

Goonewardene, KW., *The Foundation of Dutch Power in Ceylon 1638–1658,* Amsterdam: Djambatan, 1958.

Grey, C., *European Adventurers in Northern India 1785–1849,* Lahore: Govt. Printing, 1929.

Habib, Irfan, *The Agrarian System of Mughal India 1556–1707,* New York: Asia Publishing House, 1963.

Hall, Bert S., *Weapons and Warfare in Renaissance Europe: Gunpowder, Technology and Tactics,* Baltimore: Johns Hopkins University Press, 1997.

Haythornwhite, Phillip J., *The Colonial Wars Sourcebook,* London: Arms and Armour, 1995.

Hemming, John, *The Amazon Frontier: The Defeat of the Amazon Indians,* London: Macmillan, 1987.

Hogg, Brigadier O.F.G., *Artillery, its Origin, Heyday and Decline,* London: C. Hurst & Co., 1970.

Hughes, B.P., *Open Fire: Artillery Tactics from Marlborough to Wellington,* Chichester, Sussex: A. Bird Publications, 1983.

Husainmiya, B.A., *Orang Regimen: The Malays of the Ceylon Rifle Regiment,* Bangi, Malaysia: Penerbit University Kebangsaan Malaysia, 1990.

Indrapala, K. (ed.), *The Collapse of the Rajarata Civilization and the Drift to the Southwest: A Symposium,* Peradeniya: University of Ceylon, 1971.

Kolff, Dirk, *Naukar, Rajput and Sepoy: The Ethnohistory of the Military Labour Market in Hindustan 1450–1850,* Cambridge: Cambridge University Press, 1990.

Leach, Douglas Edward, *Flintlock and Tomahawk: New England in King Phillip's War*, New York: The Norton Library, 1966.

Little, David, *Sri Lanka: The Invention of Enmity*, Washington, D.C.: United States Institute of Peace, 1994.

Malone, Patrick, *The Skulking Way of War: Technology among the New England Indians*, Lanham, MD: Madison Books, 1991.

Marshall, Henry, *Ceylon: A General Description of the Island and of its Inhabitants*, Dehiwela, Sri Lanka: Tisara Publishers, 1982; 1st pub. 1846.

Methley, V.M., 'The Expedition of 1803', *Transactions of the Royal Asiatic Society 4th Series*, vol. 1, 1917, pp. 93–128.

Mills, Lennox A., *The Advent of the British to Ceylon*, London: Frank Cass, 1964.

Nanawimala, Kirielle, *Saparagamuve Parani Liyawili*, Colombo: Jinalankara Press, 1942.

_____, *Katuwana Matara Hatana*, Colombo: Gunasena, 1968.

Nypels, George, *Hoe Nederland Ceilon verloor*, S'gravenhage: Martinus Nijhoff, 1908.

Obeysekera, Gananath, *Land Tenure in Village Ceylon: A Sociological and Historical Study*, Cambridge: Cambridge University Press, 1967.

Parker, Geoffrey, *The Military Revolution: Military Innovation and the Rise of the West 1500–1800*, Cambridge and New York: Cambridge University Press, 1998.

Pieris, P.E., *Ceylon: The Portuguese Era being a History of the Island for the Period 1505–1658*, 2 vols., Colombo: C.A.C. Ltd., 1913.

_____, *Ceylon and the Hollanders 1658–1796*, Tellipalai, Sri Lanka: American Ceylon Mission Press, 1918.

_____, *Tri Sinhala: The Last Phase*, Delhi: Navrang, 1995; rpt. of 1939 edn.

_____, *Sinhale and the Patriots*, Delhi: Navrang, 1995, rpt. of 1950 edn.

Pieris, Ralph, *Sinhalese Social Organization: The Kandyan Period*, Colombo: Ceylon University Press, 1956.

Powell, Geoffrey, *The Kandyan Wars: The British Army in Ceylon 1803–1818*, London: Leo Cooper, 1973.

Raghavan, M.D., *The Karava of Ceylon: Society and Culture*, Colombo: K.V.G. de Silva and Sons, 1961.

Redlich, Fritz, *The German Military Enterpriser and his Workforce: A European Economic and Social History*, Wiesbaden: Steiner, 1964.

Ryan, Bryce, *Sinhalese Village*, Coral Gables, Florida: University of Miami Press, 1958.

Sarkar, Jagadish Narayan, *The Art of War in Medieval India*, Delhi: Munshiram Manoharlal, 1984.

Sen, Surendranath, *The Military System of the Marathas*, Calcutta: K. Bagchi & Co., 1949.

Seneviratne, H.L., *Rituals of the Kandyan State*, Cambridge Studies in Social Anthropology, Cambridge: Cambridge University Press, 1978.

Somaratne, G.P.V., *Political History of the Kingdom of Kotte*, Colombo: Somaratne, 1975.

Starkey, Armstrong, *European and Native American Warfare 1675–1815*, Norman: University of Oklahoma Press, 1998.

Stein, Burton, *Peasant State and Society in Medieval South India*, Delhi: Oxford University Press, 1980.

Stephen, Jeyaseela, *Portuguese in the Tamil Coast: Historical Explorations in Commerce and Culture*, Pondicherry: Navajothi, 1998.

Wickremesekera, C., *The Best Black Troops in the World: British Perceptions and the Making of the Sepoy 1746–1805*, Delhi: Manohar, 2002.

Zwier, W., *Het Verdraag van 1766 Tusschen de O.I. Compagnie en de Vorst Van Kandi*, Amsterdam: H.J. Paris, 1927.

ARTICLES

Abeysinghe, T.B.H., 'The Politics of Survival: Aspects of Kandyan External Relations in the Mid-Sixteenth Century', *JRAS(SLB)*, vol. 17, 1973, pp.11–21.

_____, 'History as Polemics and Propaganda: An Examination of Fernao Queyroz' "History of Ceylon"', *JRAS (SLB)*, vol. 25, 1980/81, pp. 28–68.

_____, 'Embassies as Instruments of Diplomacy in Sri Lanka in the First Half of the Eighteenth Century', *JRAS(SLB)*, vol. 30, 1985–6, pp. 1–40.

_____, 'Description of Ceylon by Antonio Bocarro', trs. and ed. T.B.H. Abeysinghe, *JRAS(SLB)*, New Series, vol. 39, 1995.

Arasartnam, Sinnappah, 'Vimala Dharma Surya II (1687–1707) and His Relations with the Dutch', *CJHSS*, vol. 6, no. 1, 1963, pp. 59–70.

_____, 'Ceylon in the Indian Ocean Trade: 1500–1800', in A. Das Gupta and M.N. Pearson (eds.), *India and the Indian Ocean 1500–1800*, Calcutta: Oxford University Press, 1989, pp. 224–39.

Barua, Pradeep, 'Miliary Innovations in India 1750–1850', *Journal of Military History*, vol. 58, no. 4, 1994, pp. 599–616.

Boxer, C.R., 'War and Trade in the Indian Ocean and the South China Seas 1600–1650', *The Great Circle, the Journal of the Australian Association for Maritime History*, vol. 1, no. 2, 1979, pp. 3–17.

Codrington, H.W., 'The Kandyan Navandanno', *JRAS(CB)*, vol. 21, no. 62, 1909, pp. 221–53.

Cooper, R.G.S., 'Wellington and the Marathas 1803–04', *International History Review*, vol. 11, no. 1, 1989, pp. 31–8.

De Moor, Jaap, 'The Recruitment of Indonesian Soldiers for the Dutch Colonial Army, *c.* 1700–1950', in David Killingray and David Omissi (eds), *Guardians of Empire: The Armed Forces of the Colonial Powers c.1700–1964*, Manchester: Manchester University Press, 1999, pp. 53–69.

Dep, Arthur C., 'Walapane Unnanse and the Walapane Rebellion 1842–1843' *JRAS(SLB)*, New Series, vol. 29, 1984, pp. 55–74.

Deraniyagala, P.E.P., 'Sinhala Weapons and Armour', *JRAS(CB),* vol. 35, no. 95, 1942, pp. 97–134.

Dewaraja, Lorna Srimathie, 'Revenues of the Kings of Kandy', *JRAS(CB)*, New Series, vol. 16, 1972, pp. 17–31.

De Silva, C.R., 'The First Portuguese Revenue Register of the Kingdom of Kotte, 1599', *CJHSS*, January–December 1975, pp. 71–153.

_____, 'The Rise and Fall of the Kingdom of Sitawaka 1521–1593', *CJHSS*, New Series, vol. 7, January–June, 1977, pp. 1–43.

_____, 'Lancerote de Seixas and Madampe: A Portuguese Casado in a Sinhala Village', *Modern Ceylon Studies*, vol. 2, no. 1, 1971.

De Silva, M.S.C., 'The Sinhalese Army during the Portuguese, Dutch and the British Periods, 1505–1815', *Spolia Zeylanica*, vol. 2, no. 1, 1971, pp. 79–87.

Gunasekera, Alex, 'Rajakariya or the Duty to the King in the Kandyan Kingdom of Sri Lanka', in Wendy Doniger O'Flaherty and J. Duncan M. Derret (eds.), *The Concept of Duty in South Asia*, London: School of Oriental and African Studies, 1978, pp. 119–46.

Hettiarachchi, A.S., 'Mahanuwara Rajaparapura', *JRAS(CB),* New Series, vol. 12, 1968, pp. 123–9.

Jonville, M, 'Narrative of a Journey to Kandy made on the Occasion of the Embassy of Major General Macdowall in 1800', *JRAS(CB)*, vol. 38, no. 105, 1948, pp. 1–18.

Khan, Iqtidar Alam, 'Early Use of Cannon and Musket in India', *Journal of the Economic and Social History of the Orient*, vol. 24, no. 2, 1981, pp. 146–64.

Nissan, Elizabeth and R.L. Stirrat, 'The Generation of Communal Identities', Jonathan Spencer (ed.), *Sri Lanka: History and the Roots of Conflict*, London: Routledge, 1990, pp. 19–44.

Paulusz, J.H.O., 'The Outbreak of the Kandyan–Dutch War of 1761 and the Great Rebellion: Secret Minutes of the Dutch Political Committee', *JRAS(CB)*, vol. 3, 1953, pp. 28–55.

_____, 'Ambanwela Appuhamy's Rebellion of 1665', *JRAS(CB)*, New Series, vol. 7, no. 1, 1960, pp. 104–12.

Pemble, John, 'Techniques and Resources in the Second Maratha War', *Historical Journal*, vol. 19, no. 2, 1976, pp. 375–404.

Perera, S.G., trs. 'Ceylon Documents at the Hague: A Latin S.O.S. from Kandy 1765', *CLR*, vol. 3, no. 2, February 1932, pp. 95–6.

Roberts, Michael, 'The Military Revolution', in Michael Roberts, *Essays in Swedish History*, London: Weidenfeld and Nicholson, 1967, pp. 195–225.

Sweet, David, 'Native Resistance in Eighteenth Century Amazonia: The

"Abominable Muras" in War and Peace', *Radical History Review*, vol. 53, 1992, pp. 49–80.

Van Imhoff's Tour of the Matara District, [March 1737]', *CALR*, vol. 1, no. 2, February 1931, pp. 83–6.

Vogt, John, 'Saint Barbara's Legion: Portuguese Artillery in the Struggle for Morocco 1415–1578', *Military Affairs*, vol. 41 (Lexington, VA), 1977, pp. 176–82.

White, Gavin, 'Firearms in Africa: An Introduction', *Journal of African History*, vol. 12, no. 2, 1971, pp. 173–84.

THESES

Kanpathipillai, V., 'Dutch Rule in Maritime Ceylon 1766–1796', Ph.D. thesis, University of London, 1969.

Kotelawela, D.A., 'The Dutch in Ceylon: 1743–1766', Ph.D. thesis, University of London, 1968.